AF477149

A Kabbalistic View on Science (Part 2)

Mike Bais

A Kabbalistic View on Science (Part 2)

By Mike Bais.
Circle of Avalon, School of the Soul (Kabbalah and Western Esoteric Tradition).
Copyright © Mike Bais 2022.

All diagrams were produced by Mike Bais in cooperation with Dennis Agterberg, and with the kind permission of Z'ev ben Shimon Halevi of the Kabbalah Society. The moral right of Mike Bais to be identified as the author has been asserted by him in accordance with sections 77 & 78 of the copyright, Designs and Patents Act 1998.
Front cover picture: Joyce Sterrenberg

All rights reserved.
No part of this publication may be reproduced, stored in a retrieval system, or transmitted, in any form or by any means, electronic, mechanical, photocopying, recording, or otherwise, without prior permission in writing of the publisher. This publication may not be sold, lent, hired out or otherwise dealt with in the course of trade or supplied in any form of binding or cover, other than that in which it is published and without a similar condition including this condition being imposed on the subsequent purchaser.

Circle of Avalon Books, Engelsmanplaat 14, 3524 AZ Utrecht, The Netherlands.
www.circleofavalon.nl
Contact the author: mike@circleofavalon.nl

Printed at Ingram Spark, USA
A catalogue of this publication is available from the British Library and from the Dutch National Library, The Hague.

ISBN: 9789082999013

Contents

Acknowledgements

I want to thank all those who encouraged me to write this book: My teacher, Z'ev ben Shimon Halevi (Warren Kenton). Even after his physical death, I experience the nurturing and sustaining influence of Halevi. In the Kabbalah tradition, the teachers who have passed on, become those who support and teach us from the inner planes. Such is my own experience in my teachings, writing and daily life. Besides, I wish to thank many other teachers who have transmitted their wisdom over the years with such care and love. I feel blessed to have met so many beautiful people who are dedicated to the Inner Work.

I am continually grateful to my family and partner, who believe in my work and always support me. I must also thank all the people within my Kabbalah community, all my dear companions, my many friends and the Circle of Avalon students. Together, all of them, directly or indirectly, made it possible to write this manuscript. Finally, I would like to give special thanks to Dennis Agterberg, who helped me with the diagrams and the technical preparations to complete the book. I am also grateful for those people who helped me to co-read the manuscript and gave valuable advice and suggestions. Without them, this book could not have been written. Also my gratitude to my editors Ramona Gault, and Aida Seguin, who have put so much love and effort in this book. The path of the writer is often lonely and solitary. It is important to have people around you that encourage you, share and inspire the process of writing.

Circle of Avalon, Spring 2022.

Prologue

After writing Part one of "A Kabbalistic view on science", published in 2019, it was clear that there would be so much more to write about and reveal on this deeply important meeting of the spiritual and scientific worlds. From my work in the scientific field of Physiotherapy, as a University Lecturer for Medical Professionals, and my almost twenty-five years of Kabbalistic training, I realized there were still so many more significant connections to be shown.

Having taught throughout the Netherlands, in Germany and Belgium, and the UK (at Hawkwood College, Stroud, England - The Centre for Future Thinking) for more than 12 years, I now realize that there are so many more questions for the reader and myself left unanswered, and even more fascinating material to be carefully explored and shared. Given that my Kabbalah workshops and the first book have been received with such enthusiasm and positive feedback, it has inspired me to continue along this journey and write this second manuscript. The knowledge of these unique teachings, once written down, will hold many keys to applying the tradition of Kabbalah for generations to come, is a challenging task for me that is well worth pursuing.

Quantum physics has countless parallels with mysticism in general and Kabbalah in particular. The modern ideas behind neuroplasticity, for example, are highly relevant to the development of today's Kabbalah. In the Kabbalah Toledano tradition, Z'ev ben Shimon Halevi (1933-2020) connected the contemporary world and humankind with the metaphysics of Jacob's Ladder and the Tree of Life. The Kabbalah Toledano tradition brings clarity and practical application into today's world. Simultaneously, I believe that science has a tremendous contribution to make in enhancing the quality of human life by connecting its scientific research and findings with the spiritual perspectives of Kabbalah.

In Part Two of "A Kabbalistic view on science", I intend to serve the Toledano tradition further so that each reader will discover the wisdom within both Kabbalah and science. Throughout the history of humankind, we find that disciplines like Kabbalah and science enable us in developing our inner journey towards wholeness. Both disciplines reveal our innate desire as human beings to consciously or unconsciously experience wholeness. In everyday life, art, music, religion, philosophy, and through many other ways of expressing our lives, we may forget to search inside ourselves to distil from the wisdom and intelligence of the physical body and psyche.

These endless possibilities lead us to wholeness and unity. This second volume further shows that our physical bodies are intelligent vessels containing all the Kabbalistic worlds. It is a temple of the Holy Spirit, and the subtle energy structures and systems of the body, such as the nervous system, testify to this wisdom and the way it communicates to us. The same goes for the scientific world of chemical substances, processes, interactions and systems that are uncovering many hidden secrets to the meaning of life.

I hope you enjoy this book as much as the first one, and that it may contribute to your own path, whether you are a Kabbalist or scientist.
May Peace be with you in all your ways,

Mike Bais

Introduction

In the 17th century Isaac Newton, and other scientists like René Descartes, gave us the physics that was based upon a material oriented universe. Reason was the development for the natural sciences. Ever since the material universe became the object of science, animals and even human life were seen as machine-like constructions. The cosmos was a clockwork mechanism that was founded on logic and sheer mathematics. This intellectual approach is part of our modern science and view of the world, which is why many school systems have these teachings in their curricula.

Living beings have a hereditary component called DNA and genes. A variation of combinations in these genes makes us different from each other. Nature selects on randomness or through adaptations to the environment. At least, that is the theory of Charles Darwin and the modern Neo-Darwinists. This leads in time to speciation. If this theory is right, and we are animals with an enlarged brain with some prefrontal neocortex activity that monkeys may not have, the question arises whether we are machines too.

DNA and genes were discovered and dissected when the techniques of microscopes developed, and projects like the human genome led to a perspective of a new universe. Until then, only the science of biology could unravel all the mysteries of the genes (that is what some scientists thought). Even biologists had to change their attitude towards life, come up with new paradigms, and put their own beliefs under a microscope. A God who had something to do with creation and the human existence was completely out of the question in these scientific approaches. Why?

Because a "God" could not be proven by the instruments and theories (hypothesis) of science. At the same time, God could not be rejected either, as it could not be proven nor scientifically rejected. Darwin, for example, had a religious (Christian) background and had a hard time believing that 'such a God' could exist and be involved in creation in the way it was promoted by the church. Scientific materialism developed out of a disbelief in a personal God so recognizable by the second-person relationship, such as the one that exists between human being and God.

According to materialistic science, the universe consists of matter, and all that is created comes forth out of matter. In other words: if there is a creator present, it is nature itself and not some invisible deity. This philosophy is a dogma and polarizes only more the differences between science and religion.
Creation, according to this science, can therefore be made in a laboratory.

All is calculated, and time-space related in a mathematical and chemical deduction. A linear way of experiencing time is part of this materialistic vision of the universe. There is no space to consider non-linear time (Eternity), nonlocality, and synchronicity, as they are not objects that can be measured by (materialistic) scientific machines. Signal-less communication, multiple localization, and consciousness outside the body can't be considered. There is compelling evidence that materialistic science cannot be the way to explain existence and answer all of the questions about life that came from the mysterious domain of quantum physics.

Objects are waves of potentiality: a world where energy is a field of probabilities. Here communication is instantaneous without signal and nonlocal. These phenomena are outside the realm of space-time-movement and therefore often stigmatized by materialistic science as vague or spiritualistic. Prejudice came about because of the connection made between spirituality and quantum physics.

Indeed, we have to be very careful not to highjack these theories and loosely connect them with metaphysics. To acknowledge that materialistic science does not provide us with answers, does not explain the universe and the presence of God. Mystically, we have all our equipment on the inside, available to experience the world, time and space, and the realms beyond. There is in fact a physics and science of God—for example: the metaphysics of Kabbalah, quantum physics, developments within biology, neurophysiology and bio-psychology.

There are plenty of scientists today, together with mystics, who work towards unity, integration, and inclusivity. Within that philosophy and mindset there can only be an approach to the different realms that leads to cooperation. We all serve the Source where all these streams of thought came from in the first place. Whether we use the same name and illustration for this Source, does not matter for those who care to look beyond the world of forms.

A human science instead of a material science (Aquarian Age) puts the soul central to our mystical-scientific enterprise. The soul is that part of the psyche that hovers between the world of Assiah and the higher Yezirah and Briah on Jacob's Ladder. The soul is like a bridge and vehicle between these worlds. It is that consciousness which wishes to return to wholeness and unity. Such can only be done when we are interested in the whole of existence and not just its parts. Matter, psyche, soul, Spirit, and God are all included in this study and journey, deep into our own microcosm and thereby into the macrocosm we all live in. We are not a soul-less machine but a soul who has taken on an earthly disguise to discover and experience who we are.

We are heart-centered creatures, although we might not experience or see this happen in the world. There is a saying in the mystical traditions: "You are born because you are Loved" (by God or Transcendence). It is that Love that lies at the foundation of our soul and whole being, as well as at the foundation of the whole of existence.

Kabbalah and the sciences we discuss within the pages of this book, are all ways of living that heart-centeredness. To gain evidence of our experiences and "experiments" of life, we depart from our own direct knowledge of ourselves, the world, cosmos, and Transcendence. Proof will mainly come through direct experience—the way of the mystic. The intellect, our feelings, our theories about the world are all beneficial and contribute to this direct knowing (Gnosis). There is a constant involvement of the human soul in the unfoldment of life. We cannot separate the objective from the subjective any longer.

The science of matter does not have to be dismissed, as it does not conflict with the purpose of this book.
We do not have to disregard this science together with the innovations of other scientific disciplines and the metaphysics of Kabbalah.

What cannot be seen is the foundation of the visible universe. The seen universe is an expression of the unseen. Yet, both are not separate or to be regarded as laying one on top of the each other.

What Kabbalah explains with the diagram of Jacob's Ladder is that all is inclusive and all four worlds are in fact within each other (fifth Tree on the Ladder). Cause and effect, Creator and created, God and cosmos are all intrinsically entangled in each other. One exists within the other, each coming forth out of the other.

Heaven, life after death, and consciousness are all experiences that are explained by these scientific disciplines that match so well with the Kabbalistic teachings. Religion is not always comparable to the metaphysics we are talking about here. Belief and Gnosis or mystical experiences are definitely not the same. How some scientific streams have rejected orthodox religion because of their dogma is easy to understand, as belief and materialistic science are opposite to each other.

There is almost no way to reconcile these views into one. Interestingly enough, from the mystical and quantum approaches alike, it is consciousness itself that has the experience from the viewpoint of the materialist scientist and the orthodox believer. We all live the Transcendence in the world: being the 'eyes and ears' of God. In this manner, we all contribute in our own way to the fulfilment of reality. We are all brought back into the wholeness of the original World (Tree), and God beholds God in the mirror of existence. Therefore we should be careful not to judge or condemn streams of thought that are outdated, limiting, or against our own way of thinking.

Do we allow that matter and energy come together and do not stay apart in our universe? Even more: is it not true that they already are inseparable? Waves and particles, energy and matter are only separate in the motion of time-space experience. This is part of the implication of our dualistic participation in the universe. Within time-space-movement, Eternity is not excluded. Like we mentioned above: the unseen is the foundation of the seen. Eternity is the foundation of time-space-movement. Could you imagine looking behind the curtain of time-space (so often mentioned as the curtain in the temple of Solomon in Kabbalah) and beholding Eternity behind it? We would look fully into the quantum domain, which would be the Holy of Holies in Kabbalah (place of the Covenant and the Shekinah).

It is an ironic idea coming from materialistic science that all that was, is, and shall ever be, is matter. A calculated, mechanistic universe is not proven at all, but rests upon a belief as well. We are all guessing in the end. The whole of existence remains a huge mystery. It is that mystery that some call God or the Transcendence. We may come to know some of the mystery through life, which is a reflection of the Transcendent. We may come to some understanding of what

this universe is all about, but the mystery remains. If we can be at peace with the idea and experience that we may indeed know the Mystery (God) but not unveil its full presence, we do not have to try to prove anything through science or dogmatic belief systems. The mystery is within all worlds and realities.
This means that we are all living within a part of reality. Some of us wish to explore worlds that complement and expand our understanding of reality.
A personal God limits us per definition as does any personal or scientific viewpoint. Why? Because our personal world is limited by its very definition.

The personal world (lower face of Yezirah) has only a partial understanding of reality: only that part which is relatable to our own personal experiences.
There are too many personal belief systems that are not based upon metaphysics and traditional teachings.

They can only lead to the personal and limited experiences of their followers. The priesthood within science and religion should be proclaiming how to free ourselves from ourselves, not how to believe something that we have found within our own dogma. We could become priests and inquisitors of our own belief systems from whatever scientific or religious discipline possible. Those possible risks have nothing to do with religion or science per se, but these are human problems in themselves in every department of life.

There can be a mechanistic-scientific development of religion and a religious development within science (credo without discernment). The paradox can be reconciled if we are open to go into that "rabbit hole" and follow Alice into her Wonderland (the way into wonders or miracles). This is the world of Briah or creation. Here, the role of the observer within the world of manifestation is of crucial importance when it comes to participation in the miracle.

Consciousness here is expressed in a wave or particle and holds both of them in their Eternal state within the middle pillar. As God came into existence and created, formed, and made itself, it (God) became the observer of its own creation. Whenever we are identified with being the observer, we are allowing God to behold itself through our eyes. Those are quite different eyes from the physical senses or the consciousness of the lower psyche (ego) looking through.
As quantum physics has shown through different experiments like the "double slit experiment", the role of the observer is exactly what makes consciousness to be wave or particle. How the universe is seen, is how the universe becomes.

This may be interesting within the spiritual idea that "Who we are is what we do, and what we do is who we become." "Who we are" describes the consciousness of being (ground of becoming) that gives rise to what we do. Our actions are coming forth out of our being as a result of how consciousness has revealed itself (identity). So, identity gives rise to action (movement). The one who observes is therefore of most significant importance when it comes to the question:

"How do I change and into what?"

Chapter 1: Kabbalah & the Kabbalistic Invocation

Throughout time Kabbalah has offered its practitioners the opportunity to reflect upon, meditate and access spiritual insights about our soul, higher self, as well as the vital knowledge about fate, destiny, and providence at work in our daily lives. Kabbalah teaches us about the connections between ourselves, the world, the universe and God.

Here, we can see in diagram 1, the four worlds of Divinity, Creation, Formation, and Action. Together, these are the four ways through which the Holy One came forth into its own creation. Kabbalah explicitly demonstrates that God not only encompasses its own creation, but God inhabits it in complete fullness.
Through the Tree of Life, we can understand the process of creation (Briah) and how these metaphysical principles, often portrayed as Archangels, present the unfoldment out of the Divine world. Both in Kabbalah and in this book, the Tree of Life diagrams reveal the many interconnected aspects of creation.

The Ten Sefirot in the world of Aziluth or the Divine world are also called the Garments of God, the Ten Utterances, the Expressions, and the Ten Names through which God communicates with its creation.
Historically speaking, Kabbalah originated in the Middle East. Many traditions, lineages, branches and expressions of Kabbalah manifested over time across the world. The main sources can be traced back to the 12th-century Provence (France) and Spain, which follows the route of the Kabbalists and mystics who fled Spain to return to Safed in the Middle East. This tradition follows the Toledano Kabbalah, based on the many influences between the 12th & 13th Centuries.

The Kabbalists who preserved and transmitted this tradition, most notably Moses Cordovero (1522-1570), who was known as a central figure in the historical development of Kabbalah and a leader of a mystical school in 16th-century Safed. Also, Joseph Caro (1488-1575), who lived in Toledo and later in Safed, contributed to the tradition of Kabbalah.

Today, we owe much to Z'ev ben Shimon Halevi (1933-2020), who has transmitted the Toledano Kabbalah teachings and brought them into the 20th and 21st centuries. Through his writing and teaching, he firstly made it possible for non-Jews to study Kabbalah and understand it as a universal body of wisdom. Secondly, he connected Kabbalah with other esoteric disciplines like astrology, and with contemporary psychology.

The teachings of Kabbalah bring us the wisdom that God can be known, and is yet unknown. As it is said in Kabbalah: "God's place is the world, but the world is not God's place", saying that while God is present in existence (the four worlds) God is separate from it. In other words: God is Immanent, and God is Transcendent. The Transcendent is the Kabbalistic idea that God is beyond existence (Ain Soph- without end) and yet God is within existence and can be known through a reflection within the four worlds, where the immanence of God is present.

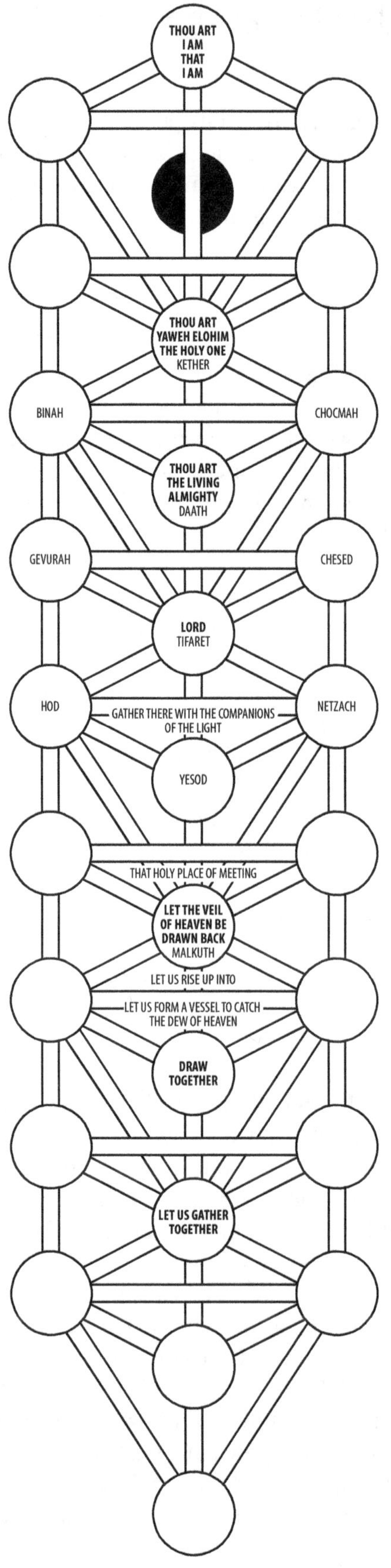

HEAR THIS
MOST GRACIOUS GOD
THOU ART
YAWEH ELOHIM
THE HOLY ONE THOU ART
THE LIVING ALMIGHTY
THOU ART
THE LORD

IF IT BE THY WILL
LET THY HOLY SPIRIT
DESCEND UPON US
THIS DAY/NIGHT
THAT WE MAY KNOW
THY PRESENCE

KETHER
CHOCMAH
BINAH
(DAATH)
CHESED
GEVURAH
TIFARET
NETZACH
HOD
YESOD
MALKUTH

HOLY HOLY HOLY
ART THOU
LORD GOD OF HOSTS
THY GLORY
FILLS ALL THE WORLDS
AMEN

THOU ART
I AM
THAT
I AM

THOU ART
YAWEH ELOHIM
THE HOLY ONE
KETHER

BINAH

CHOCMAH

THOU ART
THE LIVING
ALMIGHTY
DAATH

GEVURAH

CHESED

LORD
TIFARET

HOD

NETZACH

GATHER THERE WITH THE COMPANIONS
OF THE LIGHT

YESOD

THAT HOLY PLACE OF MEETING

LET THE VEIL
OF HEAVEN BE
DRAWN BACK
MALKUTH

LET US RISE UP INTO

LET US FORM A VESSEL TO CATCH
THE DEW OF HEAVEN

DRAW
TOGETHER

LET US GATHER
TOGETHER

Diagram 1

In the Toledano tradition, finding God's immanence is a stage within the life of the Kabbalist, where the Holy Shekinah (eternal presence) is realized, and the Transcendent is known through reflection. However, God is not a duality, so we have to be careful not to use "Transcendent and Immanent" as if it were so. For the one who knows the Immanent knows the Transcendent.

Through this inclusive Kabbalah tradition and teachings, we come to know that God is one and there is only one being. For the Kabbalist, the inner knowing of the Immanent presence or Shekinah brings us closer to the Holy One, who constantly connects with its creation. Ain Soph cannot be known and is hidden from our knowledge; God is the Mystery that cannot be known. Knowing the immanence is coming in relation to the Mystery, while the Mystery remains unresolved and hidden.

The Kabbalist knows to be one with the creator, but the Mystery will still be the Mystery. The Ain Soph is the Absolute and Perfect. There is no duality, no morality, no heaven or earth, and no word can reach Ain Soph. The Absolute Nothing and All (Ain and Ain Soph) can only be known through negatives, in terms of what Ain Soph isn't. Ain and Ain Soph are the roots of all existence, and it is through these roots that the Tree of Life (existence) grows. It is God who is the Cause of all Causes. Ain Soph cannot be named, blessed, or prayed to.

However, this mystery-teaching and practice, which is beyond existence, is not just celebrated in the obscure ancient mystic worlds. As this book will show, such mysteries are also found at the core of science today. In Quantum Physics, the reality of our material world is based on Nothingness.

Kabbalah explains that at the root of all things and beings (existence) God is the Nothing and Limitless (all). This explanation is also found in Quantum Physics when describing the core of existence as nothing. The Quantum world is empty and simultaneously full of limitless space and information.

Another example of how Kabbalah and science come together is through the Kabbalistic idea of the Lightning flash in the Divine world of Aziluth. Here, the Kabbalist speaks in analogy when God comes into existence through "light and fire", connecting Heaven to Earth. The Kabbalist finds its way back to the source of "light and fire". This is called the path of evolution or initiation. By following the way of the Lightning flash in reverse order. As we know, with physical lightning, the electromagnetic energy travels from Heaven to earth but also from earth to Heaven. Lightning is the mutual and entangled exchange of the same energy that comes into existence and moves back to its source.

The lightning flash suggests a stream of energy from Heaven being brought unto and into the earth. In Kabbalah, this process of emanation from the Godhead or Ain Soph is the way the Names of the highest world of the Divine were uttered. The Ten Sefirot of Aziluth came out of nothing and they appear out of the Will of God or Lightning Flash (Tzimtzum). Although we cannot praise and bless the Transcendent or Ain Soph, we are constantly blessed by this outpouring of Divine energy into creation.

In Kabbalah, it is said that: "Their end enters into their beginning, and their beginning enters into their end."

The lightning coming out of the first emanation or the Sefira Kether (Crown) and fills the vessels of the other nine Sefirot down the Tree of Life. This way, creation is filled with the essence of the Divine, and the Mystery of Ain Soph can be known through God's expression in creation.

The importance of Meditation in Kabbalah
In this book, several meditations will support the reader to bring the theory to life, animated through internalization. Kabbalah sessions always start with an invocation, so I would like to introduce you to this invocation and make you part of the Toledano Kabbalah tradition. Before we start this meditation and enter into this manuscript, I offer you this possibility: to engage with the Companions of the Light within all places and times.

The invocation goes as follows: you sit with your eyes closed and keep a candle ready for lighting. After some conscious breathing cycles, you read the invocation with intention and follow the described images after each part of the invocation. There is no need to hurry, so take your time with the words and images.

Invocation

"Let us gather together"

Sense, feel, and see Malkuth and the world of Assiah: be aware of your body and the four elements. The interaction of the earth, water, air, and fire in the body. Sense, see and feel within the bones, muscles, joints, the fluidic streaming substances and the chemistry of your hormones. Be conscious of the breath entering and leaving the body. Feel how the nervous system fires its electrical impulses through the body. All your senses are alert and awake to sound, sight, taste, smell, and touch. The whole inner organism is working as a whole to maintain its balance. Be conscious of our personal and archetypal physical universe.

"Let us draw together"

All our thoughts, feelings, and actions are focused as we prepare to generate a sacred space. With consciousness, prepare to enter this Holy Place and put aside worries, concerns, and preoccupations of everyday life.

"Let us form a Vessel"

Be conscious of the inner Watcher of the self: the captain of the ship of the soul; the vessel of our individuality.

"To catch the Dew of Heaven"

The dew of spiritual nourishment drops from the seventh Heaven (Kether of Briah and Tifaret of Aziluth) through all the worlds. It comes from the storehouse of life, peace, and blessings at the heart of creation (Tifaret of Briah).

"Let us rise up and go to that Holy Place of meeting"

Go where the three lower worlds meet: the Kether of Assiah, the Tifaret of Yezirah, and the Malkuth of Briah. The Seat of Solomon and the place of the self in our psyche.

"And gather there with the Companions of the Light"

Our companions, incarnate, discarnate. Our guides and teachers. The Great ones who return to assist humanity. Remember, we are a spark of the Divine, clothed in Spirit, given a form made in a body.

"Let the Veil of Heaven be drawn back"

The first Heaven or Vilon is the place where the three lower worlds meet: the Seat (throne) of Solomon. That veil protects us from looking directly into the heavenly spheres without the proper preparation (purification).

"Hear this"—Shema—Wake up! Listen!

"Malkuth"(The Kingdom)
"Yesod"(The Foundation)
"Hod"(Reverberation)
"Netzach"(Eternity)
"Tifaret"(Beauty)
"Gevurah"(Discernment and Judgement)
"Chesed"(Mercy and Love)
"Daath"(Knowledge) [this name is whispered]
"Binah"(Understanding)
"Chocmah"(Wisdom)
"Kether"(The Crown)

"Adonai,Lord"

The Shekinah, the Presence, the Immanent, the Malkuth of Aziluth.

"El Chai Shaddai - Thou art the Living Almighty"

Yesod of Aziluth - the ever-living Foundation of Life.

"Thou art Yahveh Elohim, the Holy One"

Tifaret of Aziluth— the heart of unity — Holy Oneness.

"Thou art I AM THAT I AM"

Kether of Aziluth - I am in the Now - the beginning and end.

"If it be Thy Will, let Thy Holy Spirit descend upon us today so that we may know Thy Presence. From Thee comes all Grace."
(Light the candle).

16

Meditation
Kabbalah means "to receive", therefore, meditation is key to reception and making ourselves receptive to the Mystery of creation. Kabbalah also means "inner tradition", asking us to be still and listen. It's important that we don't just listen with our physical ears, but listen with our whole being.

The Kabbalist is learning to become open and receptive without expectation. Throughout this book I will provide meditations that will support you, the reader, to achieve this. In this way, the theory becomes more alive and animated through internalization. These meditations always start with an invocation. I would like to introduce you to another meditation from the Toledano Kabbalah tradition.

First, still your body by sitting in one place, and relax through regular and constant breathing. Let your senses rest within the body, for they are allowed to follow the breathing and relaxation.

Next, go with your awareness into your subtle body and find all your thoughts, memories, feelings, and personal impressions there. Guide them into stillness and being attentive to listening. Now your physical and subtle bodies are present and aware of what might come out of the stillness.

Now, the soul and the self are brought under the conscious attention of relaxation, breathing, and stillness. Here you may become aware of the inner Watcher (the spectator of your inner movements), or silent observer who, within you, observes the meditation you are in.
You allow the whole of your being to listen in this relaxed state. Remember to let go of any expectations you may have at this point. You are only available and receptive to what might be heard through the stillness. If you remain silent and receive nothing else than silence, be content and rest within that experience.

Stay in meditation for 15 to 30 minutes. Come out of the meditation by following the Kabbalistic way of coming down the Tree of Life. If, however, you continue reading and wish to remain in this meditative state, close down after you have finished your session. Please remember that closing down and coming down the Tree of Life is essential to ground your consciousness into your physical body and bring back your inner experience to the life and being of the here and now.

Closing down
Coming down the Tree of Life at the end of a session:

"Most Gracious God,
Thou art Yahveh Elohim the Holy One
Thou art the Living Almighty
Thou art the Lord
Kether, Chocmah, Binah, Daath (whisper), Chesed, Gevurah, Tifaret, Netzach,
Hod, Yesod, Malkuth...
Holy, Holy, Holy art Thou Lord God of Hosts, Thy Glory fills all the worlds, Amen."
(Blow out the candle).

I AM
Metatron
Great
Holy
Council
Sages
Greater
Saints
MESSIAH
Sages
Lesser
Saints
Spirit
THAT
Spirit
Individuals
Soul
Soul
Self
Leaders
Ego
Masses
Body
Living dead
I AM
ADAM
KADMON
Enlightenment
Destiny
DISCARNATE
HUMANITY
Fate
ENOCH
Self-realised
Spirits
CURRENT
MESSIAH
Evolving
Spirits
Mature Souls
Developing
Souls
INCARNATE
HUMANITY
Young
Souls
Greater Mysteries : School of the Spirit
Lesser Mysteries : School of the Soul

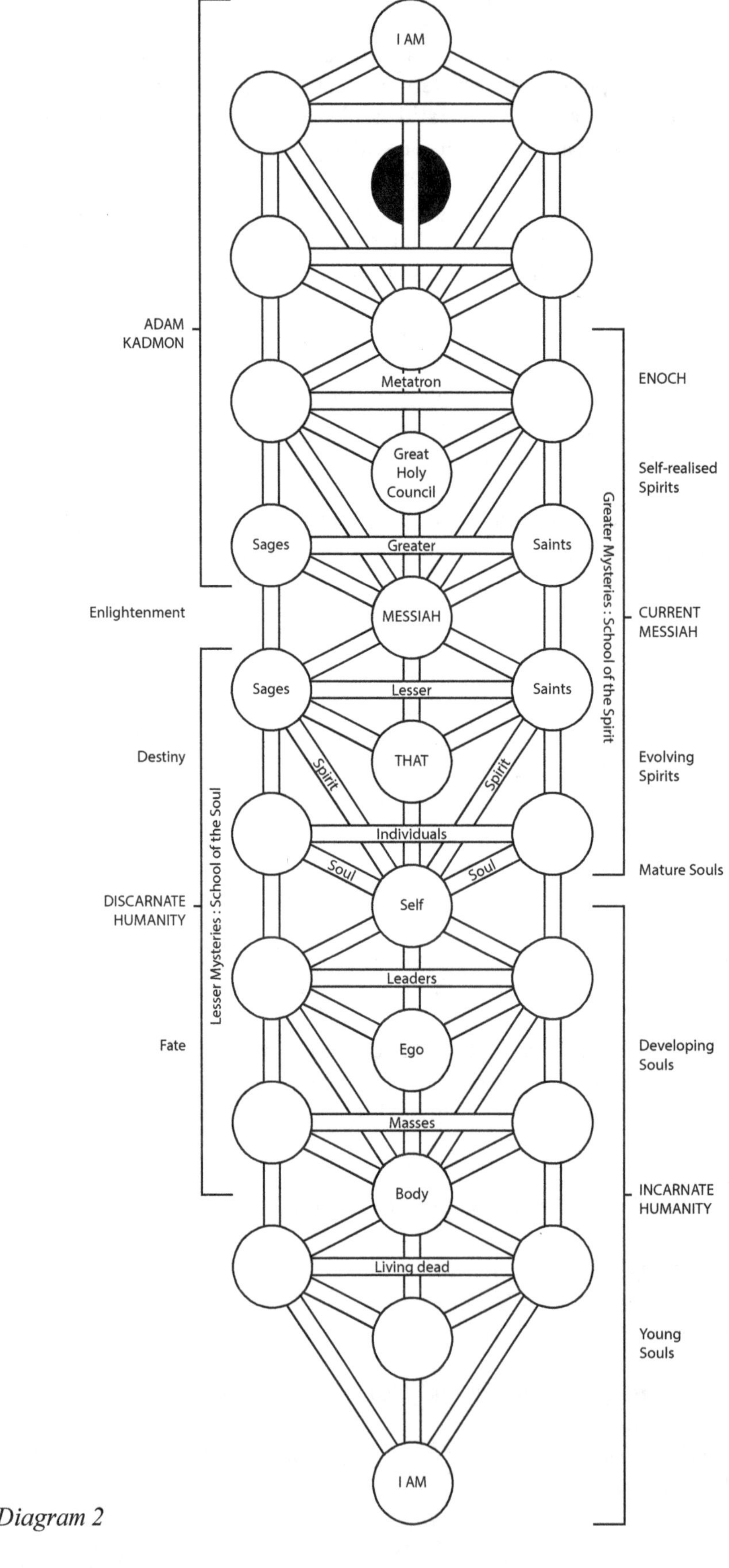

Diagram 2

18

Chapter 2: Kabbalah & Bio-psychology

The physical body in the world of Assiah is both biological and psychological, making the Human Being whole. The physical body inherently possesses all the internal & external tools to maintain its wholeness. Imagine your body as an environmentally connected instrument of wholeness. In Kabbalah, the world of Aziluth, the Divine realm, is the world of wholeness and completeness. The world of Assiah is physical existence itself, where wholeness is present. Assiah is called the world of action and, therefore, the world of movement, tension, balance, struggle, and action. Simultaneously, it is also a world of synthesis, end, and outcome.

Assiah is the ultimate world where time, space, and movement find their way into matter. Metaphysically, time-space-movement is regarded as a substance in which the phenomena of the universe can manifest as experience. The substance in the etheric body of Assiah (upper face of Assiah/ lower face of Yezirah on Jacob's Ladder) is a substance of time-space-movement which is flexible, relative, and malleable, and subject to the personal (subjective) experience of our consciousness. Although we see the physical body and the corresponding physical world around us as solid and fixed, they both move with the flow of consciousness.

Aziluth, as the ancient ground of all being, holds, sustains, and moves this substance of matter (time-space- movement) that goes in and out of existence. This life-sustaining substance in which we live and have our being is forever held in the Divine embrace of unity in the world of endless potentiality (Aziluth). Human consciousness (Yezirah) reflects the Divine consciousness in Aziluth. Through the human psyche, matter is moved (formed). In Kabbalah, we become more and more conscious that the bio-psychology of the body-mind organism we think of as 'me' is continually 'moving matter' with our thoughts, memories, energy, feelings, actions, and emotions.

To make the unconscious more conscious, firstly consider for a moment that the human being is a "mover of matter" within our physical bodies, and secondly within the physical world around us. The first consideration is easy to recognise. For example, whenever you think about something that makes you happy or sad, any chemical connected to that thought in the body is released, making the body shape into that specific quality of thought. Every thought has a chemical-electrical equivalent in the body, produced when the psyche activates certain glands to produce them.

In that sense, the biological organism has no inner moral towards what chemicals or electrical processes it brings forth. The body awaits for signals to move. Eventually, the body moves chemically and electrically, resulting in the total movement of the body, which we know as physical-motoric movements. We understand how we feel and think through awareness of body posture and behaviour. We all know how we or others behave in good, bad, or indifferent times.

Kabbalah tells us about four worlds in the diagram of Jacob's Ladder *(diagram 2)*. Assiah is the lowest world seen from a hierarchical perspective from above to below, known as the world of action. From the previous explanation, action is a forthcoming phenomenon, coming from worlds that cause this world (Assiah) to exist. Nothing moves if it is not willed from "above".

Whether they are mineral, vegetable, animal, or human, all creatures in nature are moved by subtle worlds that initiate grosser movements on the material plane of action.

Physical existence appears to be a world of effects that has no inherent causality of movement within it. The world of causation is simultaneously the world of metaphysics and the creative world called Briah. Here, the cosmic arrangements are created in concepts that are still not apparent in the substance of this existence of time-space-movement. Briah lays out the spiritual- metaphysical ground-plan or model, by virtue of what, eventually, the subtle world of Yezirah (world of formation) can formulate energetic and psychological patterns, and where the action in the world of Assiah can finally be performed.

These psychological patterns are known to the human experience as thought, memory, dreams, and feelings. Whenever energy fields manifest in the world of the psyche, an immediate identity or label is given to the activity. Your body is labelling and re-labelling, moment to moment, the story of what you are creating, even as you read this sentence. All cells, tissues, organs, and organ systems have their origin in a created conceptual design in Briah, unfolding into a psychological form that contains the properties of energy that will finally find their way into the world of action.

The movement that Kabbalah named the "Tzimtzum", or Lightning Flash, descends the world of emanation or Aziluth as the Divine action. Divine Will in Aziluth has nothing to do with some superstitious belief or fatalistic religious idea of Divinity. Aziluth is the world that "calls forth" the completeness and unity of existence. From this world, all that existed, exists now, and all that ever will exist descends through the three lower worlds, entering gradually into time-space-movement.

What is called forth is perfect because all that is created (Briah) is willed from the Divine world (Aziluth). You are here because it is willed. We are all part of the unified consciousness that pervades and contains all. All comes from unity, and all will return to unity.

That is the Will whose influence comes down the Kabbalistic worlds, constructing a cosmos that resonates with countless frequencies of that One Will. Responding to the One Will is the Kabbalistic Way of Return (teshuva), a path of reconciliation with the original world that constantly influences and moves us.

In the tradition of Kabbalah, this is the way of correction whenever the human soul goes astray from the path of unity, suffering the more extreme effects when we wander off on the path of the side pillars on the Tree of Life. Of course, it is impossible, as a time-space-movement creature, to live in unity within existence. It would draw us out of the engagement and connection with the world and all creation.

Because of the refined movement of the Lightning Flash, unity mirrors itself into existence, alternating and involving itself within its being. Unity in creation is the law of harmony, where all is in balance, compared to the scales of justice.
If you pay attention to your breath at this very moment, you may notice that while reading, there is a calm rhythm and movement of the chest and belly. But if you decide to run for five minutes, your breathing will change. After running and returning to your chair, your breathing returns to calmness.

In the tradition of Kabbalah, the primordial world of Aziluth (Divine) is the world of Principles. These are the ten Sefirot that contain the Ten Divine Names.
All other worlds that are created, formed and made from this world of emanation are based upon this world of principles. The world that is created out of this first world is called Briah, and is the world of creation and metaphysical laws.

Here is a simple example of how these metaphysical laws from the world of Briah operate through millions of physical processes in the physical world of action (Assiah):

"Action is law-bound, while action is derived from law." In other words: all our actions in Assiah are bound by metaphysical laws. The first great law in Kabbalah is the law of unity. Although our actions may lead to division and more disintegration, the law of unity brings everything back to a state of dynamic balance (unity in movement).

The world of action does not consist of random movements coming out of a rigid mechanical system. Law expresses how Divinity calls forth (Aziluth), creates (Briah), forms (Yezirah), and makes (Assiah) Itself into a likeness of movements and actions in the world of time-space. All the actions within your body and the actions without are effects of Divine influences that pervades all the Kabbalistic worlds.

Therefore, the Divine Will is present in all the worlds, and all actions in the physical world are eventually all coming from this world of Emanation (Aziluth). Your heart beats, and your blood flows, cells are generated and broken down, air is breathed in and out. All these physical actions are willed from the Divine world and made possible through the world of metaphysical Law (Briah).

Every action, whether conscious or unconscious, has its origin in the Divine world. In most mystical traditions, the unreachable transcendence can be reached and known through the Immanence that lives within creation and the ultimate world of action: Assiah. This final world is the realm of blessing as the Holy One acts through all things and beings in a fantastic theatre play.

Have you ever thought about this? That every movement and action you make is a move made first and foremost in Divine action. We do not move by ourselves, but are moved continuously by the influence of the Divine. For the Kabbalist and mystic, transcendence and immanence do not differ in their experience, except that Divinity is beholding its creation through the eyes of the Immanent beholder. This is the direct experience when the Kabbalist knows who is looking (beholding) through their being.

Every movement is a potential Divine action, becoming an actual Divine action when the beholder knows who beholds whom. The Highest Divine Name on the Tree of Life is granted to the Crown or Kether, and pronounced as: "I Am that I Am". Within that Name lies the realisation that God beholds God. Every moment in relative existence is an Eternal possibility of this realisation. All action is a movement coming out of Eternity.

Eternity unfolds from moment to moment. Eternity has nothing to do with time, except that all time-space-movement derives from Eternity.

The tradition of Kabbalah transmits that in the human experience, Eternity does not exist in time- space-movement; rather, it envelops and contains it. At the heart of the Tree of Life in the Sefira of Tifaret, the consciousness that touches upon the soul witnesses Eternity and time-space-movement simultaneously. The moment such a state of awareness dawns, the soul becomes self-aware of who is looking and brings heaven to earth through its own being.

I want to emphasize that there are no specific actions in life more Holy or sacred than others. All internal and external actions in the world of Assiah come out of Divine action, but become actual Divine actions, if the actor (doer) is fully conscious of the action and who performs it.

From this perspective, no one has ownership over or may claim what is sacred action and what is not. Direct experience is the key to understanding this spiritual idea. Direct experience can never exclude any actions in life, because we all have our moments of mystical knowing. Sports and other common activities are not just secular and mundane forms of action. When made conscious, they are as sacred as a religious ritual. Every moment of action is, therefore, transformed into a Divine activity.

Let me share some words that may be said before having a meal, transforming your consciousness in order that you come to know who is eating whom. In such a way, we can all generate a mini-Eucharist at any time. The text goes as follows: "As Thou art present in all things, so Thou art present in that which I consume, and through it I will become as I Am."

Action and the Middle Pillar
Looking at the Tree of Life *(diagram 3)* and the Divine movement of Tzimtzum or Lightning Flash (contraction), we see that Malkuth (Kingdom) is the last and ultimate Sefira on the Tree of Life. All the nine expressions of the Divine culminate and flow together into physical manifestation and the world of action.

The side pillars on the Tree of Life come together as the principles of form and energy. Therefore, Malkuth and the world of Assiah is energy (right pillar) that moves forms (left pillar). A force without form has no object or vessel to move through. A form without force is stagnant and inert. Both pillars join in the Kingdom on the Tree of Life, where mineral, vegetable, animal, and human levels all move in their particular forms. Although we are composed of the same materials, no one and nothing is the same in its composition.

Tiferet of Beriah — Keter of Yezirah
Passive Intellect
Active Intellect
Spirit
Passive Concepts
Active Concepts
Passive Emotion
Active Emotion
Soul
Self
Passive Emotional Complexes
Active Emotional Complexes
Awakening Consciousness
Threshold
Feelings
Passive Biopsycho processes
Active Biopsycho processes
Passive Electronic Processes
Active Electronic Processes
Thoughts
Actions
Ego
Anabolic
Katabolic
Metabolism
Passive Chemical Processes
Active Chemical Processes
Body Central Nervous System
Tissue
Passive Bio-processes
Active Bio-processes
Organs
Auto-nomic Nervous System
Nerves
Muscles
Skin Bones Sense-Organs
Place where three upper Worlds meet
Place where three lower Worlds meet
Yezirah Psyche World of Formation
Assiah Body World of Making

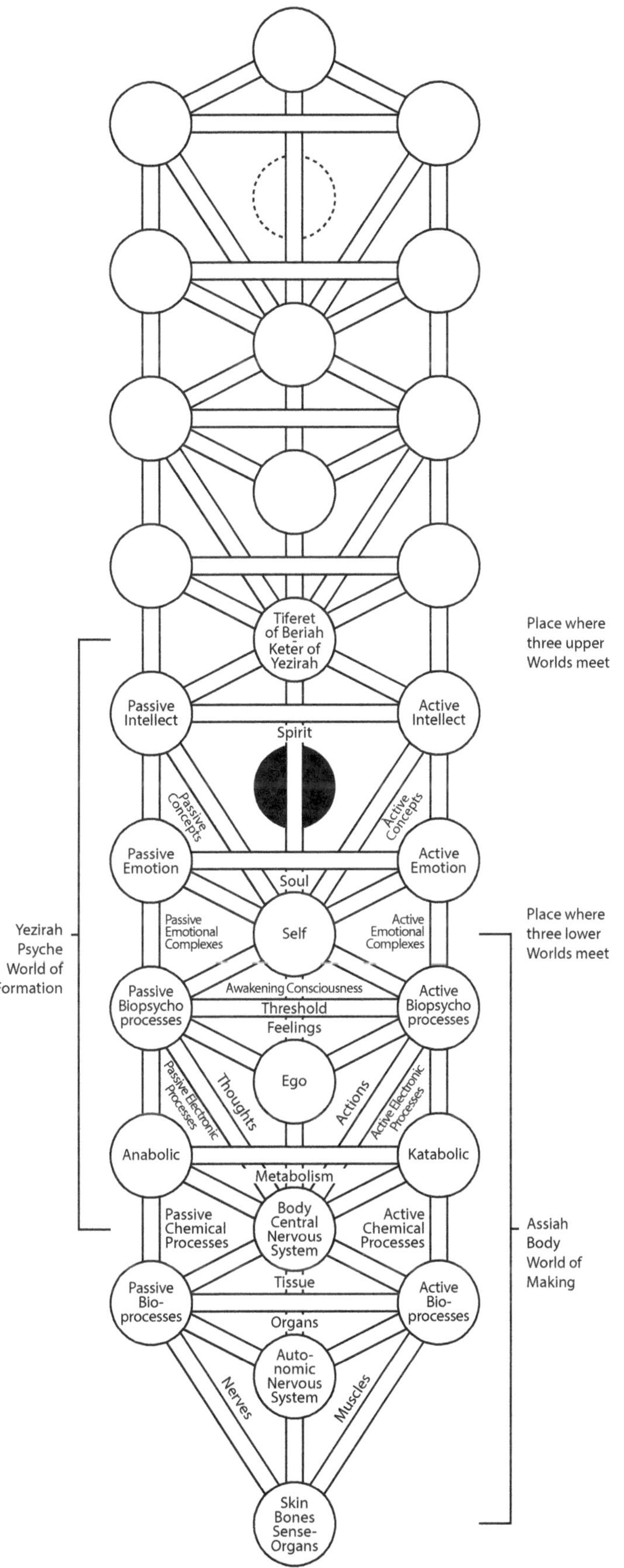

Diagram 3

Lions look the same, but they each have their distinct features. And so do Human Beings, but although they have received "coats of skin" (Genesis) or animal bodies, their psyche is much more advanced than any other animal. Force and form (Chocmah and Binah) give rise to how the energy moves, and what form it takes. Between force and form, there is a mystery (the unity of Kether), which is that ground of being who holds everything in perfect peace and Eternal stillness.

Imagine that in spite of all your actions (unconscious or conscious), there is always something that does not move and is unaffected by this ever-moving body of action. This center of unity and stillness makes sure that all returns to harmony and balance between the endless movement between force and form.

At the base Sefira on the Tree of Life, the physical body and the whole of physical existence may experience bliss through action. Whenever an action is performed with the direct experience of the Eternal in the flow between force and form, bliss is a possibility for any human being. Sometimes it is said that only creatures with a soul receive bliss and find themselves in exalted states of consciousness. Yet, when a creature experiences itself through its natural form and force, in-between this state of unity as the conscious ground of its being, a state of bliss may be known to anyone or anything.

God beholding God, or "I Am that I Am", is not reserved for the human species only, but to all creation that came down into the world of action. Assiah is the so-called last world on Jacob's Ladder, complementing the unfolding of the three higher worlds. Although this world is a completion of the Divine Will developing through successive stages into the material universe, there appears to be a new beginning within this completion.

Divine actions brings the world of matter into being. After this completion, the human being and all of the natural world are called to action to move back up the ladder. All of nature is called back to its Source. In Kabbalah, through human actions, we re-connect with the Divine action that eventually brought time-space-movement into existence. Of course, we are not so aware that our actions are Divine actions. Such a realisation can only come when we see our worldly actions in the light of Divinity moving through us. We are moved by it.

Imagine for a moment that the movement of your breath is not coming from yourself and the body you inhabit, but is the breath of the Holy Spirit who breathes through you. The Kabbalist asks: "Do I breathe, or I am being breathed?"

As soon as we are born into this world that we call earth, we are introduced to the Malkuth of Assiah, where we receive a body (vehicle) made from and for this earth. The senses that are the tools for that vehicle detect the physical surroundings on five different levels and frequencies. Each of the senses has its specific way of getting to know the world around us. Now that we have a body, the senses are directed outwardly, and they can give back the information obtained from the environment, transferring it through neurological means towards the inside of the body.

There is a continuous exchange of information going on from the inside of the body-mind organism to the outside, and vice versa. The five senses are like a window from an inside reality to an outside reality. The experiences we have as an individual shape the relationship between an inner and an outer physical world. While the senses detect the physical world of duality (force and form) around us, they are not able to come to any direct mystical experience of the world or themselves.

All senses come in pairs: you have two eyes, two ears, two nostrils, two sides of the tongue and two hands. Like the two side pillars on the Tree of Life, the senses come in pairs to be able to observe the physical world and the relationship with the inner physical world. The five senses are the perfect, physical tools to observe and become aware of these inner and outer worlds.

Imagine that you have no senses or that your senses will not function. You would become completely inert and unable to take the initiative to move. Receiving no information from your senses and the environment blocks your sensitive input that you need to interact with the world. Apart from stimuli from the exterior world and the corresponding interior reactions, the interior stimuli come from the so-called interior senses.

Kabbalistically, the interior senses are the five ways of sensitive experience to be found in the psychological domain, where the Yesod of Yezirah overlays the Daath of Assiah. Some people wonder about Daath, as its abstraction is often difficult to grasp by the thinking mind. Daath is situated around the face and head on the Tree of Life, therefore covering the interior senses anatomically at the upper face of Assiah, respectively the lower face of Yezirah.

When going into our dreams, fantasies, visualizations, and meditations, our mirror of Yesod (Yezirah) generates images coming from our unconscious mind and physical impulse system in Daath (Assiah). The physical body and the ordinary mind (Yesod) have a story to tell about our interior life. Organic life has an intelligence of its own. Each organ has a particular structure, function and development in the human body. Each of them communicates with the other. In turn, these organs and organ systems transmit and receive important information to the psychological world through the Yesod ego at the Daath of Assiah.

Contemporary times (21st century)
Stress is a major factor in the daily lives of many people on this planet. Instead of surviving under natural circumstances as our ancestors did, we have to survive in the civilization that we have made. Surely, I can mainly write from the experiences in the western (north-western Europe) part of this world. Having said this, I know that other parts of the world have different cultural structures that suffer the same problems.

There is a global tendency that the only good way forward is growth, expansion, and development (principle of Chesed), and that contraction, decline, or restriction of growth (principle of Gevurah) is bad or counterproductive to any process that leads to wellbeing. In the workplace, many jobs, environments with unhealthy atmospheres, stress and pressure to attain higher targets, profits, and production, causes an imbalance of the human bio-psychological system. This is the world of Assiah on Jacob's Ladder.

Here, the lower face of the Tree of Assiah is completely physical and made up of the four elements. The upper face of Assiah is also the lower face of the world of Yezirah, the world of the psyche, corresponding to the subtle substance known as the etheric body, which is electro-magnetic in nature.

Both parts of the world of Assiah connect with these levels of our inner and outer nature. The lower face interacts with all that is physical in- and outside, while the upper face interacts with all that corresponds to the etheric body, feeling and sensing the world around us. The human, as an organism, depends greatly on how it interacts and corresponds to the outer circumstances and changes of the environment in our daily affairs. In addition, many of the psychological-ego stresses and pressures depend on the opinions, demands, and expectations of others.

The organism that consists of the mineral, vegetable, and animal levels wishes to have consistency and a structure within living. Our bio-rhythms (Hod of Assiah) and cycles (Netzach of Assiah) and the autonomic nervous system (Yesod of Assiah) work together with the psychological cycles within the triad of Yesod of Yezirah (ego, persona, and shadow) and Hod (thoughts) and Netzach (feelings).

In current times, at schools, children experience increased pressure and stress related to the same dynamics. The so-called burnout is not reserved for the adult any longer. Many children suffer the consequences of an economy that rests upon a careless consumerist approach, meaning that we need people to produce what we wish for, and simultaneously make money to spend it on those same products. We are stimulated to buy more than we wish for through commercials and other media. Society prepares children in school to be a part of the machinery of the economy.

That often means that pressure goes up through the demands and responsibilities coming from school. The more demanding society becomes, the more demanding the school system becomes.

Children are often not stimulated by their society and culture to develop where their heart (Tifaret on the Tree of Life) is, in order to give shape to their fate. There is less time in schools to cater for children who need an individual form of attention. The mechanical system on the Tree of Life at the lower face of the vegetable-level principle within a person and the group we belong to. Stress is all around us and within us.

Stress is not a bad thing in itself, for it invites us and stimulates us to grow biologically, psychologically, and spiritually. I am mentioning here the continuous and consistent overdose of stress-related programming in our lives. In Kabbalah, you could see stress as a result of an imbalance between the two side pillars. If both pillars of force and form do not come together and reconcile, complement, and combine, then they oppose, withstand, and push away one another. The amount of tension and stress this causes depends on the duration of the disharmony and imbalance between the pillars.

The Kabbalist's work is to re-balance the pillars in the central axis or middle pillar. We experience a flow of harmony and balance in the centres or Sefirot on the middle pillar *(diagram 4)*.

There are other ways of trying to compensate for the imbalance in our lives. These are short-term solutions like alcohol, drugs, and playing games. Through modern technology, computers, and cell phones, the stream of data and information is gathered by the psyche as much as possible, and then stored on a subliminal level. Some people feel that they are missing out on something if they do not participate and gather enough information. This is an over-stimulus coming from the left side pillar on the Tree of Life and, in particular, an influence of the Sefira Hod.

The nervous system and the chemical endocrine system in the world of Assiah have a hard time digesting all these streams and quanta of data. There is hardly any time to digest and incorporate the incoming information. The more stress or tension from the opposing forces between the pillars on the Tree of Life, the more stress chemicals like peptides, hormones, and neurotransmitters the bio-psychological intelligent system will release. With enough and enduring stimuli of stress and even anxiety, our bodies become stressed and anxious. How we feel is how we chemically become.

The body and psyche "digest" this stress by producing counter-chemicals released in the endocrine glands and nervous system. These counter-chemicals are known as endorphin, dopamine, and GABA (gamma-aminobutyric acid). There are several ways to release these hormones and neurotransmitters into our bodies. Not all of them are positive in the end, like rewarding yourself with malnutrition and junk food. Sugar and salt are well-known additives that give us quick and short relief from stress, anxiety, and fear.

These products, along with alcohol and soft drugs, do indeed bring stress levels down, but they lower our ability to cope with stress in the long term. One of the causes for this is that we make our chemical system lazy by overproducing endorphins so quickly and too easily. To eat less in these times is, in general, good advice. Not only do we overeat, but we digest too many substances that compensate for our stress, anxiety, and many other emotions that we feel we cannot master. A lot of food is bad for our physical body, heart, and other organs, as well as our auto-immune system.

Dopamine addiction is also a problem belonging to the modern age. It is that hormone that makes us feel worthy, appreciated, and rewarded. On many social media platforms and fora, people post material hoping others will "like" it. Through time, a dependency on that reaction of reward will grow (Chesed as the ego-ideal in the world of Yezirah). You can see this, for example, when people "like" each other's messages and give a "thumbs up".

The more we depend on reward (ego-ideal), the more we crave a reward. Our bio-psychological mechanism that resonates with reward (centered in the ego-Yesod, and mainly leaning towards the right pillar with the active emotional complexes) becomes less or insensitive to reward and needs more stimuli to feel appreciated and rewarded. We bind our body and psyche to certain conditions of behaviour that we think will help us overcome stress and unhappiness.

Human nature in general, and particularly the Yesodic ego state of our psyche, is quite infantile in its approach to life. The ego reacts easily and directly to punishment (Gevurah of Yezirah or super-ego) and reward (Chesed of Yezirah or ego-ideal). From this system and mechanism, we like to avoid negative experiences and embrace positive experiences. If we follow these impulses constantly, the inner and outer movement shifts from our left-side pillar towards the right-side pillar and vice versa.

The more we lean towards reward and positive input, the more we become dependent on it and the more difficult it becomes to find new stimuli to feel rewarded. The more we stimulate our sensitivity for reward (success), the more dopamine and endorphins are released. The earlier mentioned substance GABA makes us feel more relaxed. The problem mentioned earlier in these times is about the dynamics between the pillars on the Tree of Life, where both side pillars receive too much pressure.

The psychological imbalance causes an electro-chemical imbalance between the pillars, thus generating a field of tension between the pillars, that is, in the middle pillar. You experience this as discomfort or stress in the body (Malkuth) or the psyche (Yesod) within your thoughts, feelings and actions. This field of tension between the pillars also generates an image of yourself and the immediate world. These images under the conditions of tension between the pillars are negative towards yourself and your surroundings. This tension overloads the reward (Chesed) and punishment (Gevurah) systems.

The more stress on the left side, the more we need to activate the right side and find stimuli that produce substances like dopamine and other opiates. The more we produce them (to prevent stress or the fear of getting stress), the more we become resistant to them. Addiction is in the making. The centre is lost, and the middle pillar has no stability and no way to re-balance the side pillars.

When we exhaust the level of endorphins and opiates in our body, we not only become less resistant to stress, we are more prone to get depressed, and are drawn towards negativity. Instead of moving away from an excessive leaning on the left pillar (which causes depression, fear, and anxiety), we are more drawn towards it by overstimulating the right-side pillar.

As the anti-stress hormones are substances like endorphin, dopamine, melatonin, and oxytocin, one of the stress hormones that function like their "opponent" is testosterone. While the first group draw us towards good social contacts and willingness to unite with others, testosterone upholds the urge to defend and stand in one's own right. Endorphins draw us towards the right pillar and the power of Netzach, which is all about social relationships and intimacy.

Tiferet
of Beriah
Keter of
Yezirah
Passive
Intellect
Active
Intellect
Spirit
Passive
Concepts
Active
Concepts
Passive
Emotion
Active
Emotion
Soul
Self
regulation
of
organism
Life
form
Life
force
Feeling
Ego /
Knowledge
of the
organism
Thoughts
Actions
Anabolic
Katabolic
Function
of the cell
membrane
Monitoring
System
Circulatory
System
Function
of the
DNA
Physical
DNA
Place where
three upper
Worlds meet
Place where
three lower
Worlds meet
Assiah
Body
World of
Making
Yezirah
Psyche
World of
Formation

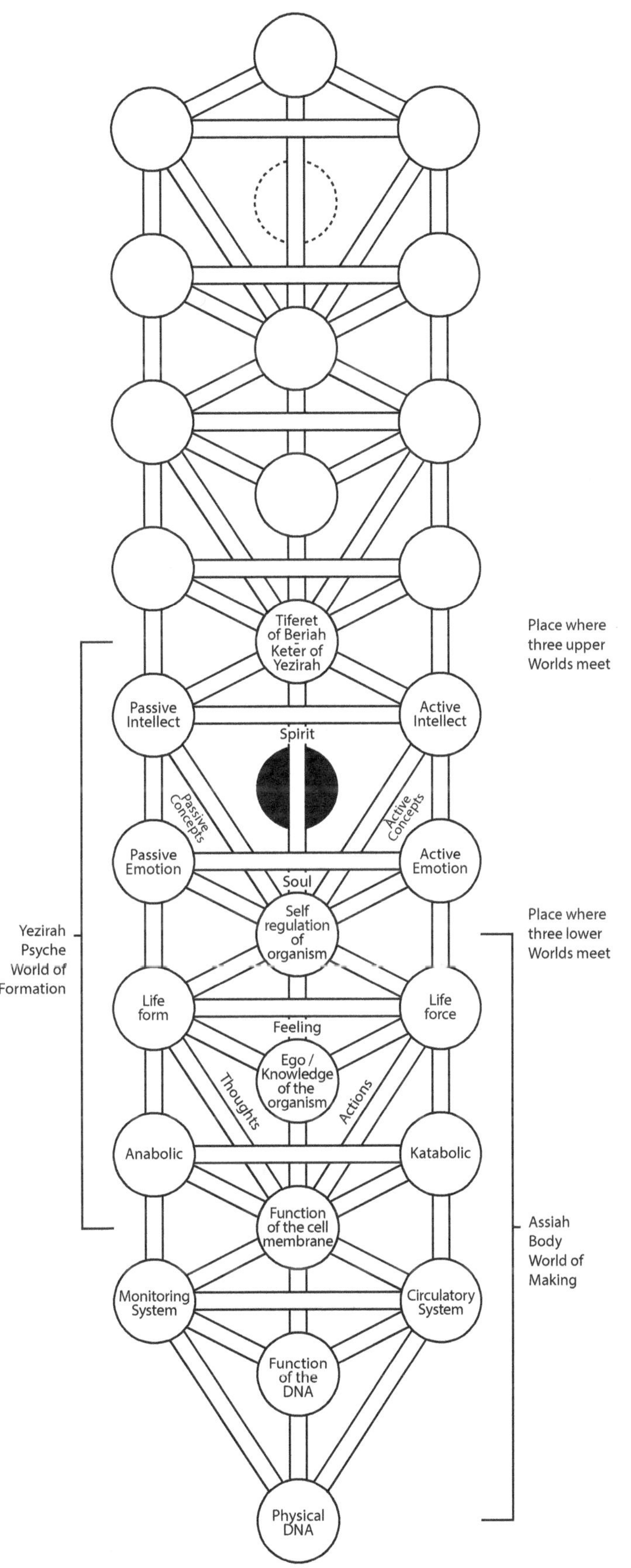

Diagram 4

Testosterone stimulates us to be in the left-side pillar, with its focus (Hod) on the individual mind and cognition. If there is a lot of testosterone in our system (world of Assiah), it will block and hinder the production of opiates. It also prevents us from changing our behaviour and moving out of our stagnation of self-righteousness and a defending attitude towards others.

Testosterone pushes us into action to fight or flee, and give a direct reaction to immediate danger. The tricky part is letting our inner system believe that we are in danger in times of relative peace. The demands and expectations of society and ourselves make us live in a kind of jungle in which we have to survive. The more we think we need to be successful and productive and live up to life expectations, the more we become stressed and even depressed, with feelings of powerlessness. As endorphins generate oxytocin and thereby generate feelings of belonging, good partnership, and loyalty, so does testosterone lead us away from a good relationship, loyalty, and trustworthiness.

Too much testosterone makes us more suspicious or paranoid (the triad of passive emotional complexes in Yezirah). Testosterone is a hormone that stimulates and activates the human being (principle of the right pillar on the Tree of Life). It gives us the ability to conquer others or a situation by force (left pillar Gevurah).

Endorphin is a hormone that sedates pain and is stress-relieving. In general, these opiate hormones make us happy and feel good. It brings us in a mode of "conquering" through love and affection. Testosterone makes us ready for the active "hunt", stimulating us to conquer a situation or a person, following the reproductive impulse of nature to propagate with anyone, as long as the species survives. Oxytocin enables two partners or friends to meet each other in mutual respect and agreement when there is a dispute or argument.

The trained Kabbalist watches the process unfold, noticing when one or the other extreme (Hod left pillar and Netzach right pillar, influences of testosterone or endorphin) takes dominance. By choice or free Will (soul triad), the Kabbalist can change their thoughts, feelings, and actions to compensate for the imbalanced situation.

People who find it difficult to attach to others and commit themselves have problems producing enough right-pillar opiates. In turn, they react defensively and, under testosterone production, become dominant in relationships and prone to addictions to release anti-stress hormones. If you look at the Tree of Life diagram in this chapter, you will see that in the Hod and Netzach of Yezirah, we find the principles of the mortido and libido, respectively.

Trans-generational influences
Many problems that we experience as human beings, and relive throughout our lives, are not always coming directly from our personal experiences. Biologically and psychologically, we come from a lineage of people who went before us. This inheritance from our physiological family has passed on their memories to us in the form of DNA.

This substance in each cell's core consists of hereditary material that stores and communicates information throughout your body. These codes of information are complex combinations of amino acids (proteins) that can present themselves in countless ways. DNA is like a library within each physical cell that stores and transmits physiological information coming from all these processes and states in the body and psyche. If DNA wishes to transmit certain information, it will make a chemical clone of itself called RNA.

DNA is a fixed and unmovable part in the nucleus of each cell in the body, and therefore, it cannot "travel" through the body to give out information itself.
It needs to send out messages through a chemical construction that consists of specific information. In return, the core of each cell and the DNA present therein receives input from chemical messengers coming from others cells. DNA is a filing system or library and is able to direct information to other cells (principle of the Sefira Hod on the Tree of Life - *diagram 4*).

RNA is the messenger chemical made by DNA in every cell in the body (in Kabbalah, an "Angel" translates as a "messenger"). RNA messages are sent to those parts of the body that need it. In turn, DNA receives thousands of messages from the organism's intelligence. The DNA structure that we have inherited holds all kinds of qualities that we may recognise in our family line.
Some may be positive or negative in your personal opinion, but these are some reflections that you can consider as a Kabbalist who wishes to learn through the body and psyche.

The physiological body on the Tree of Life, corresponding with the world of Assiah, communicates to us through neuro-chemical transmission. It transmits and receives physical messages and information throughout the whole organism, that is, information from all the three upper worlds (Aziluth, Briah and Yezirah). From this metaphysical perspective, we cannot state that biological chemicals and neurotransmitters are only physical. They are physical interpretations of Divine (Aziluth), Spiritual (Briah), psychological (Yezirah), and physical (Assiah) levels of Being.

Metaphysically, they follow the Lightning Flash or Tzimtzum down the worlds of Emanation, Creation, Formation, and Action. The metaphor of a Lightning Flash running through all worlds and the world of Assiah is spiritually appropriate. The neuro-chemical basis of all communication in the physical body is electromagnetic energy transmitted like a lightning flash.

The Lightning Flash is God's Will that runs through all the worlds as it unfolds through the ten stages of neuro-chemical intelligence. We are physically born through the sequence of the Lightning Flash, finding its way from the Crown (Kether) into the Kingdom (Malkuth), where it brings all that ever was before you into your physical Being. The physical memories that are growing throughout time, extending upon the lineage of ancestors, bring more and more experiences and information into the next generation.

The passing on of memories is the way of natural evolution. It does not mean, however, that we are talking automatically about psychological or even spiritual evolution. As a human being, you should first become aware of the chain of ancestral information that has incarnated into you. Your body is a temporary amalgam of all the ancestral history within your Being. It does not mean that you are aware of all this information and wisdom that came down the ages. Some of it may be extremely useful and fascinating. Other memories may come to you as traumas, fears, or sadness that do not correlate with your current incarnation awareness or personal experiences.

Therefore, these are not personal memories (personal consciousness in Yesod of Yezirah), but they rather come from a deeper unconscious and biological memory (DNA). Sometimes this is called transgenerational memory. You inherit certain information and experiences that your ancestors have not processed. You may inherit the karmic stains that did not get purified in their lifetime. In Kabbalistic terms, we can say that the Work (Ma'aseh) is not (yet) completed. It is possible for a generation that has woken up to ancestral "stains" to recover from them, and heal them in their lifetime.

Eventually, they are part of our responsibility. Let us not judge our ancestors, who may not have been aware of their fate and personal development. Just as we all suffer from blind spots in our own lives, we come from lineages of people who could not see, and therefore work on their fate.
There are two biological/chemical substances in our bodies that relate to our ability to engage, work, and let go of old patterns belonging to our parents or previous generation: GABA (gamma- aminobutyric acid) and Dynorphin, the opposite chemical of Glutamate.

GABA and Dynorphin make us let go of traumatic and difficult memories and experiences. Glutamates makes us hold onto things that belong in the past (even if these memories are not good for us). It's not as simple as GABA / Dynorphin is positive, and Glutamate is negative; however, people who have a considerable resistance against Glutamates and release GABA and Dynorphin easily, can go through life without realising what they could be clearing. These people bypass the difficult personal memories that are useful for the inner work of the Kabbalist. There should be a healthy mentality towards the other side, where we hold on to memories with the deeper meaning and purpose of learning from them.

If old memories (traumas included) only serve feelings of regret, guilt, nostalgia, and pain, they do not bring us any further, but stagnate and keep us away from the path of inner growth. Like so many things in Kabbalistic mysticism, we are invited to bring all things back to a sacred middle on the Tree of Life.
The nervous system works in such a way that not all information is blocked or permitted. There is a very intelligent mechanism at work here.

When you have a negative experience (tension between the pillars or a "weight" on one of the side pillars), the central nervous system (Tifaret of Assiah) with its Hippocampus, will regulate these unpleasant short-term memories and emotions. If the experience is accepted or even integrated into that short-term memory, the system can let the experience go (Dynorphin / GABA effect). If the negative experience is not accepted, the negative signal migrates to another centre called the amygdala. Here, we find long-term memories under the influence of Glutamate. From the last example, we inherit the memories from former generations and learn about dangers and complexities that we have not encountered yet. As I have described above, it may also lead to dysregulations and psychological problems that travel through generations.

Like I explained in my first volume of "A Kabbalistic View on Science", our inherited genetic properties are relatively fixed and unchangeable. In computing, we can reset our devices back to their factory settings, and we can similarly influence the "software" inscribed on our DNA. Fear is something we might inherit through former generations, but it is something that we can change by making adaptations in our inner- and outer worlds.

Changing outer conditions with our food, hygiene, sleep, social contacts, and sports is no different than changing our inner thoughts, actions, feelings, and emotions, even if at a particular level (Yesod of Yezirah), we psychologically do not believe that we can change these significant and fundamental things about ourselves.

After all, Yesod is not the psychological mechanism that makes for change, growth, and transformation. It is that part of the psyche that generates and regenerates processes and makes sure that, physiologically and psychologically, all returns within movements of cycles. With the epigenetics approach, we see the human being as we do in Kabbalah; as one being that reflects many worlds.

Any inner work or analyses of internal problems should be approached as such: the human being as a whole. The universe and all that lives in it is organic and far from being mechanical. All is connected and interdependent. Any denial of our totality leads to a division of this wholeness. Therefore, the Kabbalist is open and receptive to the possibilities within; whether they are positive or negative. It is no use to suppress or repress the unconscious content of our psyche and work only on the symptoms of what seems to be 'wrong' with us.

To come to an enduring balance and harmony within ourselves and our relationship with the world, we have to undertake the gradual journey within the unconscious. As I said at the beginning of this book: "the physical body is not here to be born and die, but to make ourselves whole". I could add that the body contributes to bringing our whole being back into balance and harmony. Although Jacob's Ladder's higher worlds continuously influence the lower worlds (Assiah), it is also possible to alter and change the higher worlds through adaptations and changes in the physical body (Assiah).

After all, we know from Kabbalah that all the worlds are within each other, and Spirit and matter are not separate. We are very responsible for our process through the body itself and by becoming awake to the complex connections between the body and psyche. Also, when we have to deal with inner problems and genetic and hereditary factors, we are confronted with the fact that we are part of that process. Healing and wholeness start with us.

Fear and anxiety, for example, lead to a deficiency in behaviour, for these constantly ask to be in control (while you are not), and the more alert you become, the more stress your system will generate. The stronger our physical and psychological stress, the less in control and the more fearful and anxious we might become. These problems come from a deep, unconscious ground that may go on for lifetimes or have deep roots in our lifetime.

Whatever the case may be, for the Kabbalist, we know that cognition (Hod and the triad of contemplation) cannot solve the problem by itself. Simply changing behaviour (Netzach and triad of action) doesn't do the trick either, nor will a fundamental change come from the feeling triad. A strong memory of sensations of fear and anxiety resides in the physical body itself and reacts impulsively to any condition related to a signal of fear or anxiety. The physical body, in that respect, is a loyal partner and gives the proper reaction to what it has learned to do through conditioning (vegetable triad).

We can easily condition the body itself to be very alert and to not lose control. This effort may cause exhaustion of the body to occur, bringing about diabetes and stress reaction through high concentrations of cortisol and adrenalin (left-side pillar and triad of passive hormones and enzymes).

To feel in danger when you do not cause an inner and outer movement of contraction (left pillar principle of Gevurah) draws us away from becoming free from fear and the urge to control. Over-activity in our inner system (on the left pillar) takes us back in time. We find ourselves reviewing our past, negative memories, nostalgia, and feelings of melancholia. Shame and guilt are other emotions that play a part in this over-activity. When the psychological imbalance enters the neuro-chemical system, the physical cells adopt and integrate the information they have received from the subtle levels of the psyche (upper face of Assiah and lower face of Yezirah). When fear and anxiety manifest and materialise in the physical body, they are rooted in our system.

Though the psychological problem might have ended, the symptoms may remain inside our physical body and behaviour. For better or for worse, the power of the three higher worlds coming down are finally being manifested in the world of action. The physical senses respond to whatever the body is conditioned to do. It sees the world through our senses, not as it is. We are made ready to face many different challenges that we have not encountered before in our lives through ancestral memories.

The heritage of our DNA gives us the ability to react to outer stimuli, and thereby, have a better chance of survival and anticipation in life. People who follow a completely different path and lead a different life than their ancestors will have to learn their unique experiences for the first time. This often happens to people on a spiritual path that ancestors never walked before. It is extremely useful to learn more about our spiritual ancestral and trans-generational memories. We are often unaware of the chain of cultural and personal memories that reveal the origins of our many unconscious, conditioned habits.

From the lower part of the Assiatic Tree, we can see that our ancestral memories
replay themselves in our actions without understanding how or why.
These dynamics you can see in the voluntary and involuntary rhythms and cycles
at the Hod and Netzach of Assiah. If your family background is known for its
soldiers and military, it will bring memories of those influences.

The Kabbalist, becoming aware (awakening triad) of these dynamics, can choose
what to do with these influences. A man who came from a generation of sailors
had an intense fear of water, even though he never had any traumatic experience
of drowning. Many of his forefathers died at sea, and these memories took root in
the family DNA. This man did not develop an urge to sail or work on a boat but
manifested the fear of drowning. As a child, he had a fear of water and could not
learn to swim. In this example, the hereditary memory was useful and practical to
warn of the dangers of water, yet, he had to overcome the absolute anxiety and
fear of water to develop a healthy relationship with water and learn how to swim.

These memories at the side triads in the world of Yezirah, interlocking with Briah,
are the passive and active cultural concepts, which are the deeper, unconscious
influences transmitted through culture and family. As mentioned above, they
contain profound motives about why we act the way we do in this lifetime.
Every family and culture, in that sense, has its karma to carry and to resolve.

The pillars on the Tree of Life could represent the nocebo (left pillar extreme) or
placebo (right pillar extreme) effect. How is it possible that children of depressed
and negative-oriented parents are positive with a happy perspective on life?
The first-generation of parents do not seem to pass on their same traits and
qualities. These parents do not teach the children how to behave positively
towards life either (as they do not know any better). Regardless, there are children
who, despite their situation (family environment), create a new and original way
of Being.

There are many different causes. First of all, a human soul does not come into the
world as an empty vessel. It carries with it experiences in memory from past
incarnations. These are not the passed on trans-genetic hereditary data (DNA),
but the psychological experiences that the soul has gathered over lifetimes.

Placebo is activated through right pillar activity, resulting in a chemical activity
by releasing endorphins and dopamine. These chemicals give us a sensation of
happiness, are life-affirming (libido), and give us feelings of hope. In situations
of pain, they can give relief, sedate, empower the immune system and support
the body's regeneration. Endorphins bring down the level of stress hormones.

Without the tension of the left pillar, these substances and chemicals would not be
produced and released. There must be tension in our nature to come to harmony
and balance. It may be needless to say, but the left pillar generates and releases
the opposite chemicals in the body that cause a negative pattern of expectations to
life (mortido). If this side of the Tree is psychologically and chemically activated,
the outlook on life is negative, low, and inclined towards depression or anxiety.

People with a tendency towards this extreme behaviour, boycott themselves and lower their psycho-physiological immune system. The hormone released under nocebo activity is cholecystokinin, which blocks the endorphins and dopamine on the other side of the Tree of Life. Glutamate is produced in higher quantities in the Hippocampus.

Normally, the Hippocampus filters out feelings of anxiety and fear, but in case of a disturbance that causes the nocebo effect, the psyche cannot turn the tide and think, feel, and act differently. Chronic nocebo behaviour can lead to problems and generate inner havoc on different levels (worlds). In some rare cases, people die of fear or languish through a hopeless situation (such as war or extreme danger). Within a psychological and physiological pathology (disease), fear can make us ill and lead to helplessness.

Victimized behaviour is a typical nocebo (left pillar mortido) effect. Victims feel they have no control over their life as they do not have an alternative perspective. With this lack of awareness, they are exhausting themselves through distress. The emotional triad in the world of Yezirah leans heavily on emotions of doubt, pain, stress, guilt, shame, and a doom scenario of their own life and future (and the world).

Memory plays a crucial part in this topic about trans-generational influences. It is our memory that brings us to a sense of identity and personal occupation. Without memories, there is no identity (at least not in the psychological and worldly sense of the word). What we remember is remembered through and within the whole body. What is often assumed to be memory based in the cortex (brain) is more complex and widespread throughout the body. Through the DNA structure, we remember all of our experiences through every part of the body.

Memory is not an effort (action); it happens to us. We do not have to keep remembering ourselves. Our bodies know who we are because of the interaction we have with the outside world. Our personalities (ego-consciousness) are not just psychological units of experiences; they are also chemical memories. The ego is extremely well defined in Jacob's Ladder. When looking at the Ladder, the world of Assiah is where the upper and lower faces of body and psyche interlock. The upper face of Assiah is the place of the Daath of the body, which is simultaneously the Yesod of the psyche (the ego).

What is remembered psychologically through the Yesod-Daath of Assiah is recalled by the whole bio-somatic body in the lower face and the autonomic nervous system. The feeling triad in the Hod-Yesod-Netzach of Yezirah mirrors itself in the somatic triad in Assiah (triad Hod-Yesod-Netzach of the organs at the autonomic or vegetable nervous system). The ego at the Yesod of the psyche has its reflection in the Yesod of the body: ego and autonomic nervous system are both functional parts of our memory.

Here, most of our unconscious processing is taking place. Likewise, the physical body is a composition of the whole physical universe. Making and processing new memories is possible by undergoing new experiences. Outside the known physical-psychological memory horizon, we can also have spiritual experiences and memories that integrate with psycho-somatic memories.

Learning and growing is the art of making new memories. Shaping new memories through self-consciousness is a particular spiritual action; we initiate our actions (karma) to remember new and spiritual parts about ourselves. It is often said that we have forgotten who we truly are, and we suffer spiritual amnesia. This kind of forgetfulness holds for most human beings, but simultaneously, like all other levels of memory, we gather our sense of self through memory in our current lifetime.

Of course, many spiritual people do testify of a deep memory that they carry along from former incarnations. These people continue their journey where it once ended in a former lifetime, and pick up these memories where they left off. Soul memories are a level of memory of the soul, consciously processing each life's experiences. Memory, however, is not identical or synonymous with identity. We formulate a part of our identity through a developing memory.

We can distil from the fact that after a trauma, like a CVA (Cerebro Vascular Accident) or other neurological pathologies, a person might lose a part of a complete sense of their identity. Because Yesod's mirror has been damaged physically (central nervous system at the Tifaret of Assiah), so has the ego-psyche. Without an inner mirror to look into, we can no longer recognise the outside world; we have no reference within ourselves, and fail to respond to our environment.

 At the same time, there is more to our identity than ego awareness. The self of the Tifaret of Yezirah, and a Self of the Self in the Tifaret of Briah, respectively, are psychological and spiritual. These memories transmigrate over lifetimes and are not bound to one lifetime, let alone one physical appearance and one ego construction. The higher life and identity clothed themselves into the forms and appearances of the lower worlds.

This is a reflection of our ancient and spiritual identity within the world, a memory connected to a temporal and mortal memory related to a relative identity. The higher identity clothed itself with the forms and appearances of the lower worlds to reflect itself. Our ancient spiritual identity and memory connect to the temporal and mortal memory as a relative identity. The higher identity cannot truly manifest (Assiah) if a personal memory in the psyche and body is not realised.

This is the Kabbalistic work: "bringing heaven to earth" or the higher worlds and higher memory into the memory of the lower worlds. The sole property of the mind, the brain, or any function of these parts of the natural human Being is not the whole of our Being. For that matter, our memory is just a temporal phenomenon of being to obtain life experience within relative existence.

God wishes to behold God in the mirror of existence, and this is possible when the Eternal remembers itself through the being-ness of transcendence and immanence. Personhood and our reflections in memory are the property and matter of the whole body. The whole body is implicated in how both personhood, and an individual, can persist or lose itself in perpetual forgetting.

It is one thing to remember, but quite another if a memory solidifies, materialises, and becomes a true part of our Being. In Kabbalistic terms, this happens when a memory becomes manifest through all the three lower worlds of the Cosmic (Briatic), Formative (Yeziratic), and Active (Assiah). If memory can no longer be distinguished from ourselves, we have become the memory, and the past becomes the present.

While the present is the ground of the future, our memory becomes our prophecy. When memories in all the worlds collide together, we become enduring and infinite throughout time, because of our continuity beyond time and space. Persistent memory is not per se a trait of the personal (Yesodic) memory, which moves in countless directions (and none) during an incarnation. If there is no persistence, there is no stability in memory, and the possibility of manifesting memories through all the worlds is small. Memories that become manifest through all three lower worlds are persistent through lifetimes; they become existential memories that carry our soul (Being) across many lifetimes and incarnations.

In the tradition of Kabbalah, they say: "God is One, there is only One God" (there is only One Being). Kabbalah does not repeat the scriptures in an orthodox sense, promoting a monotheistic idea of Divinity. Tradition here speaks about God, the ultimate Being, as One. Existence is a mirror image of God. The image is One, just as God is One; existence as being One. Kabbalah does not say that there is only one God in a personal related way. Not even in a theological sense. God is beyond any classification of thinking and deduction. God is One means that All is One!

Even relative existence and the expression of time-space-movement are One, although not experienced as most people. Even within the world of psychological and physical life, God is One. God is the backdrop or the ground of all beings. In God, nothing has come to pass yet. All is in perfect order, and nothing has manifested itself.

When I say: "in perfect order", I do not mean this in the same way we organize and order our daily lives. What it means in this context is that all that ever was, is, and will be, is present within the Eternal (timelessness) of each moment. All is as it should be but has not unfolded itself into the world that we know.
This oneness is the wholeness of our very existence, upholding all the worlds that are and will ever be. Therefore, the God of nature is the God of all created things and beings, of all religions, philosophies, traditions, and sciences. God is One and includes all things and all beings. All is an expression of that One.

God is everything, and everything is God. All is because God is. All is a manifestation of God. Without God, nothing would exist. We, and all creation exist, created moment by moment, because God is. All are connected and communicated through God. The energy you experience inside your body is God, and this energy that moves the form of your body is God.

Meditation
If you wish and are comfortable with it, you may start this meditation with the invocation described in the introduction.

Become still again, and breathe consciously. Let yourself be still from within, and listen without effort or strain. Be open to whatever may come without expectations. Now, be particularly available and sensitive to your physical body. What does it communicate to you? These might be very distinct and clear signals like pain, discomfort, or an itch, or the signals may be much more subtle. This meditation asks you to turn your senses within.

Consider this. All you can hear, see, touch, smell, and taste on the outside is now happening to you on the inside. Gently turn your attention and awareness to the physical part of your whole Being. It may be that your body communicated peace and quietness to you. Next, see your thoughts appear within your body. Realise that every thought does not appear outside of you but manifests through the physical body but in a very subtle way.

In this same manner, you may see memories and feelings float by like waves on the ocean. Any impression that you may recall is there to tell you something about yourself. Do not resist anything, and try to have a neutral attitude to whatever appears from within. Remember that the Kabbalist is mainly interested in the truth as it comes to us, not in an ego-constructed reality.

See the Tree of Life within you: all the Sefirot at their appropriate locations within. Visualise it in a three-dimensional symbol where spheres are round, and the paths are like 'tubes' running through you. See, sense, and feel what is transported through you while you behold your inner Tree of Life. Do not intend to change anything while in this meditation, merely sit with yourself and let the innate Wisdom of the Tree of Life speak to you, while you listen...

Come out of the meditation and write down whatever is of interest to your inner path and development *(diagram 5)*.

Pillar of form-structure
Pillar of form-dynamics
Source
Faith
Vision
Archetypal - transpersonal world
Inspiration
Passive intellect
Active intellect
Discernment - Nocebo
Compassion - Placebo
Soul - empty focus - free will
Conservative and maintaining emotions
Liberating and exploring emotions
Truth of Self Essence
Cognition - Introvert
Feeling - Extravert
Self image Internal vs External
Fixed assocations and memories:
- repression
- resistance
- sentiment
- repulsion
- living in the past
Free assocations and memories:
- exposure
- exhibition
- revealing
- living in the future
Body Senses Brain

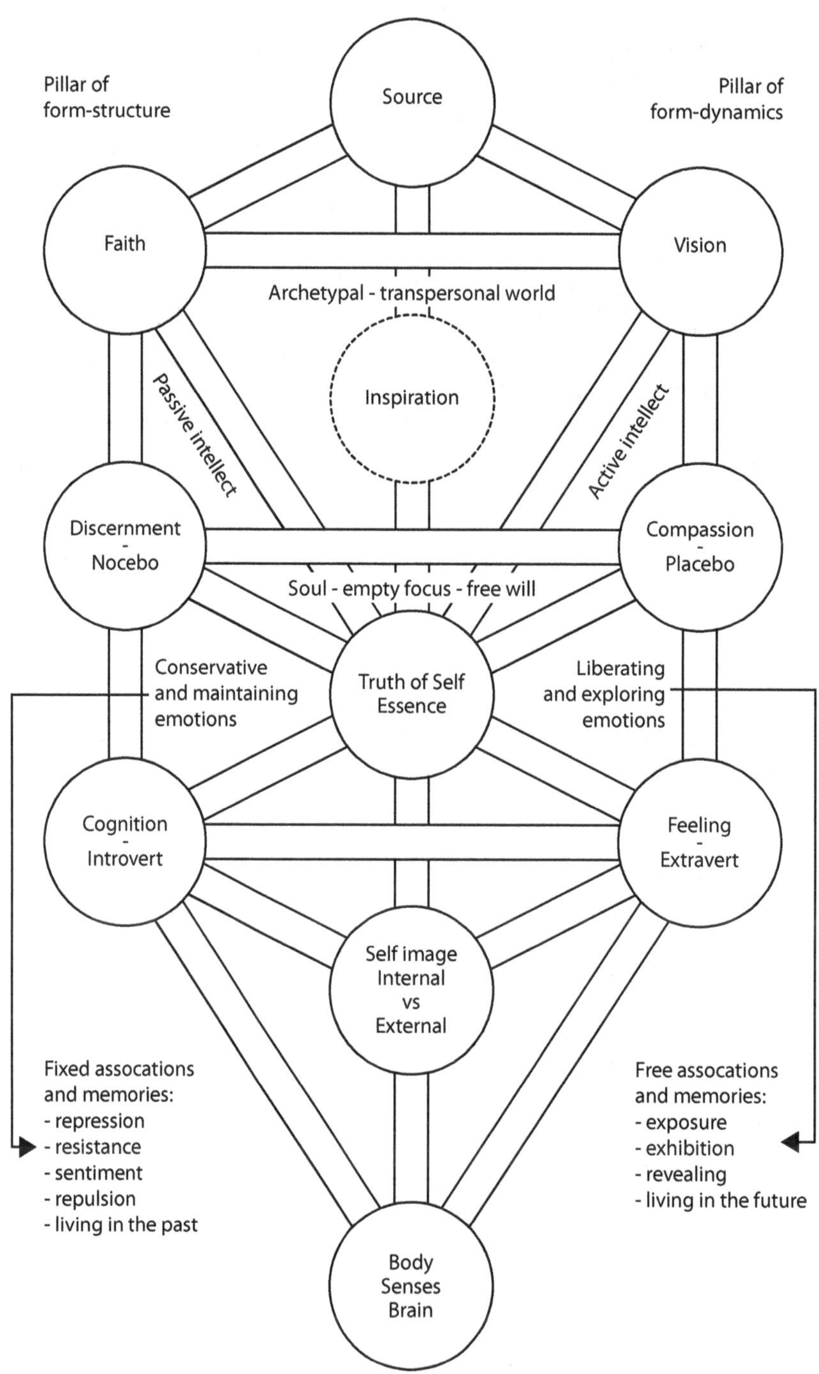

Diagram 5

Chapter 3: Quantum Physics

When the Kabbalist speaks about God, they speak about Ain (Absolute Nothing), Ain Soph (Absolute All): God the Transcendent beyond existence and God the Immanent. Divinity is the forthcoming world of Aziluth which emanates out of the infinite Nothingness and Limitlessness of God.

Aziluth means "near God, or close to God", representing the world that springs from the Godhead or Ain Soph. In Aziluth, all is Whole and One, held in ten expressions of God, all within one world. Ten names of God who have emanated in ten spheres or Sefirot. None of these Sefirot should be missing or left out, for without one (or one added to those ten), the unity and wholeness is incomplete. Ten hidden lights are named and uttered from the Godhead so that this first world of beginnings could come into Being.

Here all is "time-full", meaning all is held within the Eternal, yet, there is no time as we know it. Everything exists in the mind of the Divine (Aziluth), but there is no thought as we know it. Here all is One, but the potential for duality is present. This world is Eternal and will always be present in the three lower worlds (Briah, Yezirah and Assiah) to come (Jacob's Ladder).

Aziluth is the beginning of all being, times, and places. This "beginning" is not meant in a mythological or theological way per se, as if the beginnings of the world and the universe were a long time ago or if every beginning should be a very long time ago. Every moment (the moment you are reading this) is a potential moment of beginnings.

The potential for creation to unfold into something is ever-present. Creation and the beginning of time is not a reference to a past event, but a reminder that each Eternal moment is a new beginning. From every moment in space and time, a potential may "collapse" or fall into actuality. In quantum physics, this "collapsing" happens when potential becomes actuality in the world of action and matter (Assiah).

In Kabbalah terminology, it is said that from the world of Aziluth (infinite possibilities and the Eternal), a potential comes into the world of material phenomena (Assiah). The word "actualization" means exactly that: the potential of pure consciousness comes into the actual world of time-space-movement.

Actuality also corresponds with the word "action". Assiah, the fourth world on Jacob's Ladder, means action. In other words: what was in the beginning pure potential and Eternal, not moving but still, and in a state of pure potential, becomes actual and material.

Now, the world of potential and Eternity (Aziluth) does not disappear or vanish after the Eternal has collapsed into matter. The Eternal is always present, even when it has collapsed itself into the world of action (time-space-movement). All collapses (the physical body you inhabit in an incarnation) and is actualized through the mind of the Divine. It is being held and maintained in that state for an unknown amount of time. Every moment in our lives has potential in the world of Aziluth to be the pure consciousness of Being. Unity and wholeness are present in every moment of our lives.

Although we may feel divided in the world of action and space-time phenomena, unity and wholeness are always here. Eternity is the foundation of time-space-movement. Following the saying that God is One and there is only one Being, we could add: "And there is only One Becoming."

What can be known
How difficult it is to talk or write about who or what we are! How do we describe consciousness if we have no idea about the essence of consciousness?
We all know that consciousness is a part of us, but what it is and what it does is quite unclear.

Spiritual traditions stated some thousands of years ago that consciousness is the foundation and ground of existence. All is consciousness, and all is made of consciousness. What does it imply?

In Kabbalah, they say that pure consciousness is the world named Aziluth: the world of pure, naked consciousness, Divine love, and wholeness. A Being of consciousness, fullness, and Grace. This pure consciousness, is something different from our daily awareness, which is moving and functioning from the unconscious. We are moving all the time, but in truth, we are being moved. It seems that we do not move much by our own will.

According to quantum physics, we are held in the Divine potential or ground of Being (Aziluth). All is potential in this world. Matter in Assiah seems to be made up of particles in quantum terms, but it is also a wave and, therefore, pure potential in a domain that is always in movement (space-time-movement).

However, we as human beings, function for the greater part on the intellectual approach to life and the data we gather through the five senses. These data that we have obtained through the senses correspond with our physical surroundings and have everything to do with survival and our social structures (vegetable level) within the immediate environment and culture. The paradox for human beings is that we wish to become more than ourselves, or be limitless (immortal).

We cannot maintain the identity of the physical body and our ego, and change anything significant in a spiritual sense. Thoughts that we generate every moment are epiphenomena of consciousness. Who are you? The consciousness that is present or the thoughts that flow from that source? In many mythological stories from different cultures, we might think of two birds sitting in a tree: one of the birds is eating from the fruit of the tree, while the other watches indifferently.

These are the expressions of life in full engagement within time-space-movement (eating from life to stay alive), and the spiritual observer in the Human Being who witnesses all this and does not participate in the passing show on earth and relative existence. The bird that is observing has never entered the stream of time and is therefore not prone to birth and death. These two birds are close friends and live within the human soul: one part within the world and the other beholding the world from the realm of Spirit. One bird is the pure potential of undifferentiated consciousness (Aziluth), while the bird who is eating is the same bird, but collapsed and participating in physical reality and time-space.

From the observer in general or the position of the soul in Kabbalah (the triad of Chesed-Tifaret-Gevurah), the Human Being does not relate to life only from a second-person perspective ("I and the other"). From the soul perspective, we are the witness of our actions, decisions, and development.

There is something that every human being may discover within: the presence of pure consciousness. Presence is not a thinking process, and it is a very distinct experience that can best be explained as pure being-ness. In general, most human consciousness is occupied by personal worldly matters (Yesodic psyche or ego). The world seems to revolve around our little Yesodic ego with its needs and desires.

We are held, as it were, in the vicinity of the natural world, its instincts, and impulses. I invite you to contemplate this for a moment, if you wish to do so.

On the Tree of Life, we are talking here about the lower Garden or the lower Face of the Tree. If there was only this monitoring awareness of Yesod-ego, we would be absorbed by the natural world. This would mean that we are completely enchanted with the experience of relative existence, like the bird who is eating, occupied by eating and reproduction only. This is the philosophical idea that we "eat to become". The bird who consumes the world does not know that it is eating the world, and is oblivious of its nature and performance. After all, consummation is a survival impulse that functions mainly unconsciously. The bird who is the silent witness in the tree is the one who is aware of the relative world and the mechanism of survival. We can only know something when the silent witness awakens within us.

Tifaret is the key to the Tree of Life of becoming the observer of birth and death. The observer's experience opens the awareness of the unconscious life in the lower face and the higher or spiritual face of the upper part of the Tree of Life. In truth, these "faces" or "gardens" on the Tree of Life are not lower or higher, but expressed by their positions, the places where the hierarchy of consciousness manifests.

The lower face is within the higher face and vice versa. It is a matter of waking up to these realities within realities. The lower face with Yesod at its centre is the conscious part of ourselves although, in truth, we have only a very narrow view of the totality, because we are looking through the eyes of the ego *(diagram 6)*.

The ego's perspective is like standing in a huge stadium that is pitch dark. You hold a flashlight, and you can see small details of the stadium, depending on where you point your flashlight. The rest of the surroundings remains dark, or in other words, unconscious. The ego narrows your attention on something small, so the rest of the world "disappears"; we miss out on the bigger picture.

Pillar of Consciousness
Pillar of Structure
Pillar of Dynamic
Kether SELF of DIVINE
Consciousness of DIVINE
Binah PASSIVE INTELLECT
Chocmah ACTIVE INTELLECT
Anima Mother
Animus Father
Transpersonal Consciousness
COLLECTIVE UNCONSCIOUS
Anti-Cathexes
Passive Concepts
SPIRIT
Daath HIGHER KNOWLEDGE
SPIRIT
Active Concepts
Cathexes
Super Ego Punishment
Gevurah PASSIVE EMOTION
SOUL
Chesed ACTIVE EMOTION
Ego Ideal Reward
Conscience
SOUL
SOUL
INDIVIDUAL UNCONSCIOUS
Anti-Cathexes
Passive Emotional Complexes
Tifaret SELF of INDIVIDUALITY
Active Emotional Complexes
Cathexes
AWAKENING Pre-conscious
Mortido
Hod PASSIVE ACTION
Passive Introvert Triad
Liminal Treshhold
Active Introvert Triad
Netzach ACTIVE ACTION
Libido
Feelings
PERSONAL CONSCIOUSNESS
Yesod SHADOW EGO IDENTITY
Thinking
Sense Data
Passive Extravert Triad
Actions
Motor Response
Active Extravert Triad
Malkuth BODY
Id-Nefesh Subconscious

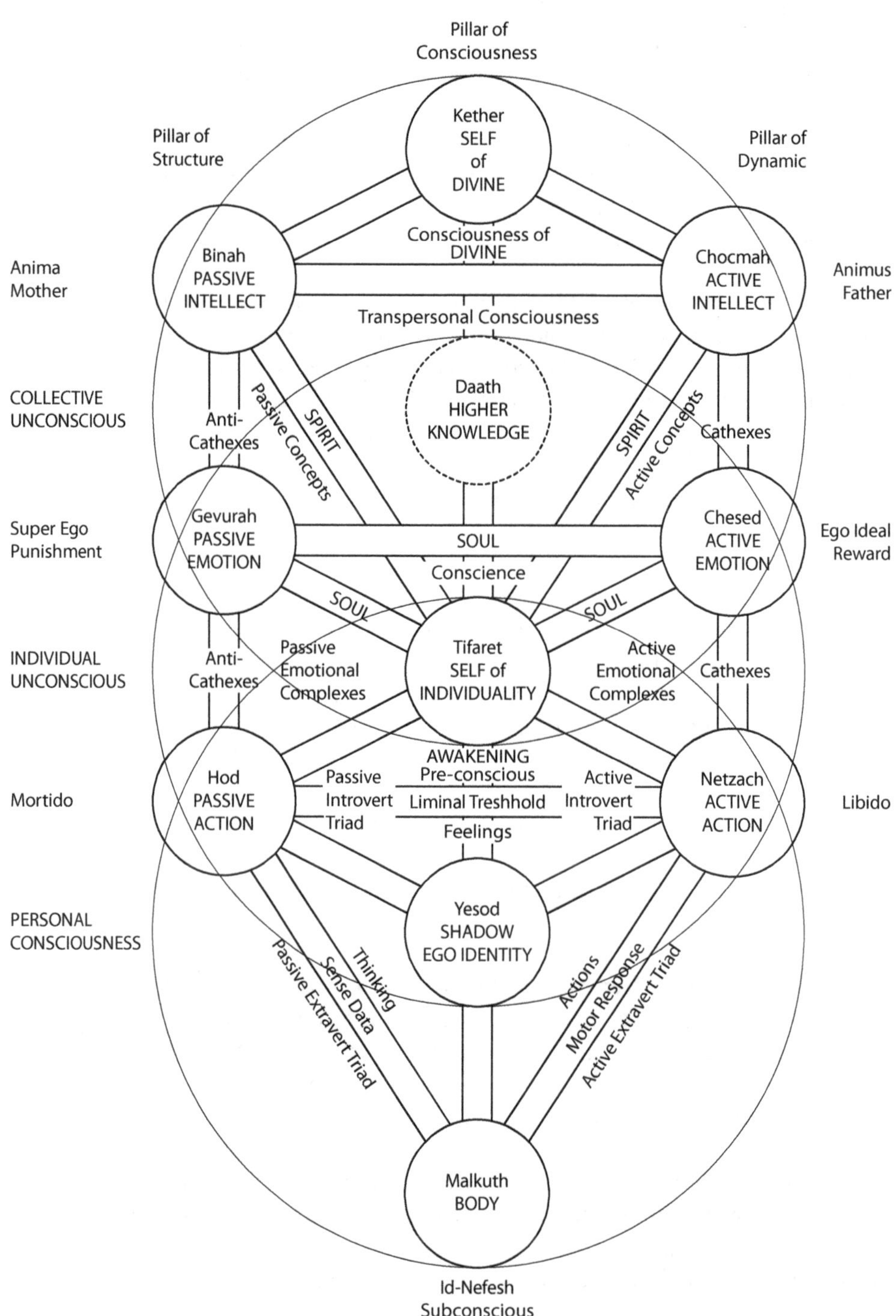

Diagram 6

This is a natural consequence of the psyche's mechanism that we call Yesod in Yezirah. This place in our psyche should function as a control centre that notices, evaluates, monitors and aligns itself to the world. The social or horizontal interaction of Yesod is meant to be flexible and agile in a psychological way. It generates pictures and images based upon the personal experiences that generate personal memories. The ego builds its power and control by all of these memories, associations and symbols, as it selects them to function in the world.

Again, the ego who is left to its own devises, actively controls the psyche (Yesod) by reducing the external world for its own ends. Through the ego, we know the difference between our personal, inner world, and the outside world, and for this reason, Kabbalah doesn't advocate getting rid of the ego. It is more that we realise the significance of the role that the ego plays at the mundane levels of our psyche. Kabbalah recognizes the pragmatic side of the Yesodic-ego, but urges the Kabbalist to see the ego for what it is.

To fully identify with the ego is to close ourselves off from the deeper levels of existence (higher Yezirah and beyond). To be open only for the eyes and ears of ego means to limit ourselves to a level that we have created, formed and made. Ego doesn't know that it doesn't know. That's why it remains ignorant of itself. However, for the Kabbalist, it is of vital importance that we do know what we know and do know what we do not know!

Being able to identify the level that we are at on the Tree of Life or Jacob's Ladder helps us to appreciate the impact and consequences that have shaped our perspective in life, pointing out in what world(s) we are choosing to live. For most of us, that is the world of Assiah. We know what we recognize, and what we don't know, we cannot recognize. We are oblivious of the things that we cannot perceive in ourselves.

This lack of self-awareness is why we do not perceive most of what is happening around us, as we have no personal recollection of the true vastness of this world. Of course, I do not mean only the physical world, but also the subtle world around us (Yezirah).

Perspective
Immanuel Kant once said: "A thing cannot be known in itself".
This can be interpreted from a metaphysical point of view. We don't know the true nature of reality, but have assumptions, based on experiments, protocols, cultural and linguistic evidence, that "something is the way it is". If there is some agreement about an object, we agree by consensus reality that "it is so".

Outside of a group of like-minded thinkers, we can have a completely different idea about the same object. Holding different ideas about the same thing not only happens in science, but also in religion, where "God" has become an "object of faith", but is seen and experienced in many different ways. Christians, for example, hold different beliefs about their God, while they speak about the same essence. We do not agree about who or what God is. In some scientific and spiritual disciplines or traditions, they say that reality is ultimately subjective.

All we experience in the relative world is subjective. We experience the world outside of ourselves, by the way we see it from the inside.

A thing cannot be known in itself, as it cannot be known in its totality, but only by its interpretations based on subjective-personal references. My conclusion of Kant's philosophical statement in relation to the similarity between Kabbalah and Quantum Physics is that our impressions and interpretations of our experiences in the world are based on psychological and sensory detection.

We cannot know a thing in itself by only seeing an object as an object and regarding it as outside of ourselves. Our interpretations of the world are both objective and subjective.

If I were to ask you where you see the letters and sentences that you are reading, most people would answer: "on the paper". But the place you are really seeing these things is within yourself. The world is happening inside of you. The whole of existence is represented in the Tree of Life. We cannot know something by assuming that they are objects that appear in the physical world. A thing cannot be known in itself as long as everything has a context. The context makes the apparently "separate" object into what it is.

Breaking up reality into little components (by the intellect alone) does not lead to knowing something completely, but only to knowing it as a separate quantity in the macro field. Kabbalah is very clear about these statements. The Tree of Life is a universal symbol that represents the whole of existence.

Wholeness encloses every apparent separate thing. Although the metaphysical glyph functions as a mirror of the Divine and all the four worlds, the Kabbalist is the subject that beholds the wholeness, which is ultimately subjective.

Mystically, God beholding God in the mirror of existence is the observer of its creation. Through observance, existence is created moment by moment, for that is the inherent power of the observer.

Let us take an example of the wholeness and context from the Tree of Life.

If we take the Sefira Chesed, we can know something about it, know its properties and qualities of greatness, compassion, growth, and love. Without its opposite in nature in relativity, we cannot fully know Chesed. So without Gevurah on the other pillar as the complementary "partner" of Chesed, we cannot know what compassion or love is. Gevurah provides us with the experience of justice, severity, contraction, and limitation. These are all opposites of Chesed which allow us to know, by contrast, the properties of one thing. We cannot know darkness (left pillar) without light (right pillar), we cannot know passivity (left pillar) without the activity (right pillar), and we cannot know the feminine (left pillar) without the masculine (right pillar).

The varieties of this dual manifestation are endless. If for some reason we do not wish to know the other side of one quality, we end up in disharmony and unbalance. Good can only be known when evil is acknowledged. If the choice is only for good or evil, we will never know that one thing in its entirety, and will always fail to bring ourselves and our actions back to a state of union. The work of the Kabbalist, which is the work of unification and integration, reaches out towards complementing our experiences and being affirmative to life.

One of our quantum physics pioneers, named Werner Heisenberg, launched the idea of the uncertainty principle, which states the following: we cannot know reality in its fullness, as matter behaves as particle (Binah) or wave (Chocmah) in our perception, and yet is both.

Schrödinger's cat experiment shows us that life and death are both probabilities in every moment in time-space. It is up to the observer what unfolds in the so-called field (implicate order of Bohm or Aziluth on Jacob's Ladder) into the manifest world (explicate order or Assiah on Jacob's Ladder). The quantum field speaks about "probabilities" rather than outcomes.

Even a collapsed probability is not final, but is always within the same field of possibilities, and therefore, can collapse ad infinitum. Although we regard the world of action as solid and continuous, the world of Assiah is always changing. Assiah may be the explicate order in quantum theory, but the mystical reality behind is an implicate order (Aziluth). The manifestation of matter is an implicate order represented by an explicate order, which is always there.

So, where do we see reality? The answer is: in ourselves. All is seen or observed inside ourselves. It is where we interpret the world and give it names. From there, we form our personalised truth and dogma. The world can be compared to thousands of mirrors in which we look throughout our lives and see ourselves eventually.

The choice, therefore, is what we like to see in the world, for what we see is ourselves. Of course, the problem with most of humanity is to get to know ourselves. We are, after all, the greatest mystery, and to explain who we really are is probably the most difficult task of humankind.

But it is of ultimate importance to eventually know what this life, and the vehicle we have received, is all about. The vehicle functions on different levels, or as the Kabbalist would say, in different worlds. A vehicle or body for every world. It is like driving a car or riding a bicycle: if you don't know how to drive or ride, you will not get far.

Our bodies (physical and subtler bodies) need to be understood before we can properly move with and within them. We could say that the whole human system or the totality of all the worlds is a complicated piece of technology. It may sound somewhat mechanical to describe it that way, but the universe works like an organism that consists of many worlds and levels.

Physicality brings forth a system of highly engineered chemical-electrical processes. The Tree or world of Assiah provides us with the knowledge to discover the vehicle we are currently living in.

Looking at the extended diagram of Jacob's Ladder, the highest world of Aziluth contains Aziluth. Briah contains Aziluth, Yezirah contains Aziluth and Briah, but Assiah contains all the worlds within the physical world of action.

To get to know the physical world and the body we received at birth is a tremendous gift, for it contains and transmits all the knowledge and intelligence present in the cosmos. As long as we do not know our vehicle, we will not be the "driver of the vehicle". The vehicle as our body is much greater than only the physical; it includes the psychological vessel, the emotions, feelings, thoughts, actions, memories, and a complicated system of energies within those levels.

As long as we do not know where all these different expressions bring us, we are not moving the vehicle where we want it to go. For example, our physical body has a memory of family identity and the "compound or tribal structure". All we have inherited in a physical way from our parents and family lies within the body. It has a story to tell, is often demanding, and directs many of our actions in daily life. This story happens without our conscious knowledge. Without growth beyond that identity, the human being will not free its own self from its cultural habits and conditionings.

To be able to develop our consciousness beyond the borders of the conditioned world of the vegetable and partly animal levels, we need to become aware of the deeper levels of our psyche, which lie within the collective unconscious or mythological domain of the psyche.

Perception on four levels
There are four functions (four ways) to perceive reality, according to the four worlds in Kabbalah:

1 Mystical (Aziluth)
2 Cosmological or metaphysical (Briah)
3 Psychological or metaphorical (symbolic) (Yezirah)
4 Literal, historical and social (Assiah)

We find a parallel dualistic stance towards life between science and religion, as both are hypothetical (that is, myths of science, and dogma of church or temple). In the west, at least, religion tends towards duality and polarity. No wonder that both disciplines are not easy to reconcile as within their frames of thought, they are in their views of life. The religion of the west is dualistic in "heaven and earth", while material science is dual in "Spirit versus matter".

In both examples, there is a division between the upper and lower part of the Tree of Life, and therefore, of the whole.

Religion and science are only maps to attempt to know reality. Reality is not a map. Maps are always paths towards ultimately understanding reality, and they are ways of leading consciousness towards a part of the truth. Science and religion shines its light of intellect or the heart on a part of the whole. So it is with education systems in the world. The Kabbalist may integrate religious ideas and science in the Tree of Life and its Kabbalistic work to come to a deeper understanding of the human being, the world, the universe and God. Dualism is a part of the natural world and came into being from the moment time-space unfolded from the world of Briah (world of Creation). All of creation rests upon the creative principles of time-space (Chocmah and Binah), and the laws of expansion (growth) and contraction (decay), respectively the Sefirot Chesed and Gevurah.

All life wishes to expand: religion and science wish to be and become authorities on the subject of ultimate truth. However, they differ in their ways of arriving at that truth. Differences about the boundaries of life can be formulated in the hypothetical question: Where does an idea of reality begin and end?

We could see two relevant questions in science:
- What is the Universe made of? (Of nothing?)
- Where does consciousness come from? (From nowhere?)

There is a tendency in science and religion to conquer, overthrow, and discard the "old for the new". Such happens with newly formed religions that discard the older ones (to be specific, from those they emerged from). Still, they hold on to conservative ideas (scriptures or old paradigms). So it is with science. We should build from the old towards the new, without disregarding older traditions that may be outdated. After all, we are standing on the shoulders of those who went before us.

We can transcend the old, but should also include it in a new paradigm. Otherwise, we might find ourselves separating nature, instead of integrating it. Is human nature only about transcending nature and "lower" creatures, or becoming more capable of supporting and sustaining life?

Some spiritual sources write about why humankind was created, formed, and made: to "tend to the Garden of Eden".

Or as the Greeks said: "...so they (mankind) can perform the work of the Gods..."

Let us not forget that the natural environment of this planet is a part of our physical nature.

Separation from our environment causes us to separate from a part of ourselves. We can set aside or disregard nature as something redundant through technology (literal interpretation) and culture (social interpretation). It is comparable to the neocortex, saying as it were to the oldest part of the cerebrum, the archaic cortex, that it is no longer needed *(diagram 7)*.

Technology is beginning to lose its grip on its intention: to regulate human life and control it. Technology finds itself at the top of the food chain. Besides, technology is becoming "God" at a high price, as the industrial market and its owners are making huge profits of the sales of technology to conditioned consumers (most of humanity).

LIFE SOURCE
Contact with the Divine
GRANDMOTHER
Family Traditions
GRANDFATHER
Family Inspirations
Family line
Family history
Leaving Home
Limiting Family Values
Liberating Family Values
Disciplined Upbringing
Liberal Upbringing
Fated Relationships
PARENTS
Mother/Father
Emotional Restraint/Abuse
Emotional Support/Indulgence
Customs
Festivals Holidays
Initations
Conditioning
Home Atmosphere
CHILDREN
Schooling
Daily chores
HOME

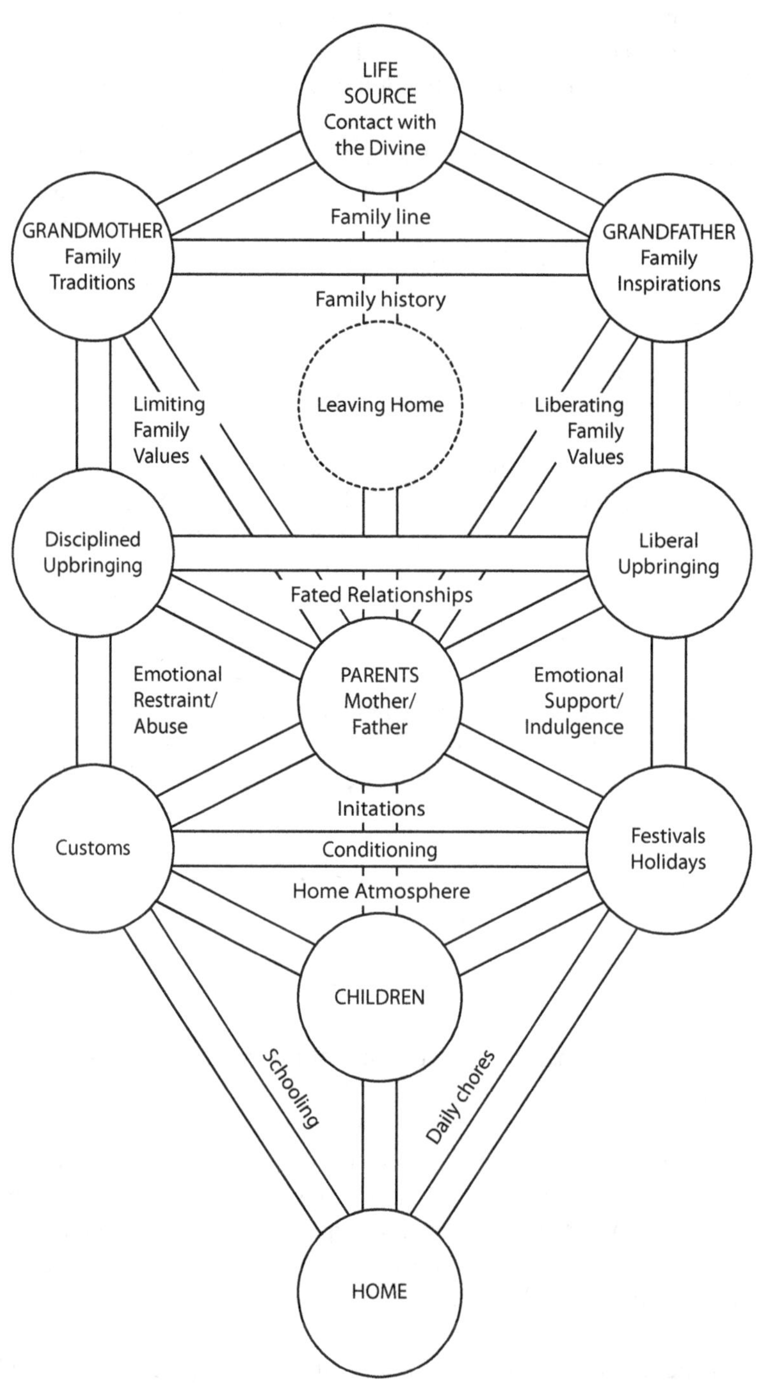

Diagram 7

The economy of the world is ruled by the dominating development and production of technology. This is the heritage of the Industrial Age, the age of technology and machines, promising to make life better, with an increase in leisure and quality of life. It's almost a pure development of Assiah (matter) but has detrimental effects on the psyche in Yezirah, and hardly promotes or stimulates anything spiritual (Briah).

In esoteric terms, this is a development that we call: "the Age of Mercury" (influence of Hod on the Tree of Life), a development in the 19th, 20th and 21st centuries. Very quick and almost elusive, like the planet or god Mercury. Technology innovates communication, accessibility, learning systems, travel possibilities, and much more.

The counterpart is the cunningness and shrewd business, politics, and a new direction of journalism and news-spreading. We are now in an age when politics is shifting from politicians to business people. Quantity-driven technology will bring us more machines and digital devices, but not a healthier and better life in quality. We may live in a world (Assiah) and age where, for most people, the material level of living (mineral and vegetable level on the Tree of Life) is well taken care of. Still, for those that find relative comfort from luxury, happiness often does not increase.

The ideal of service to humanity, promised by the dawn of the Industrial Age, is largely gone. Some are also in favor of service to the earth. If we are more fixed on making money (short-term vision and egocentric view from the ego-Yesod in Yezirah), we will make a descending movement in our growth and personal life. Science and religion still have not taught us how to manage our emotions and thoughts or energy (world of Yezirah).

The intellect (Hod) should become an instrument of clear perception (clarity), comparable to a knife, for discernment and concentration (Gevurah), not only for deduction and division. In religion, we often talk about believers and believing. Belief is confidence without understanding, sometimes called superstition, comparable to an assumption of something that is not yet experienced. Evidence-based and empirical science works via the intellect, intending to "cut open something", take it apart, and dissect it.

This urge to dissect and deduce our nature, diminishes everything into fragments, until these fragments can't be seen in their proper context. It would be the same for the Kabbalist if they would dissect the Tree of Life in such a way that the wholeness of the Tree is completely lost. Suppose there is no limit to this urge of deduction of our nature. In that case, we will diminish everything into fragments, until they are no longer explainable nor experienced, because of their separation and abstraction.

Humanity wishes to accumulate all the time. To grow and assimilate physically and psychologically (look at the number of obese people in the world: in 2020, 39% of adults in the world are overweight. One-in-five children and adolescents, globally, are overweight. This percentage is still growing). We regard what we have assimilated as our own, thinking we possess it as we have accumulated and built it up. We identify with what we have gathered and developed. As soon as we label and categorize something, we claim ownership over it.

Boredom is another problem coming from a leisure-created society. Not that we are lazy, but that we spend our time with intelligence-killing and soul-diminishing activities. Entertainment (principle of Hod on the Tree of Life) of television, computers, and cell phones is a way of technological slavery and addiction, leading to a passivity of mind and a deadening of creativity. Too much assimilation (Chesed) leads to growth without decay (Gevurah), and too much freedom for entertainment (Hod) without discipline leads to superficiality.

Technology uses the modern market system to entertain us and make us pay for it. It results in a distraction from ourselves, so we do not live our own lives, but a life dependent on the technological world. Technological programming could be seen as maximum pleasure by immediate intervention.
Through science we come closer to the idea that a "part is a fragment of the whole". Science often works from the deductive method of investigating and researching the details and "facts" to know the whole. Spiritual and religious traditions emphasize the idea that a "part is a totality of the whole". To take a part out of existence is to remove the totality. This hologram-like assumption points at the idea that Spirit is present within all things. To wish to know the whole, one needs to seek the inner world of creation itself, where we can find wholeness in every detail. That is quite different from the viewpoint and perspective that a fragment is just a detail or separate part of a machine.

When we generate a society based upon a literal interpretation of our reality, for example, through a technology-oriented society, we give square and rectangular-like shapes to the natural world (which is much more circular and oval). According to the Kabbalistic Tree of Life and Jacob's ladder, such a literal perspective is only living in- and through the world of Assiah.

Sometimes, science explains the "how", while religion and spirituality explain the "why". These days, many scientists are much more occupied with the "why". Whoever we are, or whatever ideas we sympathize with, we are all afraid of existential loss and emptiness. Through science or religion, humans try to get an understanding about existence, and how we ought to live on this planet. Some of us who wish the world to end are not always destructive in nature, but truly wish a profound transformation on a personal and collective level.

Destruction lovers are not always violent but have an inherent need for change. The fear "that the world would end" is often their need for deep transformation. In modern psychoanalysis, this fear is referred to as "Mortido". Technology is sometimes used to manipulate and accumulate the environment and circumstances (nature) to fit into our human system of living. We see countless examples of how expansion and accumulation (Chesed) without contraction and dissimilation (Gevurah) lead to an implosion of ourselves, whether economic, political, social, or personal. If we do not fear, we will only expand and assimilate (we need a measure and limit to our expanding urge).

Stopping this surge is something we saw happening with the COVID-19 crisis at the beginning of 2020. When humanity only strives to build, assimilate, and expand, something occurs sooner or later, to slow down that process of assimilation. If one pillar on the Tree of Life is dominant for too long (in this example the right side pillar of energy and growth), the other, complement pillar, will restore the unbalance in nature. In this example of Covid, the left side pillar causes contraction and slows down growth. Whole masses are effected and stopped through the law of contraction (Gevurah). People have a hard time with this, for their freedom is all of a sudden limited and they have to make personal sacrifices to live up to new rules and restrictions.

Sometimes these cosmic movements in nature are personal and in other circumstances, whole nations are influenced and contracted (slowed down). Humans can expand through conquest: conquer by force or through compassion and embrace. Compassion- expansion (right side pillar and the principle of Chesed) and severity- contraction (left side pillar and the principle of Gevurah) can go together: they make us whole when in balance. If this can happen in science and religion (and business), that would greatly help the world. Self-consciousness brings us to the growth of selfhood, and away from a life of chance. We live according to our chosen path instead of leading a life of habit (hit and miss). Do you wish to manage something in the world? Manage yourself first! For how can you manage anything or anybody without self-control and knowledge? So it is for politicians, scientists, religious or spiritual leaders.

Perspective and language
Another subject matter within the frame of science and spirituality is language. Both are highly dependent on the use of words to explain their hypotheses or beliefs. One of the first scientists who incorporated spirituality into science (that is, that he did not see any difference between the two) was Pythagoras. He held that words and numbers have meaning and correspond to "what they are" and not to what they are made to represent.

This is an important distinction - a letter, a word, or a sentence, is the meaning itself. It does not refer to something else. For example, in the Eucharist and other spiritual rituals, words are chosen because words are entities that can be invoked, rather than references to another domain. Science has the same logic in mathematical equations, as $1+1=2$ does not mean anything different than the sum code.

In Biblical and other mythological scriptures, the Word (Logos) is an Intelligence that expresses itself and becomes "flesh". The Word, or Intelligent Expression, is a source of creation and action in unfoldment. In the Biblical scripture Genesis, Adam, when created by the Word, got the position of naming all the animals coming into existence.

By naming them, they are known. In the Egyptian mythological scriptures, Isis captured her father's name, Ra, for in that name, the power to create was present. Capturing names seemed to result in ownership made by names and images. We do this all the time in our daily lives. We think that we know something when we name it.

In a sense, this is true, but only when the essence of the name is understood. If one asks: "Do you know that bird?", and you know its name, you may think you know the creature. If you do not know the name, you are ignorant. Knowledge does not come from knowing an image or a name, but by living its essence (participating in the essence of the other).

Language and perception ask for knowing through direct knowledge and experience of the thing you are beholding. Understanding the difference between knowing something through reflection (image in Yesod), and knowing its essence through experience, is vital.

When Stephen Hawking (1965-1995) wanted to develop a theory that explained everything, he wanted to know the essence of the universe, not to know a representation of it. An idea or equation may be mistaken for its essential truth. And so, we see in science and spirituality alike that forms are being regarded as the truth, leading to an identification with these forms, which in turn leads to possessive tendencies (a kind of materialism).

Similarly, within spirituality, a person does not seek representations through images and names, but essence. Language may be used organically to seek meaning, or mechanistically to put the whole of existence into categories and labels of thinking (Sefira Hod on the Tree of Life).

Are humans the first machines? Maybe if seen from the mechanistic perspective that a machine is in service of the human being by becoming an extension of human intelligence, and because of the limited abilities of the human body, tools and machines developed from the Stone Age onwards. This is an extension or expansion of human abilities through the use of machines. It is a way to transcend nature: "Use material tools and extensions to overcome the material limitations" (world of Assiah). Not only the limitations of the human body, but also of the physical surroundings.

For example: we have overcome the problems of living in open nature (weather conditions) by building houses, heating our homes, and keeping ourselves safe within it, overcoming the dangers and primitive conditions our ancestors had to face. In Kabbalistic terminology, we view this as: to transcend and control the mineral, vegetable, and animal levels in the lower face of the Tree of Life. As it was said before, these are the levels that correspond with our natural body and the natural side of human existence. Material extensions are produced by humankind to overcome physical shortcomings.

Today's development goes further into AI and computer technology, compensating and extending beyond the human psychological condition. Machine and science should be there to serve humankind. To serve is to "become a tool or equipment". As "serving God" is to become a tool in the "hands of God", in Kabbalah and mysticism in general. We have made nature into a machine (and see the body in much the same way).

According to Kabbalah, the physical body is a sacred vehicle through which we may experience the Divine. The physical universe is the dwelling place of the Shekinah. To degrade nature and the physical body to just a device is to diminish the power and essence of physical existence.

In rituals, we see a symbolic representation of a higher truth, expressed through the symbolic meaning. In animistic "religions", the natural world is not a symbol or a representation, but a spiritual fact. There are no abstractions about the symbol; the world is seen as Spirit (not as if it were Spirit). These abstractions come down from science and religion alike; they behold their experience through dualistic spectacles.

In certain religious traditions, there are no representations of Spirit or God, but what they forget is that a word and a sentence alike are expressions of symbols as well. Science and religion both work towards their idea of wholeness. Physical (sensory) and symbolic expressions are both dualistic languages.

Science suggests that force (principle of Chocmah) in whatever form (principle of Binah) is the advance of control. Because the world is inanimate without force and does not move by itself, nature needs an initiating power or force to be moved. As science categorizes the forces of nature (electromagnetism, gravity, weak and strong nuclear power), they effectively move and manipulate nature. This is control through understanding (Binah). Through the ideology that force is movement (and from this understanding comes control), also comes the ideology of reason and exploration, and the urge for discovery (imperialism).

In history, the idea was to civilize other people of a "lower nature" who did not understand the concept of the survival of the fittest; to tame the savage world through science. The resulting movement out of this ideology and imperialism was colonization, a blend of science (Hod) and politics (leadership in Tifaret). Meanwhile, the church and many other religious groups had the same urge for exploration, imperialism, and colonization. However, religion calls these urges "repentance of the unbelievers" and missionary work, all under the banner of "charity of Christ" (Chesed). The church did not support science but went in the same political direction, as they also professed power, for the church had the monopoly of force through the Holy Spirit. They claimed to be the ones to provide the Holy Spirit for the world. In other words, science and religion both claimed to have the "key to nature", and how to move and control it. Same goal, but different agendas, you could say.

People like Descartes and Galileo were believers but removed God from nature: nature (world of Assiah) and heaven (world of Briah) were divided. Matter is dead and moves only by physical force. And so, God, the heavens, angels, and the inherent flame of Divine light in the human being were exported to another place, called heaven or the sky. Other people like Darwin were believers at first, but could no longer reconcile with the religious ideas of their times (who could blame them?).

Newton was regarded as solving the great mystery of the universe (a theory of everything) by his $F=MA$ (Force equals Mass times Acceleration) formula.

Later it was clear that it did not explain everything, and that even gravity was still a mysterious force in the universe. Duality was not the problem itself; it was how human beings pushed duality (forces between the side pillars on the Tree of Life) to its limits. Even today, we see that duality in language and behaviour divides the world rather than bringing things to a unified whole. The power of words (Hod) may lead to unification, when in balance with the qualities of Netzach, the language of creativity and feelings.

Expansion of human nature
Pushing boundaries of the known and the unknown leads to discovery. We wish to discover to be certain of our life and our world. We need certainty in life. The more we encounter uncertainties, the more we ask questions. Science never stopped asking questions and answering them with deterministic formulas, and equations to quantify them objectively. The idea is that if you can materially measure something, it is true. In a way, this is true for material objects.

The Church, and many religions in general, also wished for certainty and found it in faith, another form of determinism wrapped up in the "formula of a religious credo". Do not ask too many questions, for heaven or God only knows. Determinism means that you can know the properties of something, and therefore, the present, past, and future of a thing (predictions of reality, according to science).

The Kabbalist searches for the unknown, for the sake of the spiritual work itself. From the Crown of the world of Assiah, the place where the three lower worlds meet (Kether of Assiah, Tifaret of Yezirah and Malkuth of Briah), the Kabbalist aspires to the Higher worlds of Briah, where the deep collective unconscious lies. The Kabbalist knows that without this spiritual exploration of the heavens, there will be no inner progression of growth. Questions have to be asked.

Reductionism says that by knowing the parts, you know the whole. By knowing the whole you know the universe... and therefore, everything. In spiritual terms, we say: "The sum (whole) is greater than its parts". We cannot know the whole (Spirit) by its parts, speaking in the words of the mystics. Who can separate Spirit or wholeness? Parts and separateness are perception, not reality. Wholeness cannot be divided. If we replace "wholeness" with "Love", we say: "Love cannot be broken down into separate pieces". Although we see the world as dual, and often separate from ourselves, this does not mean that this is the reality behind everything.

In Kabbalah, the world of Aziluth, or the undivided whole, does not divide or separate itself into pieces when emanating down the three lower worlds, but remains one and unique in all the worlds to be. Much of science and religion have pointed towards dualism, separation, determinism, dogma, and reductionism. Meanwhile, the mystic's experience ever has been and ever will be of an undivided whole and unity.

Science divides through labelling, numbering, determining by measurement, and control through the idea of prediction and certainty. Certainty is the counter-wish of wonder (be-wonderment and awe). The path of awe (from Tifaret to Kether on the Tree of Life) does not ask or provide certainty, but openness towards the Mystery.

Trying to put more information into a coherent and linear scheme attempts to predict and control the world. A force (will), plus information, leads to the feeling of control. More information (quantity of Hod) has not been proven to lead to growth and development (Chesed). From a quantum perspective, the more control (left side pillar) we wish to have, the less creative (right side pillar) we are. The quantum collapse of old conditionings (vegetable level) will continue as long as our minds maintain certain dogmas of living (religious, scientific, social, personal, and collective).

To dissect and take elements apart from their wholeness is a materialistic-scientific ideal. Dissection will not help us to know the whole or "the thing" itself, and all the properties are deterministically present in their fragments. Fragmentation is the result of the Kabbalist's work, who divides heaven and earth, and separates them from each other. Some Kabbalists work towards an experience of illumination, and aspire so much to the Higher worlds, that they lose touch with lower worlds (the here and now, and the objective world). Others cannot go past their personal limitations, failing to have experiences of the Heavenly world or, let alone, integrating these in their personal lives.

It is said that the parts make up the whole, and that "the parts are greater than the whole", but how about: "The whole is greater than its separated parts"? The latter would mean that wholeness is not simply a composition of its parts, but through the totality of its parts, the whole is greater than its separated units. Something has been "added" to the whole when parts come together or reunite. At least, so it would seem. The Kabbalist would say that the 32 paths on the Etz Chaim or the Tree of Life together are greater than their separate paths.

A body is greater than its separated organs. Taking these exquisite organic-devices out of the body to research and understand them is interesting, but they don't function as separate parts, and are no longer complete. The greater whole surely is more interesting. The Tree of Life as a whole is more interesting than one single Sefira on its own.

Determinism and scientific materialism shut out our awe and wonder about nature: nature should be explained and controlled through deterministic knowledge. Why? Because science serves humanity first, so we can live comfortably and securely. Science is there to deliver the conditions, so that we can satisfy our basic needs more easily. Religion is not against this per se, but regards nature often as something inferior to divinity or Spirit.

Both generate a division between worlds of experience. In doing so, they discard one world for the other, and work towards a dualistic worldview. As such, they do not engage in an effort towards unification and inclusivity. Why not? Because the goal of science or religion isn't to come to unification. They wish perfection or salvation (from sins).

Both disciplines compete to determine who will present the structure or "map" that will lead to the truth. Or even, for better or for worse, that the map itself is the truth. In material science, this theory serves as a dogma, while in orthodox religion, the scriptures are the authority of truth. Materialist versus spiritual view is comparable to a downward or upward causation cosmology. We may still be stuck in the dualistic mindset about how reality presents itself. Is it one or the other? Or are both scenarios applicable to a holistic and inclusive understanding of reality?

The way that reality presents itself is intimately related to the interaction of the observer with the world. There are endless variations on how reality presents itself. Jacob's Ladder is known as the four worlds and the four interpretations of reality: Aziluth or the Divine world is the mystical perspective. Briah, or the creative world, is the metaphysical perspective. Yezirah, or the formative world, is the symbolic perspective. Assiah, or the physical world of action is the literal perspective.

Light is both "particle and wave" in a quantum reality that's always in a dualistic form. Whoever is "watching" this reality, is both right, wrong, and neither.

Knowledge to control
In modern and postmodern times, there is an urge to control and overcome nature's "imperfections" (like disease, etc.). Both technology and social culture (Hod and Netzach) have distracted us from our true human nature. The human-animal need to control nature because of our insecurities goes back a long way in human history.

Controlling emotions and feelings is a way to enhance the economy and industry, and as a consequence, to make the natural world serve humanity without measuring its negative outcomes, or caring about it being destroyed in the process. In turn, humanity is in service to technology, economy, and the mass production industry. Orthodox religion has the same objective: to control nature and regulate life through ecclesiastical cultivation and suppression of natural instincts.

So why a schism between science and religion if they have the same objective? They explain at least a piece of the whole puzzle, and depart from a mystical and quantum physics point of view: it is all the Divine Who is beholding itself through these different disciplines and observations. All sciences and scientists, all religious and mystical traditions, believers and knowers, are the eyes and ears of the whole of creation.

Kabbalah sees the greater reality behind all these human attempts to know life and the universe. This has been transmitted through the centuries from mouth to ear (oral tradition) and through books (written tradition). Human nature is not "good", and according to science and religion, human life (nature) is imperfect or sinful and should be guided. Humans are selfish, and need a system of thought or ideology to regulate human nature (religion), and turn it into something better.

These ideas touch upon the Lurianic Kabbalistic ideas which state that creation and the universe are imperfect, and that the fallen sparks of God should be found and released from physical imprisonment. The idea behind "original sin" means to go against nature: do not eat from the apple on the Tree of good and evil in Eden, and do not disobey a higher-order or truth.

In science, they say they have found the "selfish gene" (Richard Dawkins) and claim that we have a hereditary factor inside us because we have eaten from the Tree in the Garden of Eden. We are therefore sinful, and cannot manage our own lives. Creation is imperfect, and humanity has fallen from a perfect state into an inferior and physical manifestation. Again, a dualistic stance within an ideology of the world: matter (sin) against Spirit (good). Religion portrays itself as the good (God) versus evil (Devil), and science is the good (proven, objective facts) versus evil (sin), in the lived experience that cannot be measured.

It is said that religion is subjective while science is objective. Kabbalah acknowledges that the universe is observed by a conscious witness who is within and without all things. The observer, or witness, is Immanent and Transcendent.

Whether you are a scientist, or wish to look from a more religious or spiritual point of view (or both), we are everywhere, and always, the observer and witness of this creation. Most interestingly, the observer is not outside creation, but is participating within every progressive moment.

You are never outside the process of creation, as you are the participant and observer of this universe. Our participation is ultimately subjective, and therefore, influences the so-called objective world as you are reading these words.

The Divine (Aziluth) is the ultimate observer who observes the whole of existence-as-one. To regard the Divine as something outside of creation and yourself emphasizes the duality in a vertical (middle pillar on the Tree of Life) sense. Another way of describing and experiencing dualism is by seeing "self" versus "others". Horizontally, we continuously meet the "other" in this life as someone or something else.

The world and the other person are a second or third person (a thing), and are only part of ourselves if they testify to the same ideas and ideology. Self is a construct of what we think is "me" (Yesod of Yezirah or ego), and those parts of the outside world that conform with that self. Self is used here as a psychological way of explaining the daily mode of awareness which we call the ego. The ego is the waking consciousness that monitors and supports our personal experiences.

Although the ego has a participatory awareness of what it is doing, it is not a conscious observer.
It is a complex psycho-social mechanism that works through conditioning and memory. The ego-Yesod is made to know our body-mind organism (Assiah and lower Face of Yezirah) in relation with the world outside. Conditioned patterns are physical and psychological. Almost all of your personal life is conditioned, and in that sense, is pre-destined.

Ego (Yesod of the world of the psyche) functions mostly upon the dualistic experience (side pillars on the Tree of Life), and the forthcoming consequences of that experience. The world becomes and remains dualistic. Dualism gives us a strong psychological-emotional impulse when it comes to punishment and reward (the superego and ego ideal, or the Gevurah and Chesed in the world of Yezirah).

Most of what the ego considers and decides in life is based upon what it has learned from parents, family and culture: the ethics or the sense of "right and wrong" lay deeply in the mechanism of the ego-consciousness and outlook on life. The super-ego (Gevurah) is the little devil on the left shoulder, telling you what you shouldn't do, while the ego-ideal (Chesed) is the angel on the right shoulder, telling you what you should do.

Perception of what is good or bad dictate the consequences of our ego drives and actions. Our conditioning has taught how to adopt attitudes, behaviours, and moral codes that are culturally and religiously tainted. Another way to guide and regulate the masses is through religious laws (Ten Commandments) or scientific law (rational evidence based deductive reasoning).

These dualistic laws don't need to be forced on awakened souls, as spiritual laws are transmitted to the soul. The more outside forces and people guide us, the more we lack and develop an individual self.

The ego is very sensitive to dualism and the tendency to control. Often, a form of indifference, purposelessness, and competition comes out of this state. The mind's conditioning (reason or Hod on the Tree of Life) generates dualistic and deductive psychological concepts that are always trying to dissect things or take things apart to explain them.

These conditionings of the psyche may lead to conditioned experiences that bring freedom and a clarity of mind at that level. It may also lead to more dehumanization of life, objectifying humanity, thinking and acting and seeing others as a third person (as an object). We become merely an object of faith (religion) or experimentation (science). Becoming a third person in the eyes of religion, science, or both, is to become an object of use.

In the most extreme cases known globally, people become objects in religious crusades and terrorist attacks. Similarly, in science, there is no limit to the way they test on living entities and organisms. Kabbalah is a tradition that teaches people how to become free and liberate ourselves by obtaining self-knowledge through knowing all these different perspectives of consciousness.

A dualistic God brings forth reward and punishment. God loves the worshipper for their moral duty and obedience, and punishes them for their egoism and unfaithfulness. One is loved out of moral duty to religion, or appreciated through social duty within science. Whatever we get caught up in, we are psychologically not free from these disciplines that are not concerned with liberating us from ourselves, but with binding and locking us to an ideology. Extreme ideologies are found on either side of the Tree of Life, on the right or left-side column.
In general, scientific extremes are more left-pillar oriented, while religion is more right-pillar oriented.

In such cases, the prophet is the professor or the priest. In politics, the socialist and communist parties are on the left-side pillar, while on the right side, we have the liberals and capitalists. This all shows us the extremes we easily fall into individually and collectively. These extremes find their way into the psychological and pedagogical human world, whether it is through science, religion, or otherwise.

Punishment and reward may be of use as inner moral guides. They represent the archetypes of mother and father, as they correct and enthuse us and others. The group mind is so strong, without and within, the influence of punishment and reward is always with us: it is included in our upbringing and our schooling system. There is another way to facilitate the human psyche without this emphasis on punishment and reward. That is the way of our inner conscience and self-consciousness. These levels are found on the Tree of Life at Tifaret, and the soul triad (Gevurah-Tifaret-Chesed).

For the mystic in general, and the Kabbalist in particular, punishment and reward have meaning only psychologically and socially. Karma (Mazal), from a metaphysical perspective (Briah), is a universal law of what the consequences are for our actions. It is a natural law that applies to all beings within relative existence and the world of action (Assiah). To be of the soul level means that we take responsibility for our own lives, that the consequences of each action, no matter how small, big, subtle, or gross, should be reflected upon and measured within our conscience. In other words, we need to develop our own Gevurah (super-ego) and Chesed (ego-ideal) for this subtle measurement and weighing of our soul.

In this world of relativity and duality, we speak of "winners and losers", depending on how we perform according to certain social standards. Our lives are programmed (like television and media) to compete with others and become another "top predator" or alpha leader of something. Animal people are psychologically those people that rule out of personal necessity. They rise above the need for survival, but are still dependent on others to be appreciated and revered: winning something for "me" (ego), and striving for something more. Winning/losing is a relative game, but both religion and science run that race, as they are institutions with political and economic interests.

There is, for example, in religion, the church against other faiths, or in science, they are against charlatanism. Of course, there are enough initiatives where these controversies are not present, and there is an inner work at play that strives towards union and inclusivity, instead of diversion and separation. You might ask yourself: what does all of this have to do with quantum physics?

The quantum perspective, also called the conscious observer, lies at the soul level on the Tree of Life. Only from the awareness of being aware can we come to a quantum collapse or a quantum change. If any daily and common observation and level of psychological activity were to cause a quantum change, we would constantly be altering our inner and outer realities. Fortunately, that doesn't happen. There seems to be a natural "built-in" safety measure regarding quantum changes made from an aware and conscious being.

When we rise above the stages of the mineral, vegetable, and animal levels (even though they are nevertheless still included), and operate from the soul (human) level, we rise above the conditioned impulses of punishment and reward, guilt and shame, competition and other ego-driven instincts. It does not mean we do not detect and experience the super-ego, ego-ideal, and the aforementioned psycho-emotional concepts. From the soul level, however, we are under the inner eye of the observer, where free will is present. There, the human soul can choose from the realm of possibilities that lies within us. From our Yesodic ego, we can only choose from our learned conditionings. From the soul, punishment or reward comes from the depths of ourselves.

In our conscience, we know things to be true for ourselves, and justice is a law (karma) through which we become aware of the metaphysical balance in nature. Application of Gevurah and Chesed is necessary for our inner growth, so the soul understands, and thus, takes responsibility and acts accordingly; not from a degrading motive, getting stuck in guilt-tripping or feelings of shame, but finding the balance between these opposites in our nature. The soul is interested in our evolution and spiritual endeavour. Therefore, it seeks to know how it can learn through the laws of life and makes changes correspondingly. The Kabbalist who has experienced this level will testify to the remarkable difference in perspective and consciousness.

The human effort to change something in our lives comes mostly through psychological and physical actions. The quantum conscious perspective of the observer generates changes without a process. It seems that quantum changes occur non-linearly and instantaneously. The Kabbalist may wonder what happened as certain things have altered and changed, but the process seems almost absent, because a quantum change is nonlocal and nonlinear.

Ego and Quantum physics
The conditioned mind is opposite to the quantum mind. Where fixed cycles within the psyche are present, the quantum consciousness lies dormant and asleep.
The potential of the so-called implicate order (David Bohm) is ever-present as the Eternal background of the relative and explicate order. As I have explained in the first volume of "A Kabbalistic View on Science", the implicate order is the world of Aziluth, where there is pure consciousness and potential in being. All are held here in the Eternal now in the wholeness and completeness of all that is, was, and will come to pass. The explicate order is the manifested world we call Assiah in Kabbalah: the relative existence in the realm of time-space and movement.

The ego-mind is so absorbed by the relative world that it knows no other than this reality. We become convinced that we cannot be any other person than the one the world (Assiah) has made of us (ego), or that we cannot do anything other than what we are being taught or have learned. Then we are fully in the midst of the ego and the explicate order.

From a Kabbalistic-metaphysical perspective, the world of Assiah is the literal way of looking at reality. Literalism is only one way of looking at reality, and it has its advantages and disadvantages. In quantum relation (that is, the relationship between quantum particles), a factual way of looking at reality is a disadvantage, because, from the senses, there is no way of knowing something other than from the literal approach to reality. There is a continuous discrepancy between the factual observation (the macro-level), and the observation at the quantum level.

Quantum change is the participation within relative existence from the viewpoint of the impartial observer who is without ego. To rise above the ego into the Sefira of Tifaret, we need a process of change within the psyche, where we transcend the lower face of the Tree of Life. Although we transcend on the inward way of the Kabbalist, we always include and integrate the previous levels or worlds. After all, we wish to bring "Heaven to earth" which is the work of a Kabbalist. Tifaret is the "eyes of God", as it is the medium through which an influence is made possible. The observer makes the potential of the implicate order collapse into the explicate order. The consciousness at the level of Tifaret is comparable to a doorway or a passageway for the world of pure potential to become "something" in time-space-movement.

The ego, however, is a part of the human psyche that is not made for such purposes. It has the awareness to interact between the inside and outside worlds. This psychological inside and outside is due to the working and function of Yesod-ego.

Yesod-ego works through the basic survival instincts of the physical body and the lower psyche. There is an urge for generating security and continuity in the ego. Here, you see another example of why the ego consciousness does not lead to a quantum collapse: the ego suggests a psychological continuum, and that the unfolding of time-space is always linear and continuous. Besides these survival instincts, the impulses from the animal nature for strife and exploration make way into new territory. On that "path", we start to risk things and push boundaries (leave our comfort zone), living a more individual life.

If science and scientists become predictable, safe, and controlled, then those scientific experiments are getting fossilized and dead, making no space for fresh explorations and curiosity. A religious creed could also prevent us from exploring further on a spiritual path, as we are asked to believe without questioning. Eventually, a creed and ideology-based ego is created.

Like material science, the ego needs ample proof to ensure that something is the way it is. In its subjective way, the ego claims its opinion to be an empirical proof about its own experiences. Look at the following examples: the ego wishes to replicate personal experience, to test personal ideas, beliefs and assumptions of their objectivity *(diagram 8)*.

Science says that reality should be measurable and controllable. In that way, it will give certainty to our lives. The ego wishes the same thing, and somehow functions like a scientist in subjective circumstances.

Quantum measurement is not dealing with certainties, but with measurements of probabilities. In Kabbalah, the ego is considered as a good servant, and not the master of our life. In other words, it should not be conditioned to control every situation nor continue in "survival mode" when we have already survived.

Pillar of
Form
Pillar of
Energy
CREATION
PARTICLES
WAVES
Sub-atomic
Electronic level
INERT STATE
Chemical level
ACTIVE STATE
Particular
Substance
Reaction
Mechanical level
Action
Properties
Four States
of Matter

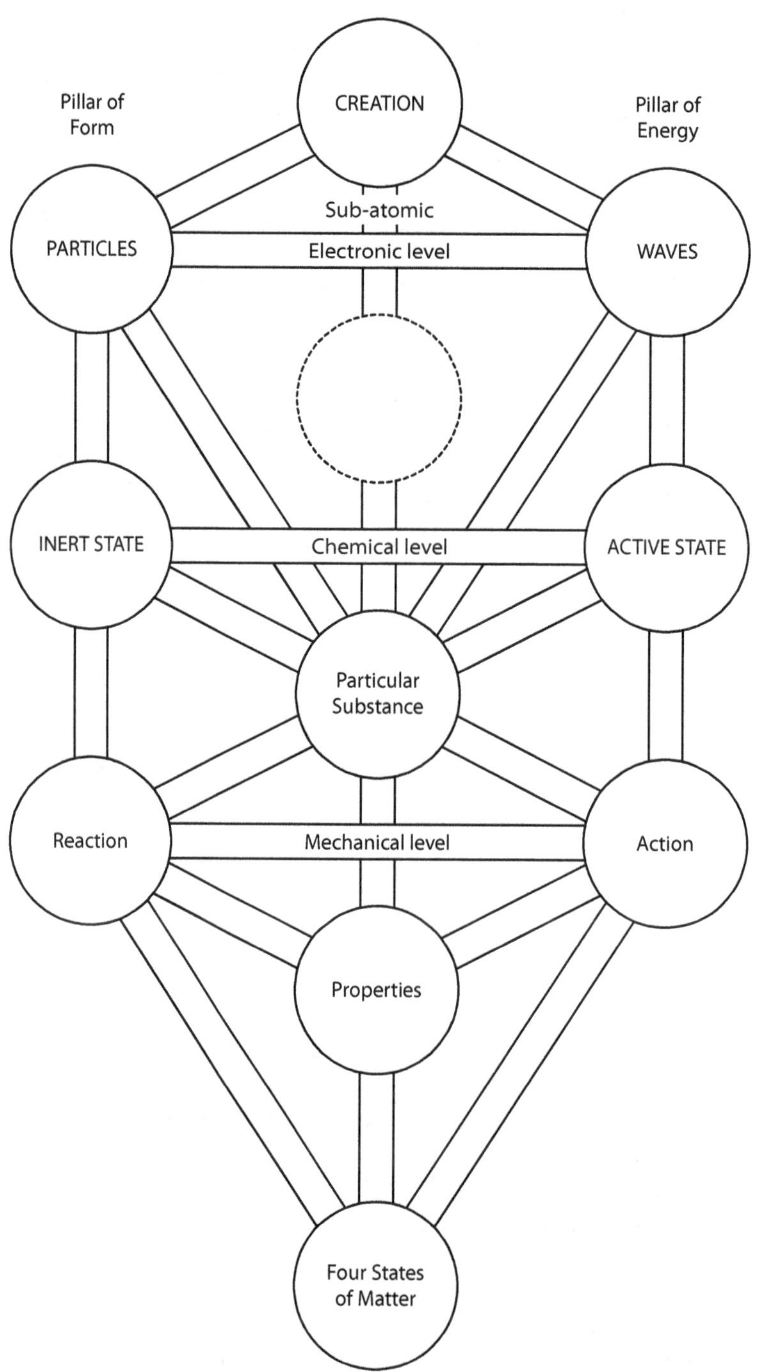

Diagram 8

Religious dogma often leads us to a "certainty through faith" with no doubt about the sacramental and liturgical authority. It is said that the words of the scriptures come directly from God. This assumption leaves no room for uncertainty, and there is no space for creative collapse from a quantum perspective. In a mere mathematical way, we can describe this equation in the following way:

1 Experiment protocol A = outcome A
2 Medical protocol A = treatment A
3 Sacrament A = miracle A

There are two ways to "destroy" materialistic, scientific, and religious ideology:
1 Mysticism
2 Quantum mechanics

Dualism in science and spirituality seems inevitable. Science is about matter and quantity, and spirituality is about the unseen and quality. In many esoteric traditions, it is said that above and below, quality and quantity, arise simultaneously from the same source. Quantity and quality are entangled like matter and Spirit. Everything comes from being and returns from being.

Although we regard and measure our human experiences into "quanta" that we recognize as quantity (left-side pillar on the Tree of Life) and quality (right-side pillar on the Tree of Life), all consist of the same being. Sometimes this is referred to as "being-ness" or "is-ness". All things in our created universe are codependent on the holism of the dualistic appearance of nature.

In other words: there is no is-ness in our experience if Spirit and matter are divided (quantity and quality are separate). Therefore, as we know from our metaphysics on the Tree of Life, quantity and quality cannot be separated. The duality in this relative manifestation is always united in the middle pillar on the Tree of Life. If this were not so in our universe, order (cosmos) would collapse and be destroyed.

There seems to be a constant in the middle pillar or the Kav (Will) of God that runs through the middle in all four worlds (Jacob's Ladder). Although this consistency is in our duality, there is simultaneously a consistency in change and probability.

As the Divine emanates, creates, forms, and makes the universe, Divinity becomes the creation process instead of "only" being an outside creator. But as soon as subject and object split, or if matter and Spirit are divided, we are immediately in the realm of dualistic and reductionist thinking ("it is all one way or the other, but can never be two ways").

Classical Kabbalah speaks about the two ways that the Divine involves itself in creation. The first and oldest is the Ma'aseh Berashith, or the way of creation the downward movement of the Lightning Flash through the worlds in the Kabbalistic Tree of Life. It describes how the Divine Will enters existence and creates, forms, and makes the worlds. Therefore the Lightning Flash is called the way of involution or creation.

The way "upwards" is the way of return or teshuva, meaning the way of evolution (initiation). The Kabbalist traverses the Lightning Flash in the reverse order. This is also called the Ma'aseh Merkavah, or the way of the Chariot, named after the mystics who travelled in their inner vehicles to journey into the Great Halls (Hekalot) or Heavenly world of Briah.

Is there a dualistic and spiritual conflict between the "upward or downward causation"? Does matter arise out of consciousness, or does consciousness arise out of matter? Or do they arise simultaneously out of an infinite source, both the same thing, only different in time-space expression?

In Kabbalah, we say that Divinity unfolds itself into Spirit-matter. No conflict is needed in such a dichotomy. The destruction of duality in time-space and the letting go of reducing Divinity to "something" brings God back to "nothing" or "No-thing", and as all springs from this No-thing, there is no real reason for the cause. God is simply omnipresent.

We could ask ourselves: Why is God? Because God is. And so all is because all is (Mandelbrot theory). God cannot be grasped and understood. Science comes to this conclusion about nature because things cannot be exactly predicted, and the phenomena of life change constantly. We seek continuity, but the facts show that discontinuity is the basis of nature and the universe. In quantum physics and mysticism alike, uncertainty means that creation is a mysterious intelligence that cannot (almost) be predicted. This uncertainty is not what the ego-mind or our human intellect (Hod) want. The intellect works through reductionism, it takes things apart in an effort to control and predict.

When combined with teleology, wanting to see things and their purpose to belong (know why I exist), or wanting to know without intervention. Teleology does not seek hierarchical or a logical causes of things, like science, but instead, it seeks to see the design and purpose of life. The cause is not important, but the process of how things came about. Theology says that God is external to nature, but regulates everything and is the designer of nature. If one does not regard God as such, we lose the world's sacredness.

So, materialistic science says that nature is without Spirit and that all is controlled by the laws of logic and reason, while theology proclaims that Spirit is above nature and controls all of nature. Spiritual and esoteric traditions say that matter and nature are not separate (and never were). We attempt to see what existence is all about and that consciousness seeks its own explanation (reciprocal loop). All is connected, and cause and effect are the same (entangled). This is how Kabbalah looks at the design and dynamics of creation, like some theories within quantum physics.

Apart from creation, Kabbalah does not suggest there is a deity or intelligence that creates and regulates life and nature by design, all in a linear and logical fashion. In this sense, Kabbalah has many similarities with the ancient animism of our ancestors. Here, we depart from the understanding that life is Spirit. Not that it is possessed by Spirit, but that there is simply no separation between matter and Spirit. All is an inclusive manifestation of Spirit.

Evolution theory - Lamarckism versus neo-Darwinism
Darwinism says that natural selection and randomness are the principles behind
creation and natural evolution. Lamarck adds that purpose and direction of will
and consciousness are included in the evolutionary movement.

Does nature simply react to the environment to change behaviour? Did giraffes
grow a long neck to reach the higher leaves in a tall tree? And because of this, do
all future generations of giraffes have long necks as genetic information implies?

Is it the gene that is the "headmaster" of the organism (and its surroundings), and
do chromosomes change, organize and regulate the cell and the gene organism?
Or is there an interaction between the organism and the organic world that moves
the "interior" and the "exterior"? Let us look at all these questions and try to
answer them.

First of all, replication of cells can only occur due to multiple stimuli coming
from the environment, and through the help of different genes (not just one);
cooperation is needed. In Kabbalah and quantum physics, the holistic view is that
a real change and transformation can only take place when all the different levels
of the total being (organism) are in conformity with that change.

In Kabbalah, the whole Tree of Life needs to be in "agreement" to come to a real
transformation within. If true, this leads to a further question: if our unconscious
is in charge of our life and its repetitive cycles, is there evolution? Or is evolution
dependent on the conscious process of creation?

Secondly, the role of DNA and RNA in our cells. The researchers in microbiology
have shown DNA to be a reproductive "organ" and not functioning like a brain.
DNA is not just a fixed program or library, but a biochemical construction that we
can alter and change according to parallel changes in consciousness and
behaviour. In these questions about evolution in a physical and metaphysical
sense, we need to consider our place in the world as human beings, and our
behaviour demonstrated on this earth.

This world of action (Assiah) asks for active participation from its organisms. It is
impossible to remain completely passive while incarnated in this world. Incarnated
in an animal body, we are also born with the accompanying instincts that ask for
competition and cooperation. Both are necessary for the participation in life.

These two animal actions correspond with the Kabbalistic principles of contraction
and expansion (Gevurah or competition and Chesed or cooperation). Although
cooperation may sound like the better of the two, competition is the vital tension in
the dynamic of cooperation. Competition is the first step in evolution before we can
realise that the "other" is a cooperative partner and not an enemy.

After centuries of warfare, we should be transcending that competition stage by now.

Cooperation is not synonymous only with "building" or "expansion", but thrives
on a mutual agreement that homeostasis (Tifaret) should be maintained between

building (expansion) and breaking down (constriction). To expand endlessly is to eventually conquer and leads to a disease of the organism and psyche.

Conquering can be done in two ways:
- By power/force (overthrowing the other, submission and slavery over the other).
- By love and compassion (including integrating, sharing).

Codependent life is more than cooperation. It may become an experience of "self" with the other. The human body consists of many different cells, tissues, organs, and organ systems, making up the "organism" or the biological self. Do the parts know that they are separate? It seems that they all have a sense of self, but they cannot regard themselves as "I" outside of the totality of the other organs.

Competition in this sense leads to tension that "invites" lifeforms to discover each other. If they do not compete, the other lifeform will take over, causing an unbalance through either uncontrolled expansion (Chesed) or contraction (Gevurah).

Cooperation should be challenged by competition and tension, so that the functions and purposes of the unit are being "tested" and brought under conscious consideration. These demonstrations of the dynamics between archetypal forces in nature can be represented by Chesed and Gevurah or Jupiter and Mars, and they should be constantly observed, checked, and corrected by a monitor. On the Tree of Life, this monitor is called Tifaret.

This solar archetype, that is, Tifaret, expresses self-consciousness, awareness of context and harmony, and has a "gathering" or unifying intelligence. Solar intelligence in nature is equivalent to the solar consciousness within the human body, which is equal to Tifaret in the subtle body, and the spiritual energy of Self known as Atman or Christ. On the Tree of Life, this is the principle of Tifaret. The message of the solar teachers is always of these qualities: unification, cooperation, integration, inclusiveness, and the way of Love.

Evolution in a bio-chemical sense seems to travel horizontally, as many species of all kinds exchange not only information through sensory ways, but literally through the exchange of DNA (genes). Of course, the simplest example is through procreation. Yet, there are other, more profound examples of exchange.

Spiritually, we should (could) also look for more horizontal ways for evolutionary exchange. Not to build towers or ladders to "climb to heaven" but to regard and behold the "next step" in the horizontal domain. We have no clue what is up or down (vertical), but we know what is inside and outside (horizontal).
What deterministic nature is interested in is the way of the so-called "selfish gene": out-competing others to survive and become better in the chain of evolution. The idea of being bad, prestigious, or striving for attainment goes hand in hand with this selfish gene.
Not being good enough is the emotional, psychological, and social input to move people to constantly attain a higher level (whatever that means), and take more out of life. Again, this is a mechanistic and linear-time related view. Nature is hard, and the only way to make it livable is to rise above it, and to conquer it.

How? By moving from a world of struggle and war, of good versus evil, towards one that embodies love, trust, compassion, and the practical side of those qualities (cooperation, empathy, support, collective effort).
This also refers to the metaphysical or spiritual constants that govern the universe, which are the natural laws provided by Briah. Human culture has the adaptability to shift from the genetic fact towards the choice (free will) of how to behave and act.

The adaptation is engineered not only by succession, but also by intelligent exchange with the environment. This can easily lead (as it does) towards opportunistic ways of making nature serve human needs, instead of living in accord with nature.

Two specific operational ways of behavioural selection can be seen in ecology and biology:
1   Reacts and responds if there is enough food etc., to survive.
2   Adaptation to shortages to cope with alterations and changes in
    the environment (just as the body does).

Type 1 functions on knowledge and experience of nature, and competition and survival strategies, if needed. Type 2, the human market strategy sets this need "for more" into motion, generating an impulse to be afraid and buy more (consume and store).

Industries compete with each other to sell more than what the consumer needs. They make the consumer believe, however, that they need more. Need is no longer coming from our natural system's information, but rather from a mechanical industry. This is the reason why we lose contact with our natural body, and we don't know what we need for true living and what our environment needs for living. Both are the same, of course. The more we are removed from our bodily nature, the more we are removed from outward nature. Industry, in turn, makes use of natural resources to make more materials that we don't need or are wasted on a huge scale.

What is needed comes from within, and not from without. Do science and spirituality still provide answers to what we need? Do they stimulate us to rediscover what humanity and the world need?

Biosphere
The biosphere of the human body and of nature in general (mineral, vegetable, and animal levels on the Tree of Life) have their equivalent on the subtle levels in the world of Yezirah, within the etheric and subtle aura of the psychological body. These two layers or worlds, interlock through the upper face of Assiah and the lower face of Yezirah.

In medical and scientific theories, these realities are separate, although they interact strongly together, as is recognized in the psychodynamic and psychosomatic conclusions that science and the medical world have drawn throughout the years. Body and psyche can no longer be separated as independent worlds or as separate functional parts of a total organism.

In Kabbalah, Jacob's Ladder is a metaphysical scheme, uncovering the different worlds or realities that are all coexistent, interdependent and inclusive. All the relative worlds (from Briah to Assiah) from creation, to formation and the world of action, form a biosphere in itself, where the universe is the total organism, and the stars and planets are the organs, while the microcosm, all life on this planet and the human being, are the cells, molecules and atoms of that organism, making up a complete biosphere.

What goes on inside the total organism (universe), determines how the complete biosphere functions and reacts. There is no independent movement or activity without an effect on the totality of the biosphere. Both the macrocosm and the microcosm are connected and mutually move each other. What is developing in the biosphere and the etheric body affects the physical organism.

This perspective on reality is very Kabbalistic- to observe from different levels such as mineral, vegetable, animal, human and beyond the different worlds, but always knowing that eventually, there is only one reality that all these worlds refer to. For example, in the world of Assiah, there is a lower face which is physical, and an upper face which is subtle and etheric, but they are not separate.
Both reflect each other, and although in substance they are different, in essence they are the same. The principles that work through the different parts of the Tree of Life (lower and upper faces) are the same, but they express themselves through different levels and worlds.

In the stream of thought called solipsism, which means that there is only one consciousness and one observer in existence, the different worlds in Kabbalah are not separate and independent units of consciousness, but are all different expressions of one consciousness. The whole of existence is one being and one consciousness. This resonates strongly with the saying in Kabbalah:
"Hear O Israel, God is one, there is only one God".

Only when one observes, can reality come into being. Multi-solipsism states that everyone's reality is real according to how we perceive it. In Kabbalah, it is said that existence is held in the mind of the Holy One, and how all is observed is how all came into being.

Through this one consciousness and observation, all the worlds are sustained.
The consciousness of the human soul has the capacity to co-create with the Divine, through both observing, and the potential and application of free will.

The brain can be thought of as a quantum computer or an electro-magnetic device where consciousness can be modified into an almost limitless amount of electro-chemical processes inside the body-mind organism (Assiah and Yezirah).
Like the Tree of Life, this is based upon a multilevel-world model of representation, depending on experience and memory of the organism. So, as long as nothing is observed, nothing is determined, but as soon as there is an observer, there is a determined, observational factor: a wave comes into being and is made up of particles. The phenomenal world is personal, determined by the subjective level of consciousness that "inspects the world as it is observed".

Being the observer is close to the notion that there is a superposition of consciousness: the human experience has a determining position. Another idea is the "inferior position", which means that we see the world from the subconscious impulses drawn from memory: a hologram-memory or personal database of the information that lives within the subtle matter of the etheric body. Our body has a natural and living memory that corresponds and resonates with the personal quality of life.

You see here how the etheric body in the upper face of Assiah co-exists with the Yesod of Yezirah and the psychological ego (personal consciousness). This is a holographic field of personalized information. The Knowledge (Daath) of the body coincides with the Yesod of the psyche, where memories of the physical body and the ego are shared and combined in a pragmatic and efficient working-unit. This function is the most dominant and prevalent within daily life. From the moment you wake up and go about your business, this system of Daath-Yesod, or body-psyche, is the main mode of operation and consciousness. It is a perfect developed and well-trained bio-psychological mechanism, although for the most part, it operates through the unconscious.

Quantum
The causal ability of consciousness lies within the soul (interface between the lower and higher faces of Yezirah). The soul's awareness can be described as: "consciousness that is conscious of being conscious". Or we could say: "the awareness of awareness itself", from which comes the mystical experience that the Universe (macrocosm and microcosm) is a self-aware Being.

God looks through the eyes of the soul into the Universe, who looks back at the one Who-is-looking! Aziluth or Divine consciousness is the potential to be. It is naked consciousness, completely whole and undivided (individual). The soul (triad Gevurah-Tifaret-Chesed of Yezirah) is the silent witness or the observer from the Seat of Solomon (place where the three lower worlds meet), who knows (gnosis) through sheer being-ness.

Consciousness is the experience of the soul. This awareness brings free will, opening a realm of potential, probabilities and choices. The soul has been described in many different ways in esoteric traditions, mediating between mind and matter, and between the higher and lower worlds: respectively, the upper and lower faces on the Tree of Life.

Self-observation from the soul leads to a realization, or at least, to the fundamental question: Who is observing? Who or what is looking through my eyes, listening through my ears and acting through these hands? This answer may come through different levels of experience, depending on who is answering.
On the middle pillar, the Sefirot tell us who is answering, and from which world. The transpersonal dimension opens up from the level of the soul where the veil of the first Heaven (Malkuth of Briah) separates. Although still aware of the Tree of Assiah, the awareness of who is looking changes into the perspective that it is not "me" (person or ego) who is observing, but there is someone else who observes the working body and mind (body-mind organism).

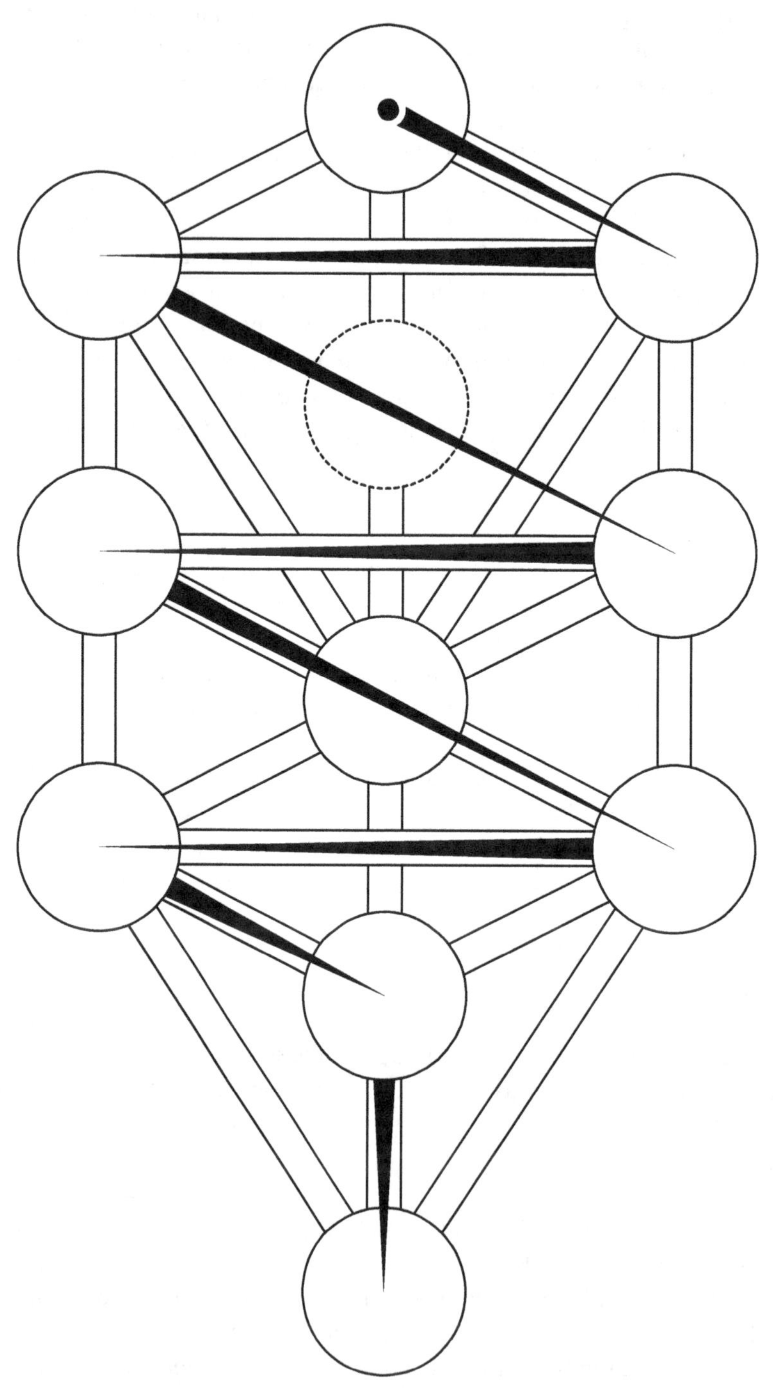

Diagram 9

From this level where the three lower worlds meet, human consciousness is a reflection of the consciousness of the Divine looking into the world.
All the senses, thoughts and feelings are becoming doorways of consciousness for the Divine to observe itself.

This takes us to the physics of possibilities, bringing into our scope the paradigm that, such consciousness, like a conjunction, parting that veil (first heaven or the place where the three lower worlds meet) that presented our separateness.
The door into the soul literally opens a new world, wherein endless possibilities reside (Aziluth) and we rediscover free choice.

Choice or free will is the process where potentiality and possibility becomes actuality through self-consciousness. Free will becomes an agent of Divine manifestation. The question arises out of this level of experience: who is choosing? If the answer to this question is: "I am", coming from the inner experience of the silent witness, there is a presence that testifies of the world. We become the eyes, ears and hands of God. This observer-effect causes waves of possibility to collapse into a particle reality: the manifestation of consciousness into concrete and solidified form. Through this process of wave becoming particle, we (the subject) create and generate (inner) objects.

Human consciousness (acting like a wave of possibilities) and the created particle object become separate, and the perception of duality is born. Only when the observer is aware of "who is looking", can subject and object return to wave-particle, as an undivided whole. This does not lead to an exclusive/dualistic, inner/outer universe, but to an inclusive perception and lived experience of reality.

Outer objects may be created by the subject-observer through the collapse from wave perception (Chocmah) into a particle perception (Binah). Created objects are never separate from the subject-observer. This quantum physics perspective is the exact same process that Kabbalah describes in its cosmology. It tells us about the Holy One calling forth the worlds into manifestation (created, formed, and made) by an act of will (Kav) *(diagram 9)*.

The worlds that emanate from the world of Aziluth (Kether of Yezirah, the Tifaret of Briah, and the Malkuth of Aziluth) are a reflection of that original world where all is held in the undivided consciousness of the Divine. Even if we live and have our being in the worlds of creation, formation and action, the world of Aziluth is always there as the potential "background" out of which the manifest world (time-space-movement) comes forth, from moment to moment (from Eternity to Eternity).

It is from this place on Jacob's Ladder, where the Lesser Yahveh or Metatron resides out of the Godhead or the Eternal, that time-wave and space-particle flows forth into movement.

It is unavoidable that the experience as incarnated beings into time-space-movement leads to an identification with the wave-particle world as moving and fixed.

Moving, because of the wave effect in the manifested world, and fixed, because of the particle effect. The whole elementary physical world consists of movement and concreteness, as we so vividly come to know in Assiah (and our personal, physical body).

Our physical body and the sensory perceptions, together with the lower psyche (upper part of Yezirah), invite us to observe ourselves and the world around us as both dualistic and separate.

In other words, we become enchanted by the world of phenomena: the passing show that is not just an object, but a living creation. The Divine Consciousness that looks through the eyes of the soul.

Difficult as it may seem, we truly are co-creators inside this cosmic potential within the world of living phenomena around us, and also through a body that consists of the same physical components. The irony behind it is that we can participate in this creative act only from that silent-witness perspective where free will exists.

Consciousness is the ground of being (Aziluth), like a sea of potentiality, where all arises from and returns to. The more we identify with this consciousness at the heart of existence (Tifaret), the more we become aware of its origin: not just being earth-walking creatures. Our sense and experience of time-space change from a linear and limited form of time-space towards an Eternal sense of being within space-time. In other words: the Eternal is Aziluth and the lower worlds are the evolving worlds of space-time (all three worlds with their own distinct time-space experience).

As it is said in quantum physics: pure consciousness or Eternity is without signal, because it has nothing to do with time-space. Yet, it is the background, as it were, where time-space-movement derives and develops.

Meanwhile, Eternity is time-space-movement-less, communicating without signal and any designated locality. Eternity is Eternity. It is all things at once. Whatever it is, it is all things at the same time. This suggests that communication (if we could call it that) from the time-space-less domain of the silent witness-observer is Eternal, and therefore, nonlocal.

Quantum-Kabbalah metaphysics explains much about God, the universe, and the human being. From this perspective we are enough, as nothing could be added unto us. Yet, without quantum- Kabbalah- metaphysics, human beings continue to feel incomplete and seek feverishly to get what they don't have.

This situation is caused through the final manifestation of consciousness, matter-consciousness, which has caused this dis-enchantment of the human being to identify ourselves as matter. Through this matter-identity, by using verbs such as "to have" and "to desire", we may be lead to the human problem for an endless search for the unattainable: "I desire what I don't have", causing a hunger that cannot be satiated by the ego-personality.

Imagine a classroom full of children. The teacher says that today the Holy One comes to visit and each child may ask for something. They all know their desires for what they don't have. One wishes for a new bike, another for infinite candy, a bigger room, new parents, etc.

The teacher is amazed and says: "Children, I cannot believe that you are asking for all these superficial things. Why don't you ask for intelligence? That is what I should wish for".

A child stands up and replies: "We all wish for something we don't have".

The lower psychological consciousness, corresponding with the lower face of the Tree of Yezirah, is not called forth, created, formed, and made, but generates what has already been processed. If the psyche could create constantly, the human being could bring forth new ideas without conscious consideration and discernment. Looking at the current state of our development, that would lead to great chaos.

The lower face is occupied with regeneration of the old (conditioning), while the upper face is the place of true creativity (not what some like to think of as creativity). The first is mechanical, predictable, and determined; the second organic, free, and spontaneous.

Quantum creativity is the participation in the creation process from the quantum level of consciousness, present at the heart of the human being: the soul.

Metaphysics like this brings us to the following story: at this age of tremendous scientific progress and development, the most brilliant people in the scientific world gathered to discuss the current state of affairs. As they could make a sheep, a cow, and even a human embryo in test tubes in a lab, they decided to arrange a meeting with God to tell Him that he was no longer needed.

The date and time were set, and they were in front of the great creator, telling Him, "respectfully", that He was dismissed from further duty in the universe. God said to them: "Well, that is fine, I see your point, but what makes you think you can replace me?" The scientists said that they could make life in their laboratory, and they offered to make a human out of the clay of the earth. They wanted to start immediately, but then God said: "No, no... First... Make the clay!"

Creation

Quantum Physics speaks about four conditions, needed for creation to occur:
- Downward causation
- Nonlocality
- Discontinuity
- Entangled hierarchy

If one of the four quantum conditions is missing, creation cannot be accomplished. In Kabbalah, choice-consciousness in the world of Assiah is too limited to cause a collapse out of the realm of endless consciousness and possibilities. According to modern psychology and science, the mind and the brain are often synonymous. Nothing could be further from the truth.

Mind is not an epiphenomenon of the brain. Intellect is rather a transpersonal and universal domain where we find humanity's cultural concepts and age-old memories (ancestral memory).

In Kabbalah, we see both on the Tree of Life, and on Jacob's Ladder, that the intellect is situated at the higher face of Yezirah/ lower face of Briah.
The brain located at the Malkuth of Yezirah does not create mind. The mind generates thoughts, and thoughts are entangled with the brain.

What entanglement means in this example is: without brain there can be no thoughts, but without thoughts there can be no brain. Consciousness holds both within its embrace, while both brain and thought are interdependent and "collapse" (manifest from a wave into a particle) simultaneously. When brain becomes thought, thought becomes brain.

In the quantum realm, potentiality and actuality are intrinsically entangled in nonlocality. Only in the worlds of relativity (time-space-movement) can we distinguish between both subject and object. We could say that potentiality and actuality are opposites. When these collapse the unconsciousness wave-possibility into conscious particle-actuality, these become opposite to each other (but are really never separate).

The way of evolution can be visualized as a Serpent ascending the Tree of Life *(diagram 10)*.

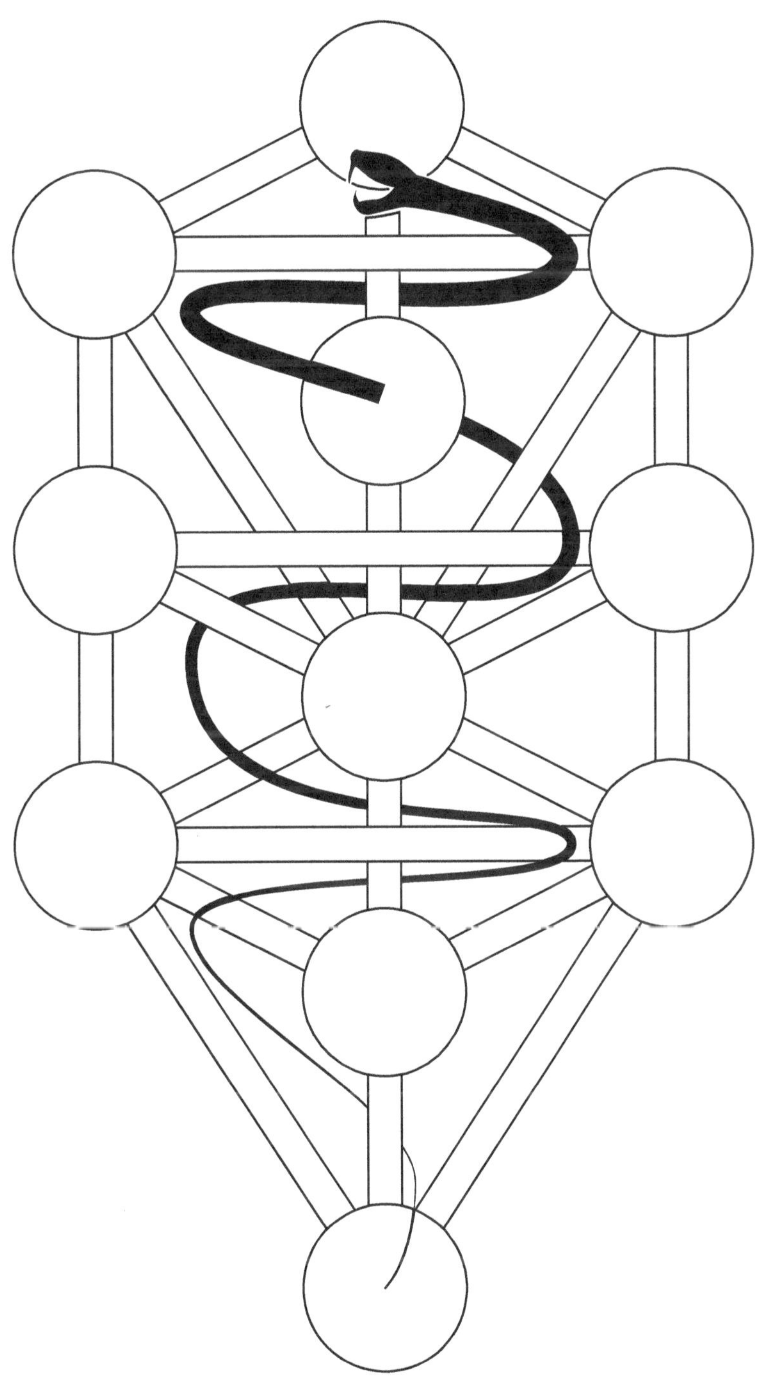

Diagram 10

Meditation

Start meditating like we did at the beginning of this book. From the stillness and the listening within you, see yourself as a being that is neither alive nor dead. See yourself as appearing and disappearing, being and nonbeing, born and dead. Be in that still place and observe all movement within you and without you in the world.

Let the timeless and the Eternal look through your inner eye, and be aware of the constant change in the world of phenomena. You remain still and observing, timeless, and simply letting the natural world unfold itself through you.

Chapter 4: The Kabbalistic worlds and Quantum Physics

Supra-mental and Archetypal

Some esoteric and quantum scientific sources, use the word "supra-mental" to mean a higher octave above the ordinary level of the psyche (lower mental capacity at the lower face of Yezirah).

As we have seen, the level of the mental on the lower face of Yezirah is the personal domain of the psyche. Here, we find the Yesod of Yezirah, the ego and personality. The lower face of the Yeziratic world contains three levels within the mental states: mineral, vegetable, and animal *(diagram 6)*.

These lower mental states correspond with the three lower chakras (Muladhara, Swadisthana, Manipura), mirroring exactly the mineral, vegetable, and animal consciousness states. The supra-mental level on the Tree of the psyche interlocks the upper face of Yezirah with the lower face of Briah, in the collective unconscious or the realm of the archetypes. These supra-mental states correspond with the three upper chakras and the three lower Heavens on Jacob's Ladder.

In between these two faces or gardens on the Tree, we find the crucial Sefira of Tifaret and the soul, being the place of self-consciousness and free will.

Our Tifaret resonates with the Anahata chakra, the place of transformation and creativity, bringing the lower mental states into the higher supra-mental states.

Or we could describe them as a psycho-spiritual process, going from generative states to transformative states.

You can see on the diagram on the Tree of Life that the supra-mental states in metaphysics are called "Heavens", the states or stages of awareness of our transpersonal nature. These three higher states or heavens are sublimated states of the three lower chakras or natural states. It is important to understand that the so-called lower levels are reflections of the higher levels functioning in the natural world.

In other words, the archetypal content that comes to us through the collective unconscious has transformative abilities, carrying metaphysical wisdom that we experience as higher spiritual morals, emotions, and values. In Kabbalah, we sometimes call these: spiritual constants.

From this upper realm of Yezirah comes a deeper and profound understanding of our innate nobility, and a vitality that is very distinct from our normal, daily life. The reason is that within the triad of the Spirit on the Tree of Life (Tifaret-Binah-Chocmah), we find the Holy Spirit (Ruach Ha-Kadosh), inspiring and vitalizing all who draw near.

In this higher face on the Tree of Life, we may also come into contact with the principle of fundamental creativity: the universal creativity that resonates with the process of how creation came into being. The word "fundamental" is appropriate at this level of the Spirit, as it is located at the Yesod of Briah / Daath of Yezirah.

The title for this emanation (Yesod) is Foundation, and therefore, it brings us a clue to this cosmic mode of creativity (which is truly creative and different from the "situational creativity" that we profess from the lower face of Yezirah).

The difference with the fundamental creativity lies within the fact that situational means to create (or generate) from old and already existent concepts. For example, a musician may compose a new song, but it is always based upon melodies that were created before.

To be original, which is possible, one does not invent a whole new tonal-scale, but creates a previously non-existent melody. The same can be done by a painter, an architect, a writer, or any individual, who receives inspiration coming from the upper Yezirah.

Being in-spirited or inspired means participating within this transpersonal consciousness where the archetypal/collective unconscious resides. For the Kabbalist, this is not a matter of "work", but a matter of readiness, openness, or what I like to call "availability" towards Spirit. The Wisdom and Understanding (Chocmah and Binah) coming from the Daath of Yezirah are a gift, rather than a product of work. A matter of grace rather than of merit.

Four Worlds
Out of four stages of Divine unfoldment come four stages of consciousness, and four modes of perceiving existence. Four ways for the soul to let God look unto Its manifested existence.
The primal world of Aziluth is the origin of pure, naked consciousness, where all four potentialities previously discussed are present in potential, or within four states of consciousness:

1 Consciousness (Divine) - Aziluth
2 Supra-mental - Briah
3 Mental-vital - Yezirah
4 Physical - Assiah

The four perceptions are known in Kabbalah as: mystical, metaphysical, symbolic, and literal. Other ways of describing these levels on a practical scale are: love, intuition, thinking/feeling, and sensing.

The worlds of Assiah and Yezirah (lower face) contain the natural world and, as such, the natural human being. These comprise the shared natural levels of the mineral, vegetable, and animal life with the senses and the vital (energetic) thought, mental, and memory functions.

As complex as the natural human being is, there is so much more to it than this. If we look at Jacob's Ladder, we see that this world (Assiah) is only one of four worlds. The physical and the mental-vital levels are close to each other, corresponding to the natural, outer world. They attune a part of our inner world and the outer-worldly surroundings to each other (bringing the interior and the exterior together).

Mental and supra-mental are the same world (Yezirah) differentiated in a lower and higher face, with their personal and transpersonal domain of operation.
In between these two faces, the soul keeps watch.

These two parts of the same world are distinct and different, but have everything to do with each other. While the lower part is occupied with personal psychological development, consisting of a general fate, the upper Yezirah is transpersonal, through which we may receive insights into our destiny. General or unconscious fate is the personal pattern that develops through direct living and participation within the world of Assiah. There, we are received from birth and immediately invited to follow the patterns and the examples of the milieu and culture.

There is a strong tendency from this lower psychological level to be influenced on the vegetable level. Life here is like a reflection of all that surrounds us, and as such, we are shaped and formed by the environment.

General fate, therefore, is not only personal, but entails a collective or group fate, giving direction and movement to the deep unconscious of that group.
Most people think (or like to think) that this process does not influence them, but no one can escape the vast pressure from the collective-general fate that moves us.
It moves masses and the individuals within it.

From this Yeziratic dynamic, located at the lower face of this world, we can easily see why there is no such thing in the ego-world as "fundamental creativity",
but only the reflective or "situational creativity".

The soul is where we start to observe the dynamics and consequences in ourselves and around us that concern general fate. First, we awake to our participation in general fate from the awakening triad of the animal level; then we see the influences of parents, grandparents, family, school, and education, friends, work, religion, society, and many more.

Besides observing this process, the soul touches, apart from self-consciousness, upon the potential to free will. Here opens a new domain, unknown to the ego, where the personality is seen and scrutinized from a consciousness that is not the ego.

One becomes the silent witness, perceiving oneself as a part of the totality, while before, the Yesod-ego assumed it was the self of the psyche (ruling the show).

Through this dawning awareness of the soul and its intricate possibilities, the soul notices that the general fate is not written in stone, and can be changed and transformed. Choices can be made that bring us out of the psychological territory of the social-emotional pressure that keeps the vegetable level in control, preventing it from growing and developing.

I AM
DIVINE WORLD
(Azilut)
Implicate order
Non-local consciousness
and a-specific potentiality
Metatron
Great
Holy
Council
Sages
Greater
Saints
SPIRITUAL WORLD
(Briah)
World of causation
Supramental level and
fundemental creativity
(higher Yezirah)
MESSIAH
Sages
Lesser
Saints
THAT
Spirit
Spirit
Individuals
Soul
Soul
PSYCHOLOGICAL WORLD
(Yezirah)
World of form
Mental & vital
Situational creativity
(lower Yezirah)
Self
Leaders
Ego
Masses
PHYSICAL WORLD
(Assiah)
World of action
Explicate order
Physical & sensory
Body
Living dead
I AM

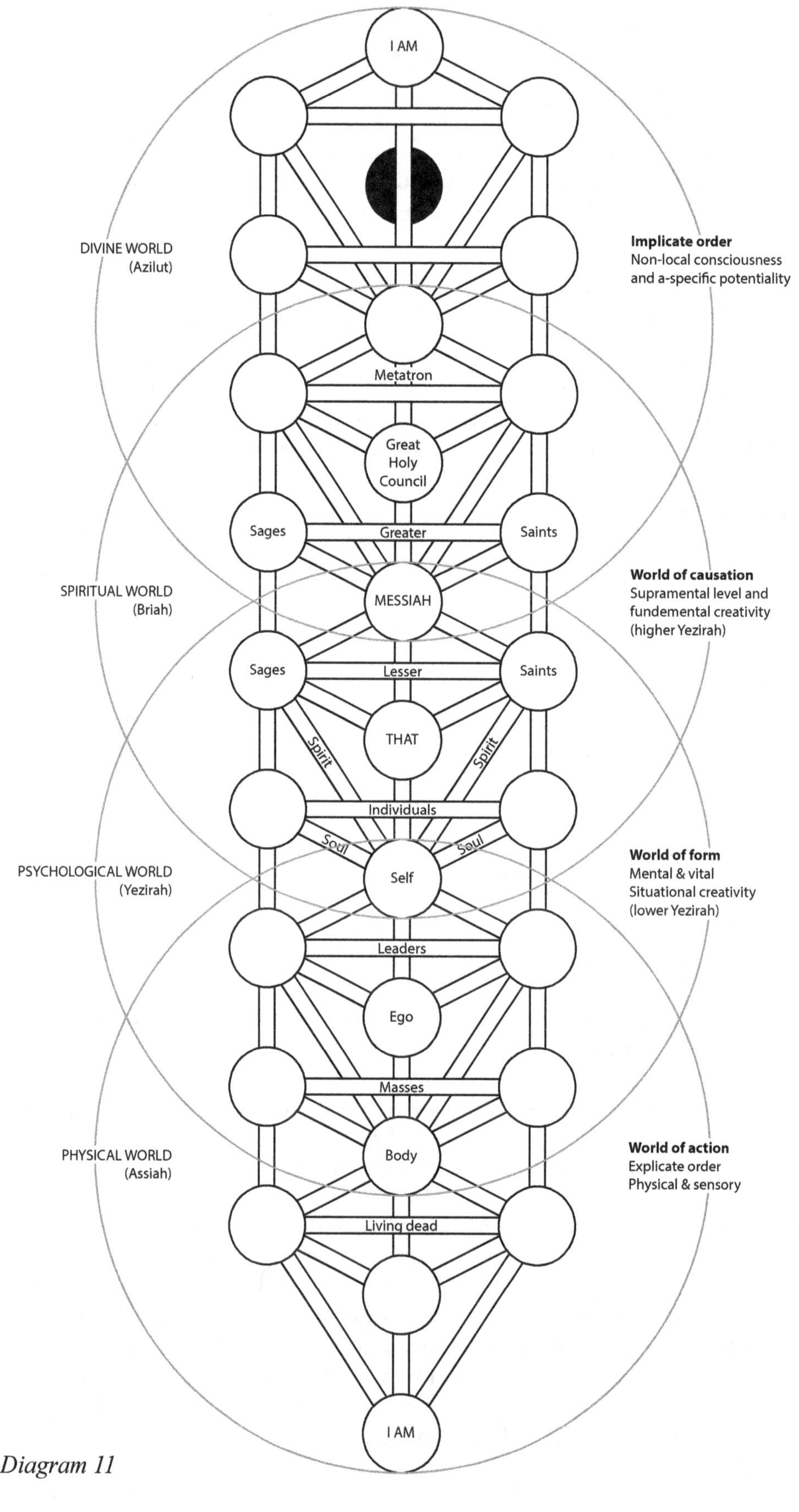

Diagram 11

In Kabbalah, we call this the specific or individual fate: differentiating one's fate from the group and initiating the self-liberating process of practicing free will. Life goes, from the sphere of activity (karma or mazal) with Yesod at its centre, towards the second sphere on the Tree of Life, Tifaret: the sphere of growth, at its centre.

The upper part of the Tree of Yezirah and lower Briah, the place of the archetypal collective- unconscious (as discussed before), is where we find the transpersonal dimension, opening to us the greater patterns that extend over lifetimes.
Here, we are introduced to our destiny (exploring meaning, higher values and morals) and our place in the world, with the specific tasks that we have developed and followed (consciously or unconsciously) over many lifetimes.

As Spirit guides us on the path of destiny, we feel inspired, challenged, comforted, tested, grateful, and stimulated to persevere through the path of awe (from Tifaret to Kether). Awakening to our destiny always leaves space for our free will, meaning that one does not have to choose to follow destiny. However, most individuals find that the path is intertwined with one's feelings of bliss and being whole.

Finding meaning, purpose, and a spiritual direction in life gives the human soul a place to "rest its head". Some call it a homecoming.

In the expressions of the deeper life, the essential meaning of the Sefirot comes to the surface. Like an inner contact with the higher world of Briah, inner creativity erupts to find expression in many forms of art. As it was discussed before, these expressions are well defined in paintings, music, poetry, architecture, and more.

The spiritual virtues (or spiritual constants) of the creative world find their way, saturated as it were, into the lower vehicle of the natural world. This process for the Kabbalist, of living these principles coming from the spiritual world can only happen if the soul has guided the lower vehicle into processes of purification, in order to prepare the ego and the body for reception.

The word "Qibel" from the word Kabbalah, means "to receive", and it is the meditation of the Kabbalist that always directs the inner attention to the reception of the Higher worlds.

The inner mode or stature of the Kabbalist departs from Tifaret (self) and the soul, a state of Gadlut, or the contact with the self, being the silent witness (sitting on the seat of Solomon). It is a virtue for the most skilled and trained Kabbalist to enter this state at will. The Gadlut state is lost as soon as the ego-consciousness (Katnut) engages with its worldly affairs.

The longer we can remain in this higher state of Gadlut, the more we are available and reliable to the Spirit (triad Tifaret-Binah-Chocmah), what we call in Kabbalah "Devekut" or the "cleaving unto God". Fundamental inner creativity is born out of love or unity (Aziluth). At the same time, from the human side (natural world and the soul), the Kabbalist starts choosing from the archetypal content of the upper Yezirah, instead of reproducing old choices, based on memories and former experiences. What does this mean?

Archetypes are the essential principles that give rise to form and, eventually, the physical world. Suppose we shift from living the personal life, based on automatic reactions (vegetable level), and reach out for the archetypal. In that case, we begin living from self-consciousness, free will, creative freedom, spiritual insights, and inspiration.

In the old jargon, the archetypes are the gods, angels, demons, and other mythic beings who express the higher creative energies in the actual structure of our world. They are the personifications of the creative principles of Briah.

These archetypal forces of transformation set into motion the world of form and action. In the word "trans-formation", we can see the meaning of what changes (namely, the world of Yezirah (lower face) and the personal structure that we have built). Of course, the outside (objective) world itself does not change, nor the psychological principles that make up the metaphysics on the Tree of Life. What does change and transform, from working within the archetypal domain, is the personal structure within our psyche: the ego and the psychological perspectives on ourselves and the world.

Time
Another important distinction between the natural world and the higher Briatic world is the experience of time. The natural world and the lower psyche experience the world as continuous in time, while on the higher, archetypal level, the experience is discontinuous.

Only through the frequencies that our physical senses detect, and the way the lower psyche works (through memory), can we know the world around us, and ourselves, as continuous.

The ego likes to think that it is continuous (immortal) by placing itself central to all activities. Yesod is central to the lower face and thereby occupies the centre between the triads of thinking, feeling and action.

Although the Yesod-ego has a central position in life, that position is relative to the whole of our being. The Kabbalist who grows into Tifaret (and beyond) starts to see this relative and mortal position of Yesod-ego.

From the soul's perspective, the body and the ego are discontinuous and mortal, but the consciousness that observes these mortal phenomena (soul) is itself immortal and discontinuous.

The soul knows, and being creative through a conscious intention (kavanah), gives consistency to the act of free will. We can will all we want, even from free will, but will is a momentum in time that loses its focus and strength (potential) if there is no intention to support it. Ego-natural consciousness knows about time in linear ways, looking backwards and forwards in time. Within the scope of this linear view, there is a limited range, because we look from the eyes of Yesod-ego.

The so called "arrow of time", that draws time in a linear and "all-at-once" fashion. Darwinism is a way of describing evolution where there is no space for fundamental creativity, based on the quantum physics paradigm that the creative world is discontinuous. Darwinism, as a theory that supports continuity in evolution, depends on fossil records and linear ideas of logic and thought.

"Logic" (Sefira of Hod) comes from certain concepts of the mental (lower Yezirah) world, and is, by definition, not creative, but linear and continuous. Our thinking cannot escape its own concepts and structures.

So, how does conscious purpose get into matter (or become matter)? Only by free choice and intention, together with choosing from the fundamental-creative domain (domain of the archetypal-collective unconscious-inspirational). The complete natural Tree of Life (Assiah) is not made to be creative, but to reproduce, repeat, form, adapt, change, and anticipate natural conditions. The creative (cosmic) world influences the natural world constantly, yet the natural world cannot "lift itself by its own arm".

In other words: the lower face of the Tree of Life (which is the natural world), and the conditioned psychological state of our psyche, is not creative. The upper face is the creative and transformative part of the (transpersonal) psyche. Meaning that the microcosm, through its inability to create, does not move or change anything in the higher worlds.

Having said all this, in Kabbalah and quantum physics, the worlds are not separate from each other. However, they are portrayed as such (even on the Kabbalistic diagram of Jacob's Ladder). The stars, the planets, the gods, archangels, angels, and nature spirits are all within the earth's sphere. The universe is not "out there", but right here.

Not only are you and the whole planet in the universe, but you are the universe. The cosmic plane that we call the fundamental creative level, or Briah, is within and around us.

The potential for creativity and the cosmic ability to transform and perform miracles are within you and everybody else. Suppose we do not rediscover our true creative potential within ourselves (part of the Kabbalistic work is to find the Heavens within and bring them to earth).

In that case, we are confined and locked within the lower worlds of reproduction and action.

How do we remember these worlds in, and about us? During the slavery period of the people of Israel (Book of Exodus), it was said that: "forgetfulness is suffering, but remembrance is liberation". We remember this by making gradual contact with our soul (spoken about above) in meditation, and moving into stillness. Those are the fundamental properties of the soul. Being the silent witness and knower of the process of life. Let us now look closer into this domain.

Grace
Justice
Mercy
EHYEH
I AM
ELOHIM
YAHVEH
YAH
EL
YAHVEH
ELOHIM
First Day
Night
Day
Second Day
Yesod
of Emanation
Firmament
Daath
of Creation
Third Day
Dry Land, Plants
Fourth Day - Celestial Lights
Fifth Day - Fish and Fowl
Sixth Day
Beasts
ADAM
Seventh
Day
Sabbath

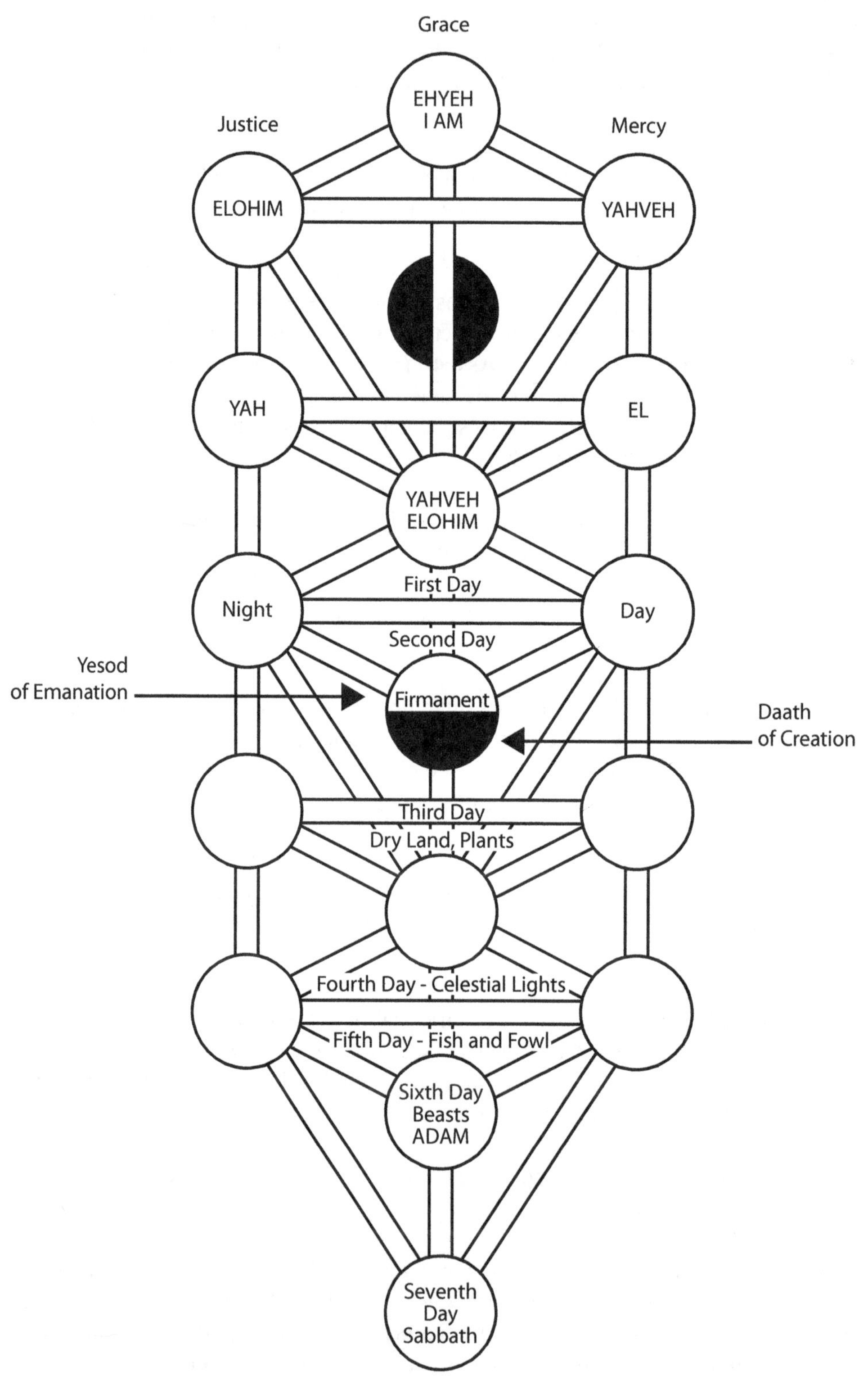

Diagram 12

Soul and reincarnation
Many philosophical concepts in East and West attempt to explain reincarnation.
Could it make matters more complicated to talk about this topic by combining
quantum physics and Kabbalah? Definitely!

The whole natural Tree or world of Assiah/ lower face Yezirah does incarnate,
and all that incarnates will eventually discarnate or move back to where it came.

The physical body disintegrates into the elemental parts that it is made from.
The lower Yeziratic vehicle will decompose, leaving no trace of the personality
and the ego structure that came together with the physical body. Both are
constructions of the world of Assiah: all that is built from and within that world
will return to where it came.

The cycles move according to law, arranging the manifest worlds (Assiah and
partly Yezirah) as they are called forth (Aziluth) and created (Briah) into being.
They are formed (Yezirah) and made (Assiah), returning to their proper place, for
nothing is lost or wasted in the universe. In that sense, the universe and life itself
are indeed immortal, changing their form and substance, but the unchangeable
will remain throughout this process.
Bodily and mental experiences, that is, the physical and lower psychological-ego
experience, are for the greatest part stored as personal (mental) memories, or
so-called brain memories. We access them through recalling events and other
personal conditionings. On the Tree of Life, we find such memories in the lower
circle or sphere of action, with Yesod (the personal consciousness) at its centre.

We built these memories gradually, passing the stages of our life with the major
influences that come to us from the outside world. Without choice, most
constructed experiences and memories are, for the greatest part, facilitated by and
through exterior conditions.

How we react to the world, and the interior response to circumstances and people,
is subjectively personal. Although we live in a very impersonal (cosmic) universe,
we make our life very personal, related through memory. This memory will not
last; it only remains for the time when our physical life is sustained on this earth,
and disintegrates after physical death.

However, these personal memories are unconscious reflections which can become
conscious when they are brought into the life-processing orbit of the soul.

The realm of the Yesod of Yezirah is a vast memory bank, storing what has been
learned, sensed, and felt. An amalgam of impressions and images, woven together
into a kind of personal timeline-timeframe, where we find references between an
inner and an outer life.

In Kabbalah, we call this place on the Tree of Life and Jacob's Ladder: "the Treasure
House of Images". There are a few good reasons why this name was given.

Firstly, Yesod is related to the esoteric principle of the moon, reflecting thoughts, ideas, images, and all present memories that you have accumulated in your life. Secondly, the reflection shows a passive kind of memory that mirrors back at us what once was. Once we discarnate (die), the mirror reflects once more, showing us the story of our life, after it shatters and disintegrates.

Beyond the mirror and the world of Assiah, the soul is operative as the vehicle of consciousness. Through this seat of consciousness, one comes into contact with the Holy One, and allows the Holy One to look through one's eyes, and hear through one's ears. In other words, free will, which is so much spoken about in esoteric circles, has the choice to turn towards the higher world of Briah or bury itself in the worldly affairs of Assiah.

Inherently, the soul positions itself in the very centre of the Tree, enabling the human being to connect "Heaven to earth", or, for that matter, to remain subordinate to the worldly influences, and live like animals. Such experiences are of a different psycho-spiritual order, taken and carried with the soul's vessel towards the next incarnation.

Through imagination, we could visualize this journey as a movement or migration from point a to point b (life a to b). However, let us not forget that consciousness itself has no properties other than presence, stillness, and the wakeful observation (silent witness). These inner qualities give the human being the experience "to be in the world, but not of this world", finding oneself time-space-free, and simultaneously, being in the world of time-space-movement. Therefore, the soul has these timeless properties while being in the world.

From this knowledge comes a new esoteric quantum idea that the soul does not incarnate again, nor does it migrate; rather, the soul remembers without the need of incarnation, through quantum collapse, the individual life experiences it had undergone over many lifetimes.

This, according to this challenging paradigm between Kabbalah and quantum physics.

We could compare this remembering with waking up in the morning and recalling the dream to waking consciousness (Yesod). From there, it is possible to recall, and integrate the dream into daily life. To incarnate is to wake up from a dream of our former incarnation. For most of humankind, the lives previously lived completely, or partly, fade away at birth, depending on the spiritual development in past lives. The maturity of the soul, and the complete human vehicle as a whole (self) in a former lifetime, make us remember what we were, where we are, and where we are moving towards (fate and destiny).

The challenging esoteric hypothesis in this book suggests that the soul does not migrate (that is, it does not go anywhere), but is indeed a vessel of consciousness that rests within the timeless dimension, where life is born and will return (Aziluth).
For this reason, it is from the soul that the spiritual experiences speak to us, giving us evidential knowledge of the Spiritual (Briatic) and Divine realms (Aziluth).

The knowledge (Daath) that is sometimes called Gnosis does not move, but it is an omnipresent knowing, as a memory in daily life that you remember wherever you are. Quantum physics talks about quantum memory consisting of a nonlocal, timeless confluence of memories that carry or contain specific thoughts and images, comprising our individual karmic pattern.

See the Seven Days of Creation *(diagram 12)*.

Meditation
As you sit quietly and invoke the Tree of Life and the presence within you, a
sense of peace comes over you. You become receptive and available to whatever
is given to you. Listen and be present.

Allow yourself to flow back gradually in time, and follow the images that appear
within you. Your inner life of this incarnation shows itself through different
moments, ages, episodes, and situations. Some are bad or good, sad or happy.
Whatever they may be, they tell a story that is the authentic story of your life.

There is a structure in all those memories, a design that is not random. Your life
unfolds according to a plan, and although you have free will, you cannot escape
the notion that all seems to be guided and leads to some deeper purpose.

Let your soul speak to you, and show you this design that presents to you the
soul's journey from many lifetimes until this very moment. From that journey of
the soul, which is the way of the seeker, you may gain insights into your purpose.

Purpose

Most of us have a purpose in life that has something to do with happiness and fulfilment of needs.

Purpose comes in all forms and shapes, according to human intention and needs. It is very dependent on where the need or desire comes from, whether the need or desire is easily satisfied, and whether that need or desire will return in time. For every need and desire returns sooner or later.

The urge to continuously satisfy the needs and desires in life (personal purpose) makes the human restless, and to be in the endless pursuit of a purpose that will never be truly satisfied (only in the short-term experiences of the lower psyche or ego).

Purpose on the Tree of Life is located in the Divine triad of Kether-Chocmah-Binah. Here we find the principle of what a human being sees and regards as a crown on one's destiny. In other words, if that purpose is achieved, life has true meaning. Some say: "I came on earth to fulfil this specific task (purpose)".

Purpose and meaning are intrinsically intertwined in the human story, for there is no other creature that we know of, that works and moves towards purpose. Of course, purpose is quite different when we start our journey in life (teshuva) from the level of Malkuth, Yesod, Tifaret, or even higher on the middle pillar of the Tree of Life.

Purpose and meaning shift according to the level or stage of consciousness one is at. This can be illustrated by growing on the central pillar of consciousness and spiritual development. Purpose is different coming from the lower face of the Tree, where we share the common or general fate of humanity. When approaching the soul level, we awake to self-consciousness, arising with a sense of specific or individual fate.

From this inner domain of the soul where free will rests, we can cause changes to happen that fall within the scope of quantum selection. Free will opens the possibility to choose (consciously) from the quantum field (Briatic Matrix), where archetypal possibilities exist as principalities, or essential beings. In Kabbalah, they are called Archangels and the Higher Angels.

From the soul level, we make decisions from the level of self-consciousness that have the potential to truly be creative and transformative (spiritual action). It is not uncommon that the soul perceives the line of destiny that clarifies the individual's purpose.

Such an insight makes the Kabbalist realise that the soul, which is receptive by choice, is inspired to live more and more in accord with higher goals and meanings. This shows that a Divine purpose (or the highest achievable one in life) is relative, depending on the evolutionary stage of development on the Tree of Life. Quantum physics adds to this that, if we wish to make a real transformation possible, we need to start choosing from higher and spiritual principles (Briatic order) like love, justice, harmony, compassion, strength, and other spiritual virtues on the Tree of Life.

We call these in Kabbalah: "spiritual constants". The natural human being needs
guidance that elevates the natural state into something more, something greater;
because it is said in the world of Kabbalah that from the level of Yesod (Yezirah),
we cannot "lift ourselves by our own arm".

Purpose and karma
How can we distinguish between particular karma memories and the accumulated
memories from a current incarnation?

What we learn through the contact with the world, the immediate family, culture,
and other direct influences, are not the same memories as the karmic memories,
which are also called quantum memories.

Naturally, these two distinct memory types, the personal and the transpersonal,
should be meditated upon and integrated. How else (as Kabbalists) could we
come to any serious integration and unity of what our transmigrated self has to
say about the continuation in a current life?

In other words, our present incarnation does matter very much, asking us to
remember what we have gathered throughout other lives, weaving, as it were,
a pattern that is in harmony with our greater (spiritual) design.

That spiritual design is known as destiny, where we come in touch with an inner
realization of what it means to be part of a greater plan. Such insight makes the
human being see that this life is not about us. Time and again, the teachers
(maggidim) of esoteric traditions have told us so.

As I have said before, a clear destiny leads to purpose and meaning in life.
Purpose and meaning give perspective to our existence, and are functioning
beacons that guide us onward, along with archetypal (spiritual) principles.

The archetypes present themselves as cosmic essences and as inner
personifications of creative and spiritual energy. Instead of leading our life
according to the impulses of worldly affairs (for example, what is in the news,
what neighbours say, how culture drives us) and personal memories only, we can
follow consciously the inner-symbolic memory that portrays our karmic pattern.
Knowing this allows for a curious and exploring attitude to flourish towards a
deeper, unconscious level (higher Yezirah).

The soul in every human being sets out on the journey for this unique exploration
towards purpose and meaning. Unique, because each individual path is made by
the decisions that one makes, based upon unconscious (generative) or conscious
(creative) fate.

Quantum thought and the opening up of free will, unveils inner possibilities to
create out of the very centre of our being: Tifaret. However difficult in its
abstractions, this creative act is called a "creative quantum leap", and can be
compared with a discontinuous jump in a continuous time- frame.

Imagine that our physical and lower psychological existence is experiencing the world as a time-space-movement continuum. It seems that our body and personal psyche wish to experience this idea, and the feeling of a never-ending life. After all, these parts of the human totality are time-space dependent and will perish in due time. They are both more or less stuck in that stage of consciousness, where they conform with the natural surroundings in which we live. We need to make a quantum leap (jump) in consciousness to be creative. After all, the quantum domain is the realm of consciousness (the all-potential consciousness of Aziluth).

From the light of this consciousness (heart of Aziluth), spring forth the two creative principles of Chocmah (time) and Binah (space), and the world of Briah (the higher creative world) starts to unfold. Kether is the pure realm of probabilities, while Chocmah and Binah represent the wave and particle functions.

The potential wave in Chocmah, the boundless wisdom in the cosmos, may collapse into a new form, or "particle", in the understanding of Binah. Suppose there is no quantum leap or discontinuity (Daath); in that case there will be no true creativity, but only a regeneration of older collapses or repetition of the same old consciousness and perspective.
This understanding is about working with an archetype or spiritual principle on the Tree of Life. One such example comes from our Tifaret, when we direct our intention and energy towards the archetype of the self.

Why are archetypes so different from personal symbols and memories? Because they belong to the creative world (collective unconscious) of the transpersonal and the metaphysical. Archetypes carry with them the intrinsic capacity (Chocmah and Binah of Briah) to transform life in all its energy and form.

What is needed to be creative is to apply consciousness, imagination, and choice (free will). Let us take this a step further, as there are multiple locations on the middle pillar of the Tree of Life and Jacob's Ladder that are called Tifaret (meaning that each world, and every Tree, has its own Tifaret).

Tifaret
Free will lies at the heart of Yezirah and touches the soul triad (free will, conscious processes of life, and conscience), but simultaneously it is the place where the "three lower worlds meet".

The Kether of Assiah is the physical maturity we may all grow towards in due time. However, to be knowledgeable of the body (Daath of Assiah), is another matter. This crown on the natural-physical kingdom means that we are conscious of our physical vehicle.

The Tifaret of Yezirah is the psychological self at the heart (center) of the psyche. The Malkuth of Briah is the so-called Kingdom of Heaven, because it is the Malkuth of Heaven, the heavenly world of Briah. At the foot of this Briatic world, we step into the Spirit realm and the first heaven. In Kabbalah, this heaven is called Vilon or veil. At this place, we encounter the experience of dawning consciousness that makes us see that we can "be aware of being aware".

Destiny
Spirit
Membrane as a barrier
Permeability of the membrane
Soul or the human level
Function of the membrane/ Selfconsiousness
Individual or specific fate
Thought
Animal level
Action
Yesod of Yezirah mirror
Sense of 'me' and awareness of in- and outside of 'me'
Personal or general fate
Physical DNA

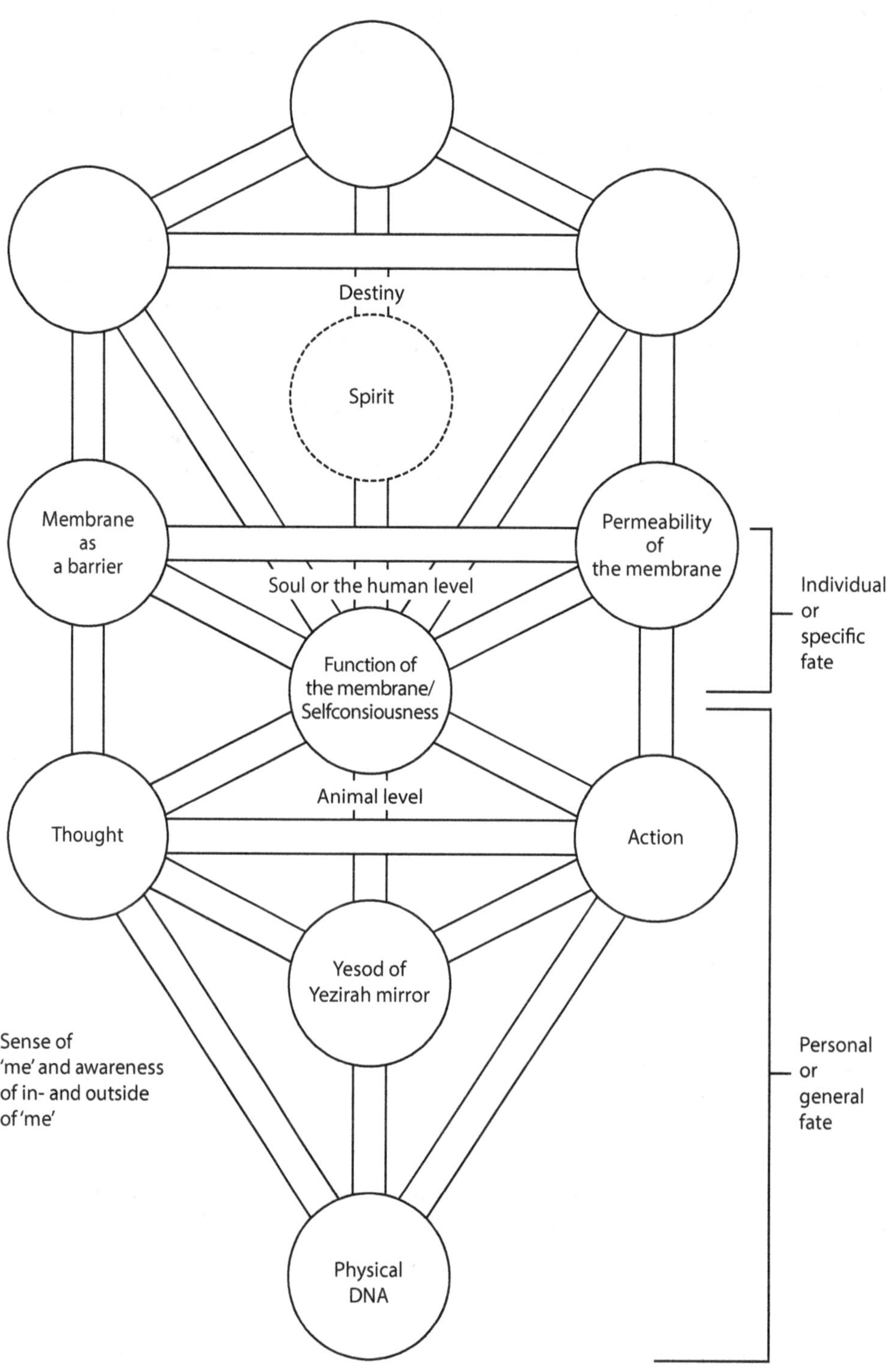

Diagram 13

Here you find the first glimpse of the quantum self, from which we can freely choose from the wave-like possibilities into a collapse of manifested particles within us. The opening (rendering) of the veil reveals a kind of naked consciousness, a self that is truly self-existent without any particular properties.

From this point forward on Jacob's Ladder, it is possible to occupy a space in consciousness that contains and embraces all three perspectives. Being of that stature of naked consciousness, one can simultaneously be in the world of the psyche and the body (meaning that spiritual consciousness does not exclude ordinary daily consciousness). On the contrary, the Spirit is the all-inclusive consciousness inherent to spirit. In quantum terms: the quantum self is omnipresent within its own manifested world.

Although it is possible to reach this summit upon one's inner mountain on the Tree of Life, it is not so easy to remain there. A nice metaphor we can extend upon is the altitude on the mountain, as we reach higher into thin air, moving into the more ethereal realm of Briah (air). The Kingdom of Heaven can be grasped, but is difficult to hold.

In Kabbalah, we talk about the state of Gadlut, when we can attain the summit, but only from an established state of Devekut (devotion) can we find stable ground in that Malkuth of Briah. To achieve this is all a matter of inner work and consciousness *(diagram 13)*.

Making the synthesis with quantum physics again, it is here that we come into an entanglement between the consciousness that creates us, as well as all other created forms and beings. We might even come to certain insights that tell us that we are co-creators, and the body and world we live in are self-created.

Even more, we give rise to these forms in a creative way, daily, from moment to moment, as we reside and are present in that creative-quantum consciousness; and if we commune with it, we are as that consciousness. This level of consciousness is pure mysticism wrapped in the modern jargon of quantum physics.

In quantum physics, they call this consciousness "nonlocal", which, in other words, is not time-space bound, but rather, it is identified with "Eternity" and is discontinuous.

For so many esoteric practitioners all over the world, it remains hard to uphold the state of "nonbeing" wished for in certain traditions. Living in a world of time space-movement implies that we cannot be permanently in Eternal consciousness (outside body and ego). We would be completely dysfunctional in life.

Kabbalists have said for many centuries that the human being is a vehicle of Divinity, rather than an illusion that we must escape (as soon as possible). Kabbalah and quantum physics are about wholeness and integration: making life complete and not dividing it into separate parts, nor excluding anything.

Karma includes purpose, for we should not forget that we generate karma all the time by living in the natural world. We are in the world of action, not only through physical activity, but also in the mental, emotional, vital, and sensitive actions, from which new effects arise that are, in turn, causes for new effects. This is why we may easily lose our sense of purpose in this vast and complicated human web of actions. We perform our life on the stage of our daily and nightly actions, consciously, or unconsciously.

Kabbalah and quantum physics both invite us to walk the way of awareness and conscious intention (kavanah), so we may more clearly know what actions we establish in and through ourselves, and thereby, into the world.

Purpose cannot arise out of coincidence, nor out of some unconscious impulse. Although our purpose may call us from the deeper depths of the unconscious (like our maggid or inner teacher calls us), we have to awake to that call, and what it tells us, so we may understand its messages, and follow our bliss.

Meditation
Relax.

After the invocation, open up yourself, and listen with your whole being.
Turn your inner attention (kavanah) towards the Holy Mystery.

Let a spark of bright light burn in your heart (Tifaret). This flame is like an inner
sun that sustains, nurtures, and keeps you. It is the source of life within you.
Sense, see and feel that this flame represents the Good, the Beautiful, and the
True. It makes yourself to shine with a beauty that needs no explanation nor
confirmation. This light extends and makes your whole Tree of Life to grow,
shining in, and through, all the 32 paths of Wisdom.

Through the essential light from your inner sun or Tifaret, all other Sefirot are
shining and alive. They seem to vibrate in resonance with Tifaret. Become aware
of the influence you have on your thoughts, feelings, and actions. By being aware
of the mineral, vegetable, and animal levels, you become self-conscious of the
possibility of choice. There is a freedom of will and choice in this consciousness
that makes you aware that responsibility comes with free choice.

Now, make an intention, and direct your will towards a certain (higher) goal and
purpose that you wish to achieve...

Tzimtzum and Quantum Consciousness

Kabbalah says that creation is a continuous process throughout time. Therefore, as the four Kabbalistic worlds unfold from moment to moment, every phenomenon in each world, every particle, force, or intelligence, has its meaning.

This process does not imply that all these things exist independently on their own. All meanings and purposes are interconnected and interdependent. The chain and web of being that weaved the worlds together, make all an inclusive whole.

Eventually, our material world in Assiah is founded on a non-material source, which is infinite in its space and intelligence (information). This is known from the classical scriptures as: "God is One, there is only One God", meaning that God is all there is. God is everything, everywhere, and in everyone and creature.

The basis of our reality and all the worlds is pure Spirit (consciousness), from which flows energy, matter, and information. What we mean with "information" in this book is not simply and only the data that the human mind can understand, but any phenomenon that came forth out of the ground of all being and existence: consciousness.

From this "naked consciousness", or what I have called earlier "the implicate world", or Aziluth, information flows down the Three Lower Worlds of Briah, Yezirah, and Assiah. Each world contains and transmits particular information.

Information interacts between a subject and an object in all these worlds. The quality of the subject and object are important to the degree that the information is transmitted and received.

If the Kabbalist wishes to be a channel between the higher worlds or Heaven, and the earth, they should be pure, and of the clearest intention (kavanah).

Apart from intention, creation needs more than an urgency to eventually materialize from pure potential into actualization (from Aziluth into Assiah). The worlds of metaphysical principles and creation (Briah), and formation or the psyche (Yezirah), are intermediary worlds, vital in understanding the process of creative unfoldment.

Although there are different theories to support these scientific and metaphysical principles, how this works from a quantum perspective is not so easily explained. One of these quantum-Kabbalistic principles is the function and role of the observer (consciousness) within this unfoldment down the ladder of creation. With the consciousness of the observer, comes what they call "measurement" in quantum theory.

A quantum particle can behave either as a wave or particle (where it is going or where it is?).

According to the uncertainty principle of Heisenberg, we cannot know a particle in two states (or stages) simultaneously. In the world of relativity, things cannot be two things or states at the same time. Outside time-space (Eternity), there are two possibilities that can exist next to, and within each other simultaneously. A wave (Chocmah), and a particle (Binah), are both the same thing within the pillar of consciousness, and stem from the same Source (Kether).

Wherever and however particles shift from wave to particle or from particle to wave, there is always this spiritual constant that keeps the whole process in the embrace of Eternity. Before observation and measurement, all particles are held in a moment of so-called superposition, or wave function of probabilities; like a moment of high expectations when something is about to happen, but you do not know what will happen.

The problem of measurement is the uncertainty about how consciousness observes the wave function. It appears through the double-slit experiment that waves of matter behave interdependently on who is watching and how the observer watches.

The subject (observer) shapes indefinitely the objective outcome of how the wave collapses into a particle (from probability to actuality). Therefore, a conscious observer is a co-creator between the higher worlds and the worlds of manifestation. In quantum theory, there are different ways of explaining this process.

First, the Copenhagen interpretation states that objective reality only occurs when it is observed. Without an observer, there is no measurement, and all will remain in a state of superposition (wave).

Secondly, we have the "many worlds" interpretation, which brings us into an interesting position in the four worlds diagram of Jacob's Ladder. This many worlds theory states that all possible states and results are realized during measurement, although in different worlds.

The result we measure, and its experience, is dependent on where we are in ourselves, or to what level our world and our consciousness reaches. We are very much present in our material world, and can easily know the measurement quality through our five senses. We often do not know where all the physical phenomena came from in the first place (worlds above Assiah).

In Yezirah (psyche) there are countless motives within the unconscious and conscious that can tell us something about the inherent observer, and why we have measured and collapsed certain things within our lives. Of course, many things are conditioned and repetitive structures within the quantum cycle of collapse. We repeat our life, day by day, and merely generate the world around and within us.

Only from the self-conscious perspective (Tifaret) can we become creative participants in bringing the superposition of the wave into a particle state with intent, and with purpose. From a Kabbalistic perspective, there are three worlds of pure potential, held within undifferentiated consciousness (Aziluth), which can collapse within and through the three lower worlds.

As a Kabbalist, you could say that the wave collapses in Archangels (Briah), Angels (Yezirah), and the material world (Assiah). Each world has a way of collapsing within this multidimensional paradigm, but it doesn't mean that it will collapse in the other worlds. For example, the world of Briah and the creative principles can exist and function without the full manifestation of the psychological and the physical worlds.

Likewise, within our human functioning, the psyche may "measure" something that remains within the realm of the psyche, and does not materialize in the lowest world. This model of four worlds suggests, like Kabbalah, that there are four realities (or more) that all show themselves in their own particular way, according to the accompanied consciousness involved (observer).

From the world of Assiah, we can only observe and interpret our physical reality, and measure our reality, from our own physical existence. We must remember that we can only create as an observer from "where we are".

Assiah can only generate the world of Assiah in the hierarchy of downward causation. From the world of Yezirah, the psyche measures through the reality of thought, symbols, feelings, ideas, and memory, and can only be understood by, and through, these qualities. Besides, this world has the capacity to know reality through metaphor, analogy, and parable. The world of Briah understands reality on its own terms, which we classify as metaphysical.

The observer (subject) is entangled (connected in mutual coherence) with the object (an electron or photon on the quantum level). This means that the observer needs an object to be the observer and the object needs a subject (observer) to become an object. One cannot exist and become without the other.

However, there is also something in quantum physics called "de-coherence", which postulates that the quantum changes in the subatomic world (subtle part of the world of Assiah) do not cause changes in the classical world of physics. In other words, subatomic collapse of physical reality on the subatomic level causes no (direct) changes on the macro-level of the molecule, tissue, organ, and organism.

It is probable that, in accord with the metaphysics of Kabbalah, such an organic change through quantum observation can only occur when the whole context of the particle is measured, understood, and brought towards a collapse.
This quantum idea behind entanglement also implies that two particles interacting with each other will always be connected, no matter what distance is between them. These particles will have predictability in which measurement and properties they might collapse into.

Aziluth and Assiah are co-existent in this theory, where Eternity (nonlocality) and locality or space- time-matter are essences in substance, and substance in essence. The essential world is coherent with the substantial world, and entangled over distances that appear "very far away" from our senses and material perspective. Matter or substance is an epiphenomenon of consciousness or Spirit.

Assiah is coming forth out of Aziluth, but Aziluth needs itself as the material substance wherefrom it will become something. Potential wishes to become actuality, and actuality wishes to return to potentiality. Instead of only thinking in dualistic terms and seeing the universe as dualistic, either as wave or as particle, or as energy (right pillar) or form (left pillar), Divine continuous wholeness (the wholeness that keeps all in check), holds together the wave-particle potential as information.

Wave and particle are two states or stages of consciousness (unlimited information) that move in and out of manifestation (manifested world). The completely mind-boggling dimension of quantum physical ideas is that the universe can be in infinite states of quantity simultaneously. Potential within the implicate order of Aziluth makes it possible that states of particles are present in multiple ways and directions.

Assiah (explicate order) is not a fixed world within time-space, but an ever-moving world within the eternal embrace of potentiality. It seems that these two realities are in search of each other, trying to come to the most coherent relationship that brings confluence and wholeness.

The Lightning Flash or the Will of God (the Transcendent) came out of Nothing (Ain) and Absolute All (Ain Soph). In Genesis, it was said that God willed "that Face would behold unto Face"; in other words, God beholds Itself in the mirror of existence.

With the Lightning Flash or Tzimtzum came a space of complete emptiness (Tehiru), deprived of Light. The Divine Light of emanation (Aziluth) became a world of Light (Reshimu), and the Divine Image or Adam Kadmon came into the Mind of Divinity. All were present in God's Light (information). All that ever was, is, and will be, was always present in this world of Divine emanation.

All that would come into existence through creation (the Sefirot, paths, letters, pillars, words, and all the attributes of God), came from this world of pure Divine potential where all is present in its fullness and wholeness (all completeness within the image of Adam Kadmon).

All is created, formed, and made from the Divine source (from the greatest to the smallest). All the three lower worlds did not just come forth out of the Divine world of Aziluth, but they are sustained by that world, moment by moment. Our material world has a deep immaterial, and eternal ground or foundation.

From the most profound, highest world, to the lowest, most superficial, there's a participatory connection to the existence of all the worlds (the Divine and its creation). The world of Light or pure "information" or Aziluth is "waiting", as it were, to be observed (to become conscious), in order to collapse into actuality. This Light (Aur in Kabbalah) shows itself as different forms of energy-signatures through the worlds of Briah, Yezirah, and Assiah.

Each Sefira is a vessel for the Light carrying this information or knowledge in its own particular quality. Each of the Sefirot in the three lower worlds transmits the

Light in its own expression. The further down we come into the worlds, or Jacob's Ladder, the more concealed the Light becomes inside the construction of matter and energy.

Adam Kadmon, and the worlds to come, endlessly and continuously communicate their information towards each other. Adam, within the world of Assiah (incarnated human being), is here to transmit and receive the Light of the world of Aziluth.

The human being is a messenger in its own right, brought into existence through all the worlds, with the ability and potential to communicate and receive throughout them.

In Aziluth, all is-as-one. All the Sefirot and their information are in complete unity. In Briah, these vessels create out of that Light, while in the world of Yezirah, the angels form and shape within subtle and psychological boundaries. In Assiah, the Light is enclosed within physicality. Information becomes "entrapped" within the materialization or embodiment of its own making.

Of course, the Light and the material vessel it has made are the same being. The difference lies within the expression of the Light, and the way the information is known to itself.

All the worlds remain a constant reflection of the primordial world of Aziluth, and God wishes to behold God in the mirror of existence. All happens through this constant participation and exchange of information through the whole of existence.

The Kabbalistic invocation that you have learned in this book is an inner way of making yourself a channel to open the vessels in all the worlds. This invocation is a preparatory work for the Kabbalist, to receive from above, and becoming a vessel for the Holy One to behold Itself.

Through the invocation, we allow the Tzimtzum or Lightning Flash (light within the void), to enter us to become a mirror. The Lightning Flash is not to be taken literally, but seen as a metaphor of how the Absolute (Ain Soph) came into being, and emanated its endless wisdom (Information) into creation.

We could almost compare this unfoldment with a being injecting itself in order to fertilize itself. Adam Kadmon has the anthropomorphic outline of a human being, but this does not mean that God is made in our image! We are made in the image and likeness of the Divine.

Our image is limitless, and ultimately complete and totally one. Nothing can be added unto us, nor taken away.

Before the Tzimtzum, in the Absolute or Ain Soph, there was Nothing (No-thing). There was no "information", as we have described and named it so far, in our quantum-Kabbalistic adventure. Ain and Ain Soph, Absolute Nothing, and

Absolute All do not mean that there is nothing there, but its mystery is beyond any classification of thinking or reference.

Down the worlds, the complexity increases as the Laws that descend down the worlds with the sequence of the Lightning Flash evolve, and gradually solidify into matter. From the highest, inner world of Aziluth towards Assiah, the process of entropy decreases. Through this law, the worlds become more structured and predictable.

In quantum words, the worlds become more determined through a collapse of repetition (conditioning), from a more chaotic state of randomness and probabilities, towards states of predictable, and actual manifestation.

The Lightning Flash is the way of God pouring Itself into its own space (Tehiru or Pleroma). The Divine Light that comes down the Tree of Life is not the fullness of God, otherwise, the Presence of God would be Absolute, and there would be no time, space, and movement.

Within the Absolute, there cannot be any unfoldment or movement. Therefore, the Light (Ain Soph Aur) is coming down in a temperate way, following the sequence of the Lightning Flash and the primal law of octaves.

Through this continuous sequence, God (the Absolute) transforms nothing into something, from a state of apparent chaos (entropy), into a state of order (within chaos). This process has to be constantly supported by something that lies as a foundation under this progressive motion of creation. This "something", that is the Eternal "constant" within creation, is God.

God is the mover and the sustainer of all that was, is, and shall ever be. From Ain Soph, the world flows into being, and thereby, the arrow of time comes into existence. Even the world of Aziluth is time-full, although there is no unfolding of time as we know it, or how we experience it in relativity.

From our Kabbalistic perspective, it seems that Ain Soph is our "past", flowing into the future through all the worlds. This linear, relative and cognitive perception of time and existence is not applicable to our personal experience of time.

Ain Soph is neither beginning nor end; it is everywhere and nowhere. It is all at the same time and every moment, but is not in time and space. The Tzimtzum, or Lightning Flash, is the Will of God becoming Eternity "clothing" itself into four worlds. This Will of God is also expressed as a straight line through all the worlds, depicting the fifth Tree on Jacob's Ladder, where all Sefirot (Ten Eternal Expressions of God) are aligned into one line (Kav).

This line is not there to explain time as a linear process because it has nothing to do with time, for it expresses the Eternal through all the worlds. Eternity brings all the worlds into the Holy Now within the middle axis of existence.
Therefore, being aligned to the earthly Adam Kadmon (incarnated human being) through the Will of God (Kav) attunes the Kabbalist to the four worlds, and the whole of existence.

The work of the Kabbalist is to "return" along the reversed path of the Lightning Flash (way of experience through time), alternating through that middle axis where the Kav of God is present. This momentum on the middle pillar is where we find the timeless and spaceless dimension, or the nonlocality in quantum physics.

On each Sefira on the middle axis in the four worlds, human consciousness comes to experience how the Eternal has expressed itself through time.

Working inwards or upwards on the Tree of Life or Jacob's Ladder (four worlds) is to retrace our steps back to the Divine Source: from complexity to simplicity, from structure towards the essence, and from ordered states that are predictable to chaotic states of pure potentiality.

Fulfilment
Purpose
Destiny
Experience
Vision
Realisation
Constraints
Fate
Opportunities
Decision
individual
Compulsion
Social Pressure
Talents
Drives
Ordinary
Person
Life
Basic Needs

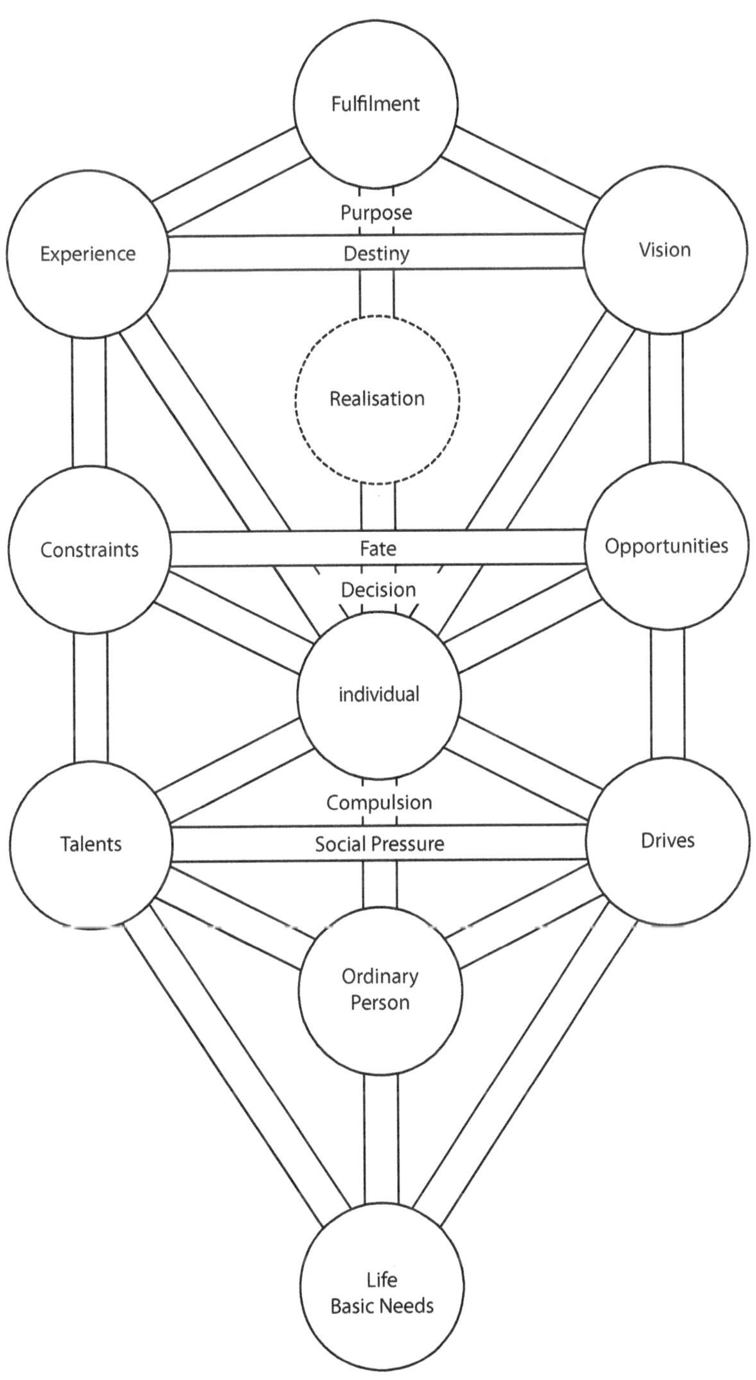

Diagram 14

Meditation

Sit down and relax.

Start regular breathing and make contact with your physical body. Realize that your physical vessel is always in the "now"; it cannot be otherwise.

Aware of this unique moment in time and space, you breathe through all Kabbalistic worlds within you. From Assiah into Yezirah, Briah, and even Aziluth. You are reminded that the breath is the movement and essence of the Holy Spirit (Ruach Ha-Kadosh).

Slowly, you visualize a light on top of your head. That light takes on the form of a hollow crown of brilliant white light. In that hollow ring of Holy Light, a point of concentrated Light begins to form and you feel pressure, as if a thousand suns were contained within that single point at the top of your head.

The pressure of Light starts to move in a straight line, from the top of your head (the Crown or Kether) to the right side of your head into Chocmah, crossing over horizontally into Binah at the left hemisphere of your head, forming an upward triangle.

The pressure of Light is still there, although somewhat lesser. The Light is continuous in a diagonal line to your right shoulder. When it crosses before your face, you feel a sensation of some kind. At the right shoulder, the Light is known as Chesed, and it seems to expand even more, and crosses over horizontally to the Sefira Gevurah, where you feel the Light contract.

The Light comes into balance when reaching the heart centre or Tifaret; but quickly, the Light pursues its way into the area of your right hip, known as Netzach, where all energy goes around in cycles.

The Light reaches your left hip at the Sefira Hod, where you feel the power of reverberation. At the pelvis or genital- level, the Light comes to a pause in Yesod, and you feel the life energy inside your body. The last movement of the Light goes vertically down between your feet in the Kingdom or Malkuth.

Feel the complete receptivity, and release of all that Light, as it came down under such tremendous pressure, and has now released itself into physical existence. Realize that this is the movement of the Lightning Flash coming down the worlds every moment. Creation happens all the time.

Take a few breaths, and come out of the meditation. Write down anything that you perceived in this meditation.

Adam Kadmon

The incarnated human being is a creature that arrived from the four worlds and is born into the material world of Assiah. Born into a body of four elements and five senses does not mean that all the worlds have fully and consciously manifested into the physical world. It is the sacred task of Adam (humanity) to enter the Garden and bring Heaven to earth.

Adam is the guardian and caretaker of the Garden of Eden, the Holy Place where the light and peace of God is upon all creation. The mythological story about the fall from Eden, suggests that Adam has eaten of the Knowledge of the Tree of Good and Evil (information), and thereby "falls" into the world where good and evil (duality) dwell. This is the realm of Assiah and the world of quantum actuality (explicate order).

According to this myth from the Book of Genesis, and some of its theological interpretations, we have to return to a state of wholeness. It appears that our fall happened a long time ago, when the world was created. According to the Kabbalistic tradition, and even quantum physics, this scenario is much more profound. The fall from, and return into Eden, is potentially happening at any moment, at any time and place. As soon as we are aware of our duality inside and outside of ourselves, we "fall" into relative existence (again). Our physical birth is the physical fall from our soul's journey over many lifetimes.

The so-called mythical fall (which we can experience every possible moment while incarnated) is a psychological fall. When we are preoccupied and distracted (unconscious) from our internal and external duality, we are blind to the Eternal and the Garden of Eden. From our psyche's distracted, dualistic and deterministic consciousness, we witness the world of strife, competition, polarity, and all the processes that make this duality increase or decrease.

The Eternal within us watches this spectacle as time and space unfold, merely observing from the un-manifest what happens in the manifest. Implicate order watches the explicate order. For example, let's imagine that two birds are sitting in the Tree of Life: one eating of the Tree, and the other watching. These two birds are vast friends, belonging together (like fingers belonging to a hand). Through entanglement, the one exists because of the other, and one arises out of the other.

From the legend of Genesis, Adam ate from the Tree of Good and Evil, and took this knowledge into the incarnated, material world. Because he obtained this knowledge, Adam (the undivided human being) lost its purity and innocence. Some Kabbalistic sources speak about the Kelipat, or the remnants (shells) of creation, which are the evil remains that manifested with us in this world. In truth, evil is a necessary consequence when creation unfolds.

When good exists, there must be an opposite force and principle in nature; otherwise, evil cannot be known. The human soul of Adam inherited the potential for free will (choice), and when the soul rises out of its sleep (lower psyche), the psyche's self enters the possibility to choose.

The relationship between good and evil is regarded here from a metaphysical perspective, and not from a moral-psychological point of view. In classical Kabbalah texts it is said that only Good comes from God.

The sages and teachers of old told us that the whole of creation is Good, and all is created because it is Good (Tov). Evil is to go against the natural order and laws of creation. If one does not understand these laws (ignorance), it is easy to go against (sabotage) oneself (within or without), and act against the world.

Free will is a vital "ingredient" within the human psyche (soul) to make a quantum change (collapse) happen. Ignorance leads a human being disconnected from the will of the Almighty to all kinds of evil.
Evil is the way of the wanderer and the lost souls, not a superstitious-religious point of view. The seeker (Kabbalist) directs their life towards the knowing (Daath) of God, and participates in the great Mystery.

To obey the Commandments of the Torah (as they say in Judaism) and orthodox ways of Kabbalah, is not simply to obey rules from old scriptures. The living Torah evolves over time through the human soul and the process of conscious development throughout the four Kabbalistic worlds. The esoteric Torah follows the way to "reveal the Shekinah within the world".

In Kabbalah, the spiritual (esoteric) interpretation of the Torah is the metaphysical symbol and teaching of the Etz Chaim, or the Tree of Life.

It is the teaching that leads towards God, and not towards a life that is directed and interested in the natural world and instincts (lower human nature).
The Kabbalist transforms their natural and incarnated being into a vessel to receive the higher worlds.

In other words, the Kabbalist invites a quantum impulse and collapse(s) to happen through the inner process of the teachings and their application. This transformation is almost impossible if the soul is only occupied with the natural world of instincts and impulses. Within the natural world (mineral, vegetable, and animal levels), the behavioural dynamics of conditionings, cycles, and repetition from Netzach and reverberations from Hod repeat old, personally-generated patterns.

Only when the soul reaches out, and aspires "upwards" into the heavenly world of Briah and beyond, the world of awe, wonder, and inspiration, can we come to transformation (quantum collapse).

The Kabbalist is aware, through the Tree of Life and Jacob's Ladder, that this universe and creation as a whole is inclusive and entangled. The old, dogmatic, and extreme assumption that good and evil are "God's opposites" in nature, is not valid any longer. These ideas answer to a personal God who has personal preferences and resistances. Those ideas and images of God are made in the image of men (the human being makes God in their own image and likeness). God has called forth, created, formed, and made all this creation- the whole of existence. No working, dynamic, or law is separate from the other.

All systems are interconnected as one system, one movement, under the Will of the Absolute. We cannot know and understand the parts of this existence without knowing the whole.

The seeming paradox lies within the metaphysical idea that the whole is present, and can be known through its parts.

Like a hologram, it can be seen that the whole is not made out of parts, but is present in what we selectively think of as parts. This universe (and therefore creation) is not divided, but each part mirrors the wholeness of the other, so that wholeness looks upon wholeness within the endless parts of relative existence. The sum is greater than its parts, and there is nothing separate or outside the whole.

Whatever happens in creation effects the interconnected wholeness inherent to existence. Does that mean that all things work towards wholeness and unity?

Certain ideas and theories in science and Kabbalah have said different things about this. There is no agreement or final word about how we interpret Divine Providence. However, the closest we might come to understand what the Divine Will wishes, and how it provides for this existence, is that It (God) makes all to return to Itself.

All that develops throughout the universe, in all times and places, is under the influence of Providence. Whatever the subatomic world does (and whether we understand it or not) is directed towards wholeness and inclusivity. The human being chooses to follow and live a life in accord with Providence. Choosing does not mean that all our life experiences will be thriving with good times. Providence also means that we are moved towards our limits, resistances, and shortcomings… all from our human perspective.

The way that the Kabbalist can direct their will and attention towards Providence is to turn inwards, on the way of teshuva (or what the Greeks would call metanoia). The inward movement we are making on the Tree of Life is "upward" or inward, towards the upper face or higher garden on the Tree. In Kabbalah, teshuvah also means "answer", and is called this way because it is the soul responding to the call from the higher worlds (to return). In psychological terms, this is the transpersonal archetypal part of Yezirah, and the collective unconscious.

In Kabbalah, the path that leads from Tifaret towards Kether is often called: "the path of Awe". To the human experience, it may seem that what happens in this interface between the psyche and Spirit (Yezirah and Briah) is of the miraculous and supernatural.

According to Kabbalah, we emphasize that, although in the eyes of the ordinary mind this appears as unnatural or supernatural, the higher worlds are far from unnatural; on the contrary, the world of Briah is where we find the laws of nature and how the universe is governed (physically and metaphysically).

From the everyday human perception, the higher worlds are separate from our personal world. Therefore, the miracle is "out there", and something apart from this world. Not so for the mystic and the quantum scientist, who regard the subatomic world as a spiritual world where all is possible.

We encounter miracles every moment (often without knowing), as miracles lie at the basis of our material world. The creation we are living in, making up the very substance of our bodies, testifies to the miracle of the universe. The laws that govern everything in little and great, the stars in the galaxies, and the electrons in an atom, are truly miraculous.

Quantum physics teaches us to redirect our attention inwards towards the miracle, not outside ourselves. Out of the Source of Oneness, duality and all phenomena within existence are created constantly. Creation happens all the time, and every moment in history, and the future to come. As I said earlier: the human being can create from the existing conditions, building new forms and concepts out of what already is.

But the miracle of creating new things out of nothing, or sustaining creation over long epochs of time, is a different matter. Kabbalah explains that all is created out of a single Light, and one single Law. It is said in the Toledano Kabbalah tradition that the first, and main Law (one of the four great Laws), is the Law that "All is One": existence is made out of one piece. There is only one God, and there is only one being.

Some scientists have stated that the four main forces of physics (gravity, electromagnetism, and weak and strong nuclear forces) originate from one force. The Big Bang brought all into existence (the expansion from the dimensionless point from Kether into the second Crown or Chocmah). Therefore, all are connected, and nothing is separate from the other.

Albert Einstein brought mass and energy together into a single whole with his formula for the theory of relativity ($E=mc^2$): Space and time into a single whole, just like the metaphysical law that energy (Chocmah) and form (Binah) cannot be separated (although depicted separately on the Tree of Life).

Space and time (Chocmah and Binah) are one of a kind: Spirit undivided, yet expressing itself in a twofold manner. Miracles evolve and unfold as soon as the world of creation (Chocmah and Binah) emanates from the heart of the Divine (Aziluth). When creation is born, the universe expresses a "miracle", which happens every moment in history, now, and in the future.

As long as the Holy One wills it, the whole of existence is created again and again.

From both the metaphysical and quantum physics point of views, creation is not simply a linear process that started somewhere long ago and ends someday. Creation is held in the world of Eternity (Aziluth) and therefore, creation is Eternal in its sequence and movement.

The miracle begins (or unfolds) when the human being perceives the Law of One, which holds everything in creation in the Eternal Now; and yet, all is created according to the laws that include space-time (law of the supernal triad and sequence). All is full of time-space and movement in the worlds to be, and simultaneously still, timeless, and spaceless. A miracle is something that is seen from the human perspective.

Archangels from the world of Briah are those that bring forth the lower worlds. For them, creation flows naturally from their being and consciousness. Quantum physics tells us all about the working of creation and archangels - the principles of metaphysical law.

Downward causation, nonlocality, discontinuity, and entangled hierarchy are the quantum and metaphysical principles of creation. These four laws are all coming forth and kept within the first and most important law - the Law of Oneness.

We cannot add to or subtract from whatever is created. All is one, and no other being or process can undo it, or change the course of the unfoldment of the One. Only when it is made in their nature can the course of creation be changed.

A miracle, in the Briatic-Kabbalistic sense, is when Aziluth becomes a creative probability, making the metaphysical principles unfold. Certain things that we experience as human beings may seem to be very improbable, but do not go against the laws of nature.

That we can't believe certain things to happen doesn't mean that they are unnatural or not probable; because we do not understand fully what the laws of nature are all about, we cannot comprehend certain phenomena. It is important to explain here that miracles are subjective experiences of how we understand the "improbable" nature of the Higher Worlds (Briah and Aziluth).

For us, and the whole of relative existence, things may seem improbable and unlikely. Some things occur only once in a lifetime, and the time when it occurs is unpredictable. For the Holy One, all things are probable and predictable. The universe is an extremely fine-tuned organism where all is under the influence of the will of the Holy One.

Existence is directed towards certain ends and beginnings, most of which we do not know about. Kabbalah says that the more we approach God through our Kabbalistic work (Torah), the better we understand God's ways. Because of this, our lives will become much more probable, well-tuned and timed, determined and predictable. If we work in accord with the will of God, all that we will, shall happen. For God, probability does not exist, and for those living and working the will of God, there is no probability. Einstein said: "God does not play dice with the universe".

The religious (and sometimes dogmatic) idea that God intervenes with creation should not be taken as a personal intervention based upon personal preferences, such as the way we human beings intervene with each other, and the world.

Intervention from the Divine world of Aziluth is constant and continuous. If the will of the Divine were to cease, at any moment, the three lower worlds would cease to exist. We may understand the intervention of the Divine through the laws described above. The Divine world appears to us as that realm of endless probabilities and uncertainties, we speak about in quantum physics. Yet, all is willed and expressed in certainty and determined through the Providence of the Divine will. Providence is a difficult subject, and even within the history of Kabbalah, not all Kabbalists agree what that means and entails.

The way we approach Providence in this book comes from the world of Divinity (Aziluth). That world is all of existence that was, is, and will ever be (a world without end). Providence is first and foremost the will that all is One, and although the worlds evolve out of that oneness, all remains one and will eventually return to one.

To work as a Kabbalist in the ways of Divine Providence is to live the way of unification, the way of oneness. In all aspects of life, the Kabbalist is directed towards the way of Providence, to participate in the work of Divine unfoldment. From this way of being with the holy intention (kavanah), we can use our free will to be deterministic and predictable.

All will evolve towards the same end: unity. Omnipotence cannot fail, as the Law of One is determined to work through all the worlds. Although we can separate, divide, and break up the unity in our experience, the Law of One will prevail.

Meditation
Start with the previous meditation of the Lightning Flash.

The whole Tree of Life is now gradually coming into your being. Not just the Ten Sefirot of the Lightning Flash, but all the twenty-two paths in between start to shine with that same brilliant Light. These thirty-two paths make the Tree of Life.

In and through you, the Tree of Life is shining forth. Slowly but surely, the silhouette of a human being takes shape inside the Tree of Life.

It has no particular features at first, and no form you can recognize ... Just the rough outlines of a human being in that shining, white Light. As the Tree of Life shines in and through you, you can see and feel the particular shape and form of your human features and constitution out of this anthropomorphic form.

Adam Kadmon, the Divine Human Being, appears now through your relative form and being. Sit with this image for a few more minutes and then come out of the meditation. Write down what you might need to remember.

The four worlds and Quantum perception
In Kabbalah, there are four different ways of perceiving reality, as we have already seen on Jacob's Ladder and the four worlds. These are the mystical perception from Aziluth, the metaphysical from Briah, the metaphorical (or symbolic) from Yezirah, and the literal from Assiah.

Quantum perception has its effect on the world of Assiah. Technically, all that happens in the quantum world happens within the world of Assiah (Malkuth of Malkuth). Here within the material world, the wave function is always present, appearing as if the collapse (particle) is the only worldly state.

According to Von Neumann-Wigner, the quantum collapse can occur from every possible observation in quantum mechanics; even the lowest and most subjective observations can cause a quantum collapse. This idea supports the statement that all perception leads to all forms of creation, dependent on what level we observe. The observer functions from the world of psychological conditioning, participating in the collapse of what has already been created.

Another hypothesis of quantum perception is that the wave-state (superposition state) does not describe reality, but that the collapse in the observer's consciousness is what eventually leads to an objective reality (coming from the subjective reality of the observer).

This touches on the Kabbalistic principle that nothing truly happens (wave), and all that manifests or collapses (created) is eventually there (only because of the presence of the wave and the consciousness that observes the wave). Consciousness remains the ground of being upon which the whole of existence rests. When it manifests or collapses, the wave will support the particle manifestation for a certain amount of time in relativity after it vanishes again into the wave from where it came. At every moment that information is exchanged, we can speak about a measurement process. The change is a de-coherence between the micro-quantum and macro levels of all physical manifestation.

In Kabbalah, not all things that move are created in the upper worlds to manifest in the physical world, nor do physical forms change (although at the quantum level, there is a collapse measured).

Quantum physics also brought forth other hypotheses about the quantum measurement of creation. It is said, for example, that all possible results are realized during a quantum measurement, although the results or effects are spread across the multitude of the lower worlds. In Kabbalah, that could mean that a collapse of wave function could manifest in one, two, or three (lower) worlds.

Again, a collapse does not mean that the observation happens only within the world of Assiah; after all, observation or involvement of consciousness is present in all worlds, consciously and unconsciously. Whatever we mean by quantum collapse and measurement, the interaction between the subjective observer and the quantum object (universe as a whole) is the basis of all quantum-theories.

The Kabbalistic worlds are constantly observed by those who inhabit them, and thereby, these worlds are contained and preserved in consciousness, and manifest accordingly. The creature and the created are eternally entangled in this process of being (consciousness) and becoming (created being).

Every created being (in any world) is a being of consciousness, observing the world designed for it. In this quantum symbiosis, the worlds, and all the created phenomena, are created repeatedly. Providence wills that all is directed towards wholeness and inclusiveness: all are held in cycles of being and becoming.

All the worlds are one, and although throughout creation it appears that worlds become separate and divided into different parts (through the Sefirot and the thirty-two paths of the Tree of Life), all remains a single whole. Quantum entanglement agrees with the statement that although particles (electrons) are separated from each other, their properties remain the same, "as if" they were the same particle. Well… that's because they are!

As we can see through the process of emanation (which means "to count"), all remains within the unity of Kether. Kether is not divided nor duplicated when the Lightning Flash descends through the worlds. The One remains the One.

In Chocmah, the One is mirrored into "another" One, which appears as two. Chocmah comes into being because the One observes itself in movement and space (energy). Binah is known through the One who appears as three because of the One who observes itself as time (form). In Malkuth (the Kingdom, the tenth emanation) the One returns to itself through the entanglement of all the created numbers.

All the three lower worlds, from Aziluth downwards, on Jacob's Ladder (Divine) are identical with the world of Aziluth, but appear in their own energy and pattern, according to the Will of the Divine. All these three lower worlds contain the whole of Aziluth. All information of all that was is, and shall be is present in every world.

Of course, this does not mean that we can know and observe all this information at once. The beauty of it all is that, when all the worlds are held in the Divine Name of Eheiheh Asher Eheiheh, I Am That I Am, the highest world (or the Implicate Order) consciously becomes the Explicate Order in Assiah.

Creation (Briah), coming down the worlds into Assiah, is based on a hierarchical pattern (system) on Jacob's Ladder. Every world interlocks with the next world where quantum measurement happens through the interaction of the worlds (where face touches upon face). All that comes down the worlds (downward causation) is uninterrupted (Lightning Flash or Tzimtzum) from Crown to Kingdom, and from Kingdom to Crown.

All that comes down into the world of particles (atoms or smaller particles) in Assiah are entities. These entities within the physical world are acting on the edge of physicality and non-physicality (material and immaterial), and are therefore, often called Angels in Kabbalah.

Let us remember that Angels are messengers from the worlds of Briah (Archangels) and Yezirah (Choir of Angels). Their content and expression can only be altered and changed by the creative act down the worlds (not from the level at which they live and operate).

All the worlds down into Assiah contain and "transport" the same patterns of wisdom (information from Aziluth), as long as there is no other pattern willed by the world of Origin (Aziluth).

In Assiah, every atom is sustained and preserved in the pillars (energy and forms) of the higher worlds. This makes it possible for the material universe to be stable and reliable. All particles know where they came from, and what they need to do (we do not need to instruct electrons to move in certain ways). In the world of Assiah, time-space and movement are measured through distance, but in the higher worlds there is no distance in that same quantitative way, and energy and form change according to their interactions, or constant blending and separation.

The soul is that particular (unique) part of the human psyche, functioning as a vehicle of consciousness, and is the conscious observer of the spiritual journey, the path of the Kabbalist. It has the power and the ability to learn, guard, and direct our inner processes, and furthermore, to be self-aware.

Kabbalistic journey
At birth, we are given a vehicle made of the same materials and elements as the world.

That vehicle (physical body) has five senses which we can use to get to know the world around us. These five physical senses are a primitive part of the human body: they incarnate as long as we have a body and correspond with the oldest parts of our brain and nervous system.

Most of what we detect through the senses is done through automatic and conditioned systems. The body and the lower part of the psyche (world of Yezirah) use these senses daily, yet we are hardly conscious (aware) of what the senses are telling us. Most of what we take in from our environment, and the world, is unconsciously selected by our inner body, and psyche. This simply means that there will be hardly any growth or inner development.

Only through upheaval and crisis will the flow of conditioned use of the senses be broken. For the Kabbalist, conscious use of the senses of the soul leads towards a new horizon. Now, the senses can become spiritual tools and equipment for the higher vehicles of the psyche.

In the tradition of Kabbalah, the soul has different positions on the Tree of Life, and is sometimes described in different fashions. The Toledano tradition is very precise about its meaning and functional presence in the life of a human being. After the self-awareness and consciousness (observer), which gives us the ability to become aware of being aware, there is the individual's self-responsibility. From the soul, we take matters into our hands and shape our journey as we go. This is more than just social responsibility. Here, we take on the responsible attitude towards our spiritual life and service to something greater.

The soul makes the difference between normal (mundane) living, and observation from conditioning, and the clear awaked state of the soul. If you wonder whether you have experienced this, I can say that you probably haven't, because if you did… You would know!

Another attribute of the soul is its immortality, incarnating through lifetimes to learn what must be learned, and undergo what one must face. As I said before, the soul is stationed between worlds, and can be lost in the worldly things of your personal life and society, or it can reach into the world of spiritual being.

To prevent the soul from being caught up in some dualistic position, we should not forget that it is the soul that can, by choice, direct itself in both worlds at the same time. This ability is exactly the spiritual task of the Kabbalist while incarnated: to make of oneself a "bridge" or a channel between the worlds.

In this way, the soul can become the guide and teacher of the lower vehicle or world of Assiah. The incarnated vehicle's mineral, vegetable, and animal levels do not move to spiritual evolution. The soul is that consciousness in us that can make it happen. As the vehicle and observer of consciousness itself, the soul has creative and "measurement" qualities. The soul is the vehicle of quantum-creative measurement.

While the lower psyche in the Yesod of Yezirah is bound to conditioned cycles (Netzach) and reverberation (Hod), it cannot escape its own limitations. The soul knows that it has a choice at any possible moment in life.

Every moment is a potential creative moment. This is not a matter of belief but direct experience through the application of our conscious awareness.

As the soul is in the midst of the human psyche (Jacob's Ladder and the world of Yezirah), its position is partially in space-time relativity (world of Assiah), and outside our human experience of time (higher Yezirah and lower Briah). The soul is the one who observes from that timeless dimension, and yet, is engaged with time-space.

If we talk about de-coherence in quantum physics, we mean to say that, although there is a change measured on the subatomic level (collapse), it does not mean that on the macro-level (for example, cells of the body) things are changing physically.

Things may change at the timeless sub-atomic and quantum level, but it takes time before this change manifests through the world of time-space. The soul is between the timeless and time-space realms, and knows this to be true. Not all changes on the inner planes are directly noticeable on the manifested level of Assiah.

The soul is the vehicle to make sure that the timing (Kairos in Greek) is right to manifest something into the lower worlds. The soul should practice and often engage with the inner planes or higher worlds to determine if something is right to do, and if the timing is right.

The soul itself is not outside the possible dangers of corruption and inflation. Being in-between the animal level (nefesh) and the Spirit, the soul may get lost in either of them. If the human-animal nature dominates, the soul is lost through the instincts and desires of the world (world of the dual impulses of attraction and resistance).

The soul who directs the attention only towards the Spirit will equally get lost in the abstractions of the Heavenly world of Briah. The subtle task for the soul is to live in several worlds simultaneously, and "stretch" itself, as it were, between the three lower worlds. From the Kabbalistic and quantum perspective, the soul is time-space engaged, and yet, within the realm of Eternity.

As it is said in some of the older texts in the Kabbalah tradition, the soul is in between the evil inclination and the heavenly world. Both of these are demonstrated daily within the inner world. So, although the soul can engage in different worlds, we may understand that it can do this because it is timeless and consists of a very subtle structure.

In its deepest essence, it reflects the light of the Divine (supernal triad), and as soon as we remember this to be true, the soul starts its journey or spiritual quest. How can the soul be Eternal and in time and space? On the Tree of Life diagram, the realm of time-space is represented by the two side pillars, while the Eternal is the middle pillar. These two pillars are the realm of the relative and time-space dependent world (implicate order), while the middle pillar is the Eternal pillar or axis in between (explicate order).

As we are an image of the Divine within this diagram of the Tree of Life, we have inherent in ourselves (and contained) the worlds or levels of time-space and the Eternal within us. To be within the fullness of our being within the whole Tree of Life means participating in time-space (our daily life), and simultaneously, being within the Eternal, witnessing consciousness.
Again, implicate (Eternal or Quantum) can co-exist with the explicate (time-space-relative and realm of quantum collapse) order.

The creator and the created co-exist. The soul knows (or at least starts to realize) that we are co-creators with the Source of all. For the soul and its pure nature, the journey leads on to serving the Holy Presence within creation. In Kabbalah, that means "doing good", and not leaning to the side of evil (that means to not sympathize with the forces of destruction and chaos). It also means that we do not allow ourselves to be "eaten up" by the forces of society and the demands of others.

The soul has a priority that comes from the world of the Spirit. When the soul is the main navigator on our spiritual journey (the Work), the Kabbalist is aware of the mental powers that draw us towards Spirit, or away from it. When we are drawn towards mental images within the world of Yezirah (Treasure House of images in the Yesod of Yezirah), we repeat and recycle old ideas and memories. These are enforced and reinforced for goodness' or evil's sakes.

If there is too much space psychologically (Chesed) to allow all these images to enter and reenter our psyche, we will get lost on our path. We need Gevurah and Chesed to discern and be clear about what mental activity to follow, and which activities to abort. Every mental activity is likely to lead to physical activity.

Unconsciously, we are moved by thoughts coming from deep archetypal motives within the personal and collective unconscious. We are able, as human beings, to shape our journey by consciously giving direction to these inner motives and impulses. That means giving rise to thoughts you want to think and have chosen to think.

From there, you direct your actions in the way that you have chosen. These changes in your inner and outer choices and actions may come from an intention from the level of situational creativity (we change something in our Yesod) or from the level of fundamental creativity (Tifaret). From Yesod, we change something in behaviour, while from Tifaret, we change our consciousness and perception. These changes in consciousness and perception lead to a fundamental transformation, as we now know from quantum physics.

Meditation

This meditation is meant to make you aware of your "quantum activity" throughout the day. If that awareness is present within you, there is an awareness that is "aware of being aware".

Therefore, begin this exercise by sitting still and meditating on your breathing, while you become familiar with the consciousness that is observing the process of breathing.

Once you feel this presence within you, gently open your eyes and go about your immediate business within or outside the house. Stay with that awareness that observes all that appears and disappears within and around you. Thoughts, memories and situations come and go. Do not try and change anything about what is unfolding. Be aware and observe. When possible, you may close your eyes between your daily activities to come back to that observing awareness if you have lost it.

All that "rises and falls" within your consciousness is the potentiality of quantum-creation within your being. This may manifest anytime soon (or already may have). Optionally, you may write down what has occurred and what reoccurs within you.

Now that you are aware of your inner activities, you also become aware of how you give rise to your inner and outer worlds (your personal life).

In the triads of thinking, feeling, and action, all you do within that lower face of your Tree of Life around your psychological ego, shapes your current life structure. Even if these are conditioned activities, it means you reshape and strengthen them time and time again.

In this way, you get a clearer view of how you generate your own journey.
It all starts from within.

If you find certain inner activities sabotaging, compromising, and blocking you, you can choose to change them from within the observing consciousness of your being.

Remember that repetition is not the key for real change and transformation (quantum collapse) to happen. Success for change lies within consciousness (observer), and bringing all of your being (thinking, feeling, and actions) under the change you wish to make.

Chapter 5: Kabbalah & Neuroplasticity

Anatomy
In the world of Assiah, there are, esoterically speaking, two realms: the gross-physical, and the subtle-psychological.

In classical Kabbalah, the upper and lower parts of the Tree of Life are called faces or gardens (Pardes). In the Zohar they are called "countenances": compositions of paths that give rise to a kite-like shape on Jacob's Ladder. The key point between these two faces in Assiah is the Tifaret of Assiah, located at the region of the human heart; this is where we find the function of the central nervous system.

The central nervous system includes the brain, spinal cord, and a complex network of neurons. This system is responsible for sending, receiving, and interpreting information from all body parts. The central nervous system monitors and coordinates internal organ functions, and responds to changes in the external environment. Let's remember that our nervous system is divided into the central nervous system, and the peripheral nervous system. Sometimes, the CNS is compared to a control room from which tasks and actions are delegated. The reality behind this system is more complicated.

Together with the Sefirot of Gevurah (anabolic) and Chesed (catabolic), Tifaret forms a triangle in which the metabolism occurs in the body.

However, the Central Nervous System's (CNS) position on the Tree explains a lot more about its functions and properties.

First of all, it lies centrally in the human anatomy on the Tree of Life. Its position is central at the Tifaret on the middle pillar, halfway between the lower and upper faces of Assiah. Tifaret has many possible ways of describing its qualities. The name Tifaret reveals harmony, balance, truth, and even goodness.

The physical brain functions mainly on chemical-electrical impulses. Data are being transmitted towards and away from the CNS through the peripheral nervous system. The sensory and motor neurons within the CNS organism make this data-transmission possible. These neurons allow the organism to receive information from the milieu interior and exterior.

Together with the Autonomic Nervous System (ANS), or vegetable nervous system, the organism is maintained in a biological balance or equilibrium. This system is occupied with automatic processes that do not directly reach the level of self-consciousness.

The ANS is also responsible for the subconscious triggering of physiological memories (a phenomenon which has already been discussed in this book). And then, only when there is urgency (like pain), or when we choose to become aware of our vital processes (like breathing, heartbeat, blood pressure, etc.), do we become aware of them.

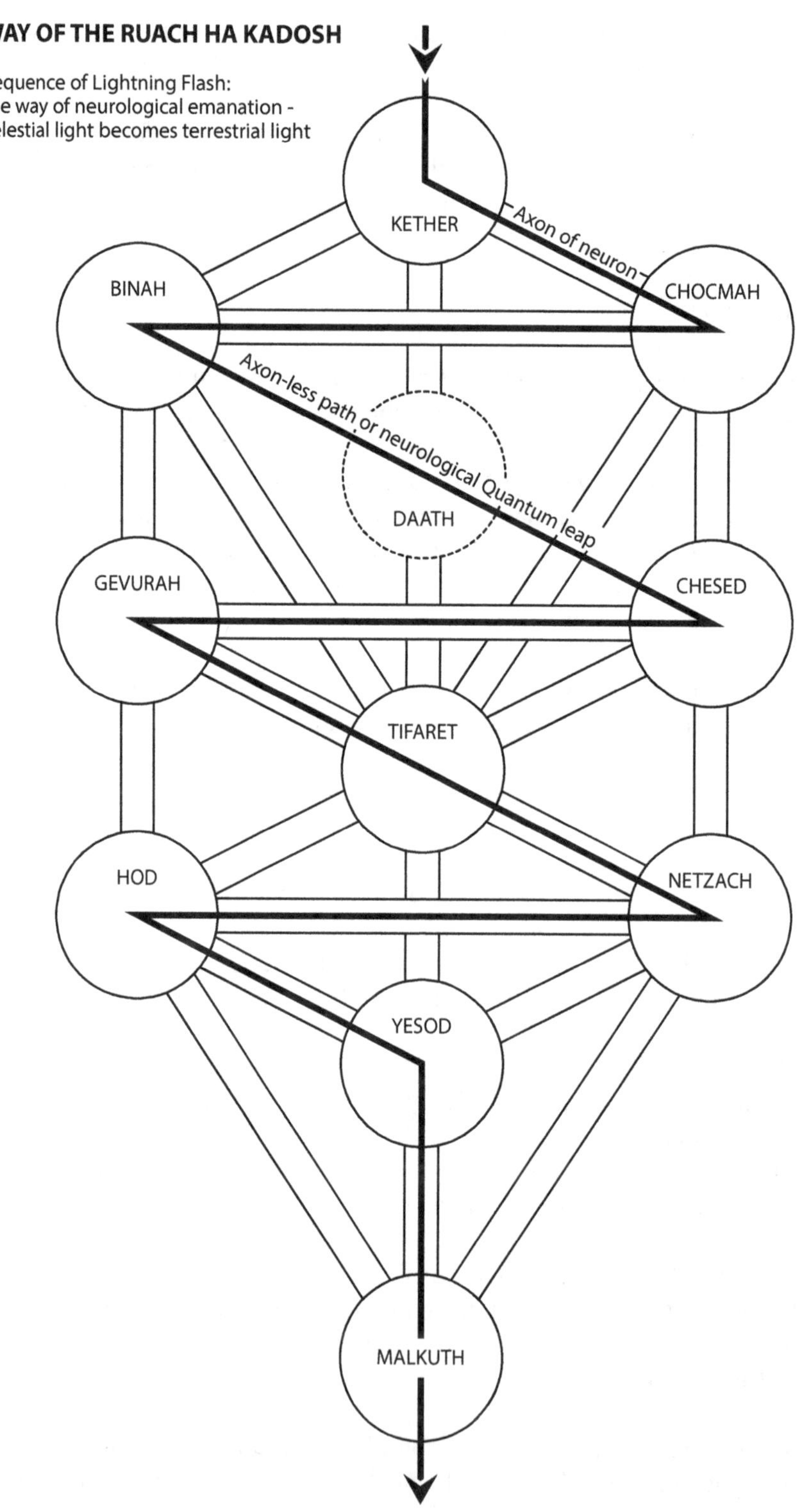

Diagram 15

122

Awareness enables us to participate in, and alter, these processes. For example, when you are stressed with a high heart rate, you could bring that rate down using relaxation exercises and meditation.

The Yesod of Assiah reflects the same metaphysical principle as the Yesod of the psyche, in the upper face of Assiah. It is here where the Yesod of Yezirah and the Daath of Assiah coincide. By developing our daily awareness of consciousness, we can become acutely aware of the unconscious ANS processes triggering the body (like bodily memories, heat, heart rate, breath, and many others).

This is very important, for it is through these everyday experiences that we gain the sense of how the body and psyche work together. Daath is direct or mystical knowledge of how body and psyche work together, derived from direct experience. While growing up, and at a later age, we can grow and integrate the developing psyche and physical body through the Yesod/ Daath complex.

The Tree of Life is therefore present in our own bio-psychology, which is the ground that makes this development possible. Just below the CNS, in Tifaret of that same world, we find the Yesod/ Daath-complex in Assiah, operating as a physical monitor (but still mainly unconscious).

Parts of that CNS have neurons which pass through neurological centres that make us aware of our bio-psychological processes, and other neurons that pass through more unconscious (reflex) centres.

In the Hod of Assiah, monitoring bio-impulses are voluntary, unlike the Netzach of Assiah, where involuntary cycles and biorhythms are found. The potential to become aware of these processes is always present. It would be impossible for an organism to be continuously aware of all processes within the physical and subtle bodies.

Likewise, the psyche also has quite a small part that is conscious. Most of the physical-psychological content is dormant, and lies waiting. Naturally, awareness kicks in whenever it is necessary: for instance, the moment that something or someone pushes our buttons, so we are forced to wake up from our slumber. At such a moment, there is a possibility for change. We can detect when and where to change through self-awareness of our bio-psychological conditioning.

The Kabbalist does not wait for a natural change to happen through necessity (stress, pain, anger etc.), but is very aware of what needs attention, and eventually, what needs change. These may be physical and psychological processes. On the way towards unity, which is the path and work of the Kabbalist, we move ourselves on the Tree of Life, to live not only from necessity, but from the soul level.

The soul is that vehicle of consciousness that can reach out into the natural world, and the higher worlds simultaneously; it is very interested in integrating the totality, bringing back our whole being within the vision of one consciousness. The soul on the Tree of Life is between worlds; a place where the three lower worlds meet.

These three modes or levels of consciousness come together in one: firstly, the Kether of Assiah (the crown of our physical existence), knowing about one's full potential within the physical world.

Secondly, the Tifaret of Yezirah (or the psyche's self), where we capture an experience, and how our physical body, ego, personas, and shadow parts, come together under a sense of identity that is aware of itself.

Thirdly, the Malkuth of Briah (the first Heaven, and last Day of Creation or Sabbath), where we receive a spiritual glimpse behind the veil.

Only at this level can we have an experience of the Higher worlds (Briah), or Heaven. The Veil of Heaven is lifted through the work of the Kabbalist, and through grace.

In Kabbalah, we say the soul has two faces that behold Heaven and earth in one vision.

In my first book about quantum physics and biology, I discussed the soul in this same way. The soul is a crucial seat of consciousness in the total vehicle (Tree of Life), because of its ability to mediate and process the exchange between the natural world (Assiah), and the metaphysical world of Briah and Aziluth. In both the Tree of Life and Jacob's Ladder diagrams, you can see that, below and above the Tifaret of Yezirah, there is the Daath of Assiah and Yezirah, respectively.

The knowledge of the body and the psyche at the foundation of the Yesod of Yezirah and Briah means that the soul is present in between these subtle centres of knowing. It is here where we obtain direct experience and knowledge: the true mystical knowledge, or gnosis (Daath).

Now let's have another look at Jacob's Ladder, and see the same geometric relation between the Tifaret of Assiah with the Yesod of Assiah below, and with the Yesod of Yezirah above. The CNS has the same central position as the Tifaret in Yezirah.

The nervous system and the self in the psyche are different in substance, but are the same in essence. Down the whole of Jacob's Ladder, from the world of Aziluth to the very world of manifestation in Assiah, each principle of the Divine reflects itself into all three lower worlds.

In each world, Tifaret is located in between these Yesodic-Daath complexes. Notice that the first Yesod on the Tree of Life and Jacob's Ladder is a Yesod without a Daath. Through this Yesod of Assiah, or the ANS, we can become aware, only indirectly, through the CNS and the Yesod/Daath of Assiah/Yezirah.

At the very top, there is a Daath of Aziluth with no connection to a subsequent Yesod. There is a Kabbalistic way of seeing Jacob's Ladder as vertically circular, rather than linear. The Malkuth of Assiah would form an ecliptic whole with the Kether of Aziluth, and the Yesod of Assiah with the Daath of Aziluth.

Well, what does this all mean?

Metaphysics of this kind can become extremely complicated, while it should simplify matters. I will therefore break any complexity down into three simple elements.

First of all, Kabbalistic metaphysics shows us that the Universe is not divided, but that everything is interconnected, interdependent, and is a reflection of the other. Spheres, which we call Sefirot in Kabbalah, are potential principles within and without the human experience. They may be known as states of awareness (they come and go), or as stages (prolonged states).

Secondly, all centres on the middle pillar are Sefirot of consciousness, connecting to the functional side pillars of the left and right in the Kabbalistic diagrams of the Tree of Life and Jacob's ladder.

Thirdly, when we speak of hierarchical levels in Kabbalah, there is no sense of a higher and lower value system. We are referring to different levels of awareness in the sense of evolution.

At each Sefira on the middle pillar, Kabbalists can see the consciousness level below it, and its awareness capability in other words: we cannot know what is above our stage of knowing, but we can see what came before it. We know for a fact that most of humanity live out their lives on the vegetable level at the Yesod/Daath of Assiah and Yezirah.

The animal level is certainly present at the triad of Hod-Netzach-Tifaret of Yezirah. With some individualism and freedom of will, many on this earth move their social status above the average vegetable level (triad Malkuth-Hod-Netzach).

The soul level is quite rare for most human beings to experience, yet many may have state experiences that are more fleeting and not very continuous (as a prolonged stage of knowing).

Nature in general, and the human organism in particular (with its frontal-lobe capacities in the brain), grow and develop through shorter or longer periods of time (according to the biblical account and the evolution theories). The ladder of evolution, or Jacob's Ladder, depicts both an image of physical evolution, as well as a spiritual influence (Holy Spirit or Ruach Ha Kadosh) throughout life that moves all in the worlds of Yezirah and Assiah.

The creative centre within the human being (Adam Kadmon) is the Tifaret on the Tree of Life. Astrologically, Tifaret corresponds to the cosmic object that we know as the sun. From sources in astronomy and astrophysics, we know that the sun is the creator of the solar system (gathering about itself dust, debris, gasses, and other elemental materials), pulling it all in its electromagnetic orbit.
In a literal and physical sense, the sun, as our day-star on the earth, is a creative, nurturing, and life-giving centre. Although it seems that the sun is separated from its "children" or planets, they are all connected within a subtle, refined, but powerful nuclear network.

I want to draw the analogy here with the central nervous system within the Tifaret of Assiah, as it operates and functions in a similar way. Please remember that the CNS at the Tifaret of Assiah represents the function of the central nervous system, but is not its physical location. How the synapses of the nervous system work is through fiery impulses between the nervous cells (neurons). Chemicals are released depending on the type of electrical input between the synapses.

Life in this solar system is based entirely on the sun's nurturing, creative, and life-sustaining force. All the levels in nature (like mineral, vegetable and animal) are what the Kabbalist can find on the lower face on the Tree of Life. All of them are born of the sun.

As a metaphysical metaphor, the sun has a network, like a nervous system, identical to all organic life. Aside from this metaphor, the actual function of the nervous system has many literal and physical attributes that can be directly compared to the impact of the sun.

We have a literal and a metaphorical sun within us; a solar system that we know within the body, and have named a "neurological system". Likewise, as the cosmic sun has unlimited energy and unbounded creative capacity, so our nervous system is the physical core of those same faculties.
Potentially, the inner sun or heart has a reach in the totality of the body, and the personal part of the psyche. In the world of Assiah, the central nervous system has its influence over the bio-psychological organism, consciously or unconsciously. If you regard the physical sun in our solar system, and compare through analogy the inner sun or the heart, you see the parallel principles at work through the electromagnetic network that holds all other systems (planets or organs) together.

The sun (a central organic and spiritual "device" of high intelligence that organizes and orchestrates all functions in the body) is represented in our bodies as our heart and nervous system (which are central organs of the macro and microcosm). If we look at the CNS, the brain is the Tifaret of the body, which is, together with the physiological heart, the most important organ of the body.

Through MRI studies, we see that the whole brain (part of the CNS) is active throughout daily functioning (even when the actions are not complicated, and when not all parts of the brain are responsible for certain actions). We have different patterns of learning in our brain that are activated (chemically and neurologically) when something is used in a physiological sense, and so, it develops. What is not used remains undeveloped or even decays. The brain itself asks to be used, you could say.

We know for a fact that, in the microcosm and in the human being, our physical nervous system has interneurons which connect with many other neurological structures. These interneurons or glial cells, are hardly used or "wired", as far as we can see. Connections made between the different neurons in the central nervous system (or brain) and peripheral body are like the sun connecting to the objects and planets in the solar system (the complete body of the sun).
The brain and the nervous system do not search for these connections themselves

when they are not stimulated and invoked to do so. In that sense, the brain may have a hierarchical position in the world of Assiah, but it is dependent on stimuli from higher levels and worlds.

From a causational-materialistic viewpoint, "upward causation" assumes that all creation comes from matter. Creational activity does not come out of a higher dimension (called spiritual unfoldment or downward causation). Kabbalah explains through Jacob's Ladder that both downward and upward creation unfold, and have their place in existence. It is not a competition between scientists (upwards causation) and creationists or theologians (downward causation). Up to this very day, the described controversy between downward and upward causation is still going on.

The brain is not the soil from which all creation flows forth. Although it is an amazing piece of biological equipment, the brain is not the sole core of creation in the human being. Rather, it is a magnificent organ that functions partly independently (in accord with physical nature), but is sensitive to conscious stimuli and suggestion. We can teach the brain to connect with the interior and exterior worlds through the seat of consciousness, Tifaret (the place where the three lower worlds meet, and the connection with the soul).

Here, we choose what to think, feel, and act upon, and how best to respond to life. Instead of reacting to the already existing patterns in the brain and the nervous system, we have free will and self-consciousness to make changes in these patterns, and form new neurological patterns. To create new neurological pathways in an electro-chemical sense, we have to lay down new patterns and levels of consciousness. To achieve this, we must begin exploring how Kabbalah and neuroplasticity come together.

A deep understanding of the Tree of Life and Jacob's Ladder will significantly help to follow the next chapter. It is not that neuroplasticity is incomprehensible without Kabbalah, just that the metaphysics held within Kabbalah, as previously explained in this book, is important to be mastered before continuing.

Neuroplasticity: what is it?
For many centuries, the ruling idea about the brain and neurological tissue was that it could not be regenerated. Neurological tissue once damaged or traumatized was thought to be completely lost and may never recuperate. Even with exercises, it would not be possible to recover the brain and make healing possible.

We know that some experiments in the eighteenth century indicated that neurological tissue could be trained, leading to growth and recovery. Charles Bonnet and Michele Vincenzo Malacarne came up with evidence about the plasticity capacity of the nervous system. Although recovery is slow and frustrating, the nerves are capable of finding ways to grow new neurological pathways or redirect themselves via stimulation using nearby pathways.

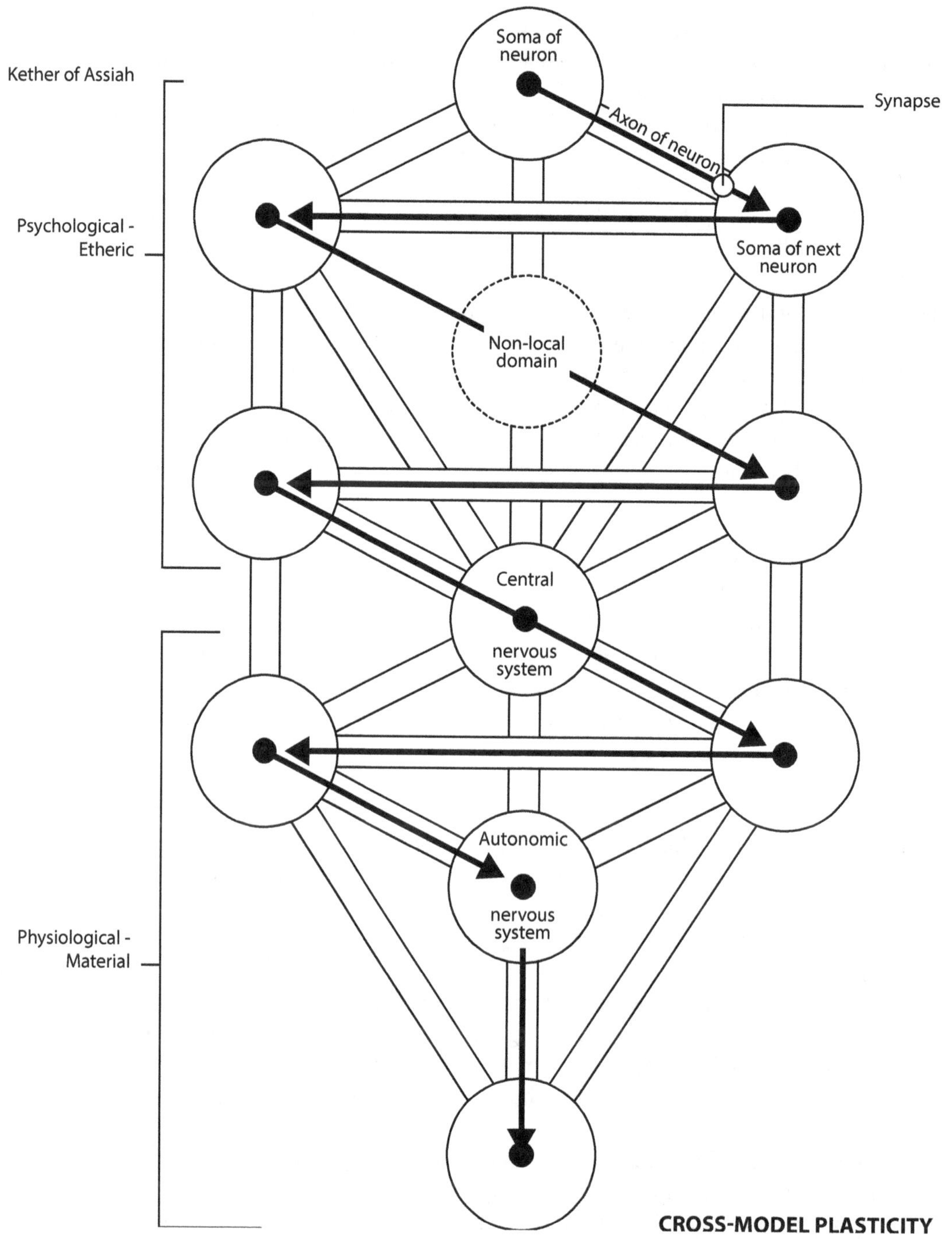

Diagram 16

128

Kabbalah has transmitted in its teachings that the human being is complete, containing all the possibilities to come to wholeness (healing). As it is said in Kabbalah: Adam Kadmon is complete and whole.

The famous Jean-Baptiste Lamarck said in his time (early 19th century) that the parts of the brain developed through using them. His insight agrees with a law in biophysics, saying that "function forms the organ". If we wish tissue to develop, we need to put that tissue and organ in their proper function. Of course, this is the whole idea behind sports and revalidation.

Interestingly, another discussion was going on in the 19th century about the anatomical structure of the nervous system. In those times, microscopic techniques were not yet so advanced to fully distinguish how nerve cells look like. One group argued that the nervous system was made up of multiple cells, as was later proven through better technological developments. The other group was more convinced in their hypothesis that the nervous system was like a sheet or matrix: one complete system that was undivided.

We know that the latter seems wrong in an anatomical sense when we look at the neurons themselves. In between the cells, there is a gap called a synapse (synaptic cleft), where neuro-chemical reactions lead to the transmission of information. When we understand the totality of the visible neurological system, and the invisible neuro-chemical system, we can appreciate that the nervous system is a continuous and unbroken whole.

There is an interesting analogy when we look at Jacob's Ladder, and, in particular, at the world of Assiah. As discussed earlier in this book, the world of action consists of one physical or lower face of that world, and the other subtle or psychological, upper face. According to the combined stories of the scientists of those times, the nervous system was a broken and unbroken whole, partly physical, and partly energy (electrical and chemical).

These principles return in our Tree of Life and on Jacob's Ladder, where the lower face is the visible and broken part, and the upper face represents the unbroken energetic part. Of course, this is one system that consists of structure (left pillar) and energy (right pillar). The energy talked about here has a relevant Kabbalistic-synchronistic relation.

There are no coincidences: the physical energy that science has found within the nervous system is purely electromagnetic, and the energy at the upper face of Assiah is also electromagnetic.
We call it etheric energy in esoteric language, which is a field, rather than a current. The etheric energy is known for its malleable, flexible, and form-giving properties.

Besides this, the etheric energy-field and energy is known in Kabbalah as the Nefesh (the Vital Soul). Nefesh is a life force that animates all things, and sets nature and all life-forms in motion. It is said that the Nefesh moves the stars in the macrocosm, and also the electrons around a nucleus in an atom (both in the macro and microcosm). This force is transpersonal, cosmic and personal, all at the same time.

We experience the Nefesh in our personal world of Assiah through the vitality of the physical, and in our mental-psychological body. Feeling low in energy does not only come from the physical body, which does not generate that much energy by itself. Food "fires up the furnace", so to speak, but when we look at the capacity of the energizing system within the body, we can see that our vitality and energy comes from the Nefesh.

In physical science, electromagnetic energy is a closed circuit in the nervous system, while the nervous system is the generator of that energy. This may not be the whole story.

In esoteric traditions in general, and Kabbalah in particular, there may be a difference in the substantial expressions of energy and form, but in essence, they are the same. Besides, the physical body is not a closed system in the way that material science sees it. However evident it may appear to the eyes and the other senses, the skin is not the final boundary between the physical body and the outside world.

The energy within the nervous system is connected with its physical electromagnetic circuit to the more free-flowing substance of the etheric body. As can be seen on the Tree and Jacob's Ladder: the physical reality of the human body and the subtle-etheric is one world, one system, one energy.

This is quite obvious and evident at birth and death, when the physical vehicle is charged, as it were, with the Nefesh vitality. At birth, the baby shines with this energy, in full bloom and awakened to a new world. All senses and organs are ready to direct this energy to live. At death, the Nefesh body gradually detaches from the lower face of Assiah. One cannot exist without the other.

The Kabbalist on the mystical path gradually realizes that their energy is not that personal. We are part of a great energy field that we think of as "personal". Human beings have this urge to make things personal and connect with the world in order to make the world in one's image (Yesod of Yezirah). Within the etheric body, we connect with different energies and memories that seem to have their place.

Be that as it may, our associations within the field of the electromagnetic energies (etheric field) are only personal for the time being. We gradually develop these associations and personal energy patterns (memories), but must let them go when we discarnate and leave our physical identity.

So, let me draw a little conclusion here, which is, by no means, written in stone. If the nervous system (in its energetic-etheric manifestation is like a field), the physical part of the nervous system might be a field as well. Not by ignoring the anatomical facts, but by seeing the nervous system as a unified whole (because it behaves that way). We know the cells are separate, but the network gives rise to a sheet-like (matrix) structure or tissue.

Returning to the plasticity story, around 1890, William James said that:
"The possession of a structure is weak enough to yield to an influence ... but

strong enough not to yield all at once!" Although James was not Kabbalistically trained, he made some interesting commentaries. His ideas were often more than superficial observations. Every structure is made out of energy patterns. Forms do come into the world by themselves, whether they are psychological-subtle or physical-gross forms. At first, they are compositions of energy, molding into physical reality, and clothing themselves, as it were, in matter.

Any change in the composition of energy (Nefesh) may lead to a change in the physical structure. Remember that energy is not separate from the material form, but is inherent and inclusive in physical existence. The way your body is composed, how it looks, and how it functions has everything to do with the energy patterns within the body. So, structures and forms are dependent on the influences of energy.

Although quite a general remark, the influence mentioned has direct impact on our story here. Influences can come from thoughts, feelings, inner and outer actions, memories, sensitive impressions, and so on. A structure in our body in the form of a molecule, cell, tissue, organ, or totality of organs, can be changed through energy (an influence). Now comes the second part where James says: "but strong enough not to yield all at once".

Imagine changing something within the body by just having a single thought. That would lead to chaos and random outcome of our physiology. We will see later in this book that thoughts and feelings do cause neuro-chemical reactions, and have an influence; but it takes many more of those thoughts and feelings (influences) to truly come to a change, or even a transformation of the organism.

In neurophysiology, this is called an action-potential, when several influences or neuro-chemical reactions are needed to cause a movement along the nerves. There seems to be a delicate balance between the possibilities of change (right pillar) and the stability of the organism (left pillar). Harmony or homeostasis is a matter of the middle pillar, with emphasis on the central Sefira of Tifaret.

The CNS in Assiah, and the psychological self in Yezirah, both have that role to play in the natural human being. Homeostasis is not a fixed state in our biopsychology, but a fluid balance of constant movement. Now, nerves in themselves do not decide much in our general nervous system and our organism as a whole. Decision making has to come from the central nervous system, but daily decisions are mostly based upon conditioned and learned programs within the organism.

Although the nervous system has the potential to learn endlessly and beyond limit, the organism remains in its inert situation of comfort and predictability. If the nervous system is therefore not triggered and stimulated to come to new situations of learning, there will be no new growth of nerve cells, or new neurological connections.

The nervous system needs unknown impulses and information in order to be stimulated and grow. This is the so-called "plasticity", which occurs mainly at those anatomical parts of the nerves where the junctions or synapses are present. These are the ends of the nerve cells, where the electro-chemical information is transmitted from one nerve cell to the next.

The place of neuro-chemical transmission of the synapse is the location where electrical impulses are translated into chemical substances called neurotransmitters. These substances have a Mercurial-Hod function in both form and energy (neuro-chemical): they provide the complete organism with information.

The plasticity, or transmission function, of the nervous system occurs at the point of these synapses where two or more nerve ends come together, causing a neuro-chemical reaction that modifies the signals. Plasticity may happen in the CNS and/or the peripheral nervous system. If this plasticity were not possible, our bodies would not be able to adapt to new situations. In Kabbalah, the human being is like a Tree (Adam Kadmon).

The Tree image, as metaphor, is not chosen by accident (as nothing is in Kabbalah). It is the Tree that communicates to us the possibilities of growth and development: a connection between Divinity (roots) and its branches (whole Tree of life), spreading into existence, where its fruits manifest eventually in the Malkuth of Assiah. The deeper the roots of a tree in nature, the higher it grows, and its fruits will show in accordance with that process of growth.

The human being, and especially the nervous system, is not rigid nor unmodifiable, but malleable and changeable. We have to admit that in the current state of affairs, the theory of neuroplasticity does not have a working method from A to Z on how to actually change something.

Kabbalah could provide us with some answers, but always in relation to the reasonable possibilities of our reality today. I would not like to take you into a New-Age kind of book where you are told that all is possible, and that we are "creators of our own reality".

Let us remain scientific about it in a classical and metaphysical sense.

The central nervous system, and in particular, the brain (which looks like a cauliflower), is itself like a tree, or an orchard with many plants and trees. With the aid and knowledge of how to cultivate that garden or orchard, we could come to a greater understanding and use of the nervous system.

What is even more interesting is the response within the synapses.
The word synapse is derived from the Greek "syn", which means together. It is the place of probabilities for learning, and the transmission of consciousness, clothed in thoughts, feelings, and energy.

Like the conditionings in the psyche (energy patterns in the upper face of Assiah/ lower face Yezirah), the nervous system contains many electrochemical conditionings that were generated through the repeated use of those nerves and synapses (through the influences of your upbringing, culture and background).

Conditionings in the personal part of the psyche and physical body join hand-in-hand.

The forming, and generating of our personal psyche takes place through the Daath of Assiah (ego-Yesod), where we learn through the environment, culture, religion, family, and origin of the ancestral line. If we do not become aware of these patterns, we will not open the possibility to move away from them. Moving away in the Kabbalistic sense does not mean to escape or flee, but rather to spiritually transform what is blocked in the psyche/body.

The natural organism (physical body) that we inhabit most of the time or all of our lives (world of Assiah) is largely occupied with regenerating, strengthening, and reproducing itself.

We mostly become aware of these personal growth patterns when we experience an unexpected crisis, or through other people, or challenging situations. If we are not on some kind of interior journey or quest (for it is there where we meet ourselves more directly and intimately), then, what does not come up to the surface in our consciousness, will present itself through the outside world. It is in the world where we meet ourselves.

Kabbalah tells us from its mystical philosophy that all is there, held in a perfect, Divine embrace. Nothing needs to be added to the universe, nor to you. All you need to become whole is right there, within you. The physical body contains all the possible tools to grow spiritually.

This is fascinating from different points of view. First of all, the body does not need more cells. The brain does not need more brain cells, or nerve ends to grow in consciousness. It is much more a matter of exploration and discovery. As it is said in Kabbalah: the work of unity is like a remembrance. Forgetfulness about ourselves, and who we are leads to an exile from our true nature: what it means to be truly human.

The scientific dogma that the brain and nervous system cannot learn or regenerate was founded upon the outcome of some research and survived until this very day. During my own medical and paramedical training, I learned that certain tissue does not regenerate, especially nerve tissue.

Meanwhile, since the mid-1900s, there has been enough scientific evidence to prove consistently that the nervous system and brain can be trained, and can develop. One of those discoveries was "long-term potentiation", or LTP (Bliss and Lømo), formulating a mechanism where synapses were strengthened for prolonged periods of time.

We also know that the nervous system can learn by sensory input. This can be through touch, sight, smell, taste, or hearing. On the Tree of Life, this would be the lower triangle in Assiah, between the Malkuth-Yesod-Hod (place of the nerves and sensory input).

At the other side of the Tree at the triangle of Malkuth-Yesod-Netzach, we find
the motor functions and muscles. We know that the nervous system can learn and
develop as a whole, through physical exercise; even those parts of the brain that
have no direct influence over the motor-muscular system.

Concerning neuroplasticity, these two systems (the sensory system and the
motoric system) are regarded today as the main learning systems in science.
Of course, when we look at Jacob's Ladder, locating the triads mentioned above,
they are at the very bottom of the Ladder, attached to the Malkuth of Assiah.
We are talking about an upward causational way of creation.
However, as it was discussed before, there are two ways of looking at creation:
upward and downward (through matter or Spirit). In Kabbalah, these ways of
creation are known as the Ma'aseh Merkavah, and Ma'aseh Berashith: the works
of evolution and creation. The mystical vision behind these two ways, is that they
do not contradict each other like two dual, irreconcilable principles.

Creation comes from Spirit, and Spirit (Ruach) is present everywhere.
That Immanent presence of the Transcendent Divine is called Shekinah, present
within Malkuth-the Kingdom, the physical world and body in which we live.
Causation is potentially present within the very manifestation of existence.

The foundation of scientific evidence for neuroplasticity came from the sensory
and motoric body movements that stimulate the nervous system. Let's expand
upon these ideas.

Deeper meaning
Neuroplasticity, like Kabbalah, is a vast subject. There are many layers or worlds
and endless discoveries to be made. A story without an end.

There are different levels in the nervous system where plasticity can occur, such
as on the molecular level and the individual cells, the nerves and their endings
(synapses), or within whole fields where neurons gather. Also, in networks and
clusters of neurons, and in the very central nervous system and the cortex (brain).
(For further reference, look at the diagrams in this chapter).

It seems that there is a possibility of plasticity at every level of the cortical nerves
which arrange an enormous number of functions in the body. Experiments have
proven that not all these neurological structures can be stimulated in the same manner.

Broadly, there are three forms of neuroplasticity:
- Functional: Here we look at how we can release inter-synaptic chemicals
  through the right stimuli. This works if we know how to release the right
  neurotransmitters. Physiological changes can be established through the right
  frequency or rhythm of the neurological impulses, stimulating stronger or new
  chemical signals to the nerves and nervous system.
- Structural: The attempt here is to enhance the growth of new neuro-fibres.
- Tissue and synapses and the growth of new cells: this method brings
  connections between different parts of the nervous system and individual
  neurons, to generate new neurological pathways.

DIVINE
Passive intellect
Active intellect
SPIRIT
Knowledge
Passive concepts
Active concepts
Negative and positive charge of conceptual intellect
Passive emotion
Active emotion
SOUL
SELF
−
Emotional complexes
+
Emotional complexes
Passive bio-psycho
Active bio-psycho
Awakening
Threshold
Feeling
EGO
Thinking
Senses
−
Ions
+
Ions
Passive and active IONS
Anabolic
Katabolic
Metabolism
CENTRAL NERVOUS SYSTEM
−
Hormones enzymes
+
Hormones enzymes
Tissue
Bio voluntary
Bio involuntary
Organs
AUTONOMIC NERVOUS SYSTEM
Nerves
Muscles
SKIN BONE SENSE ORGANS

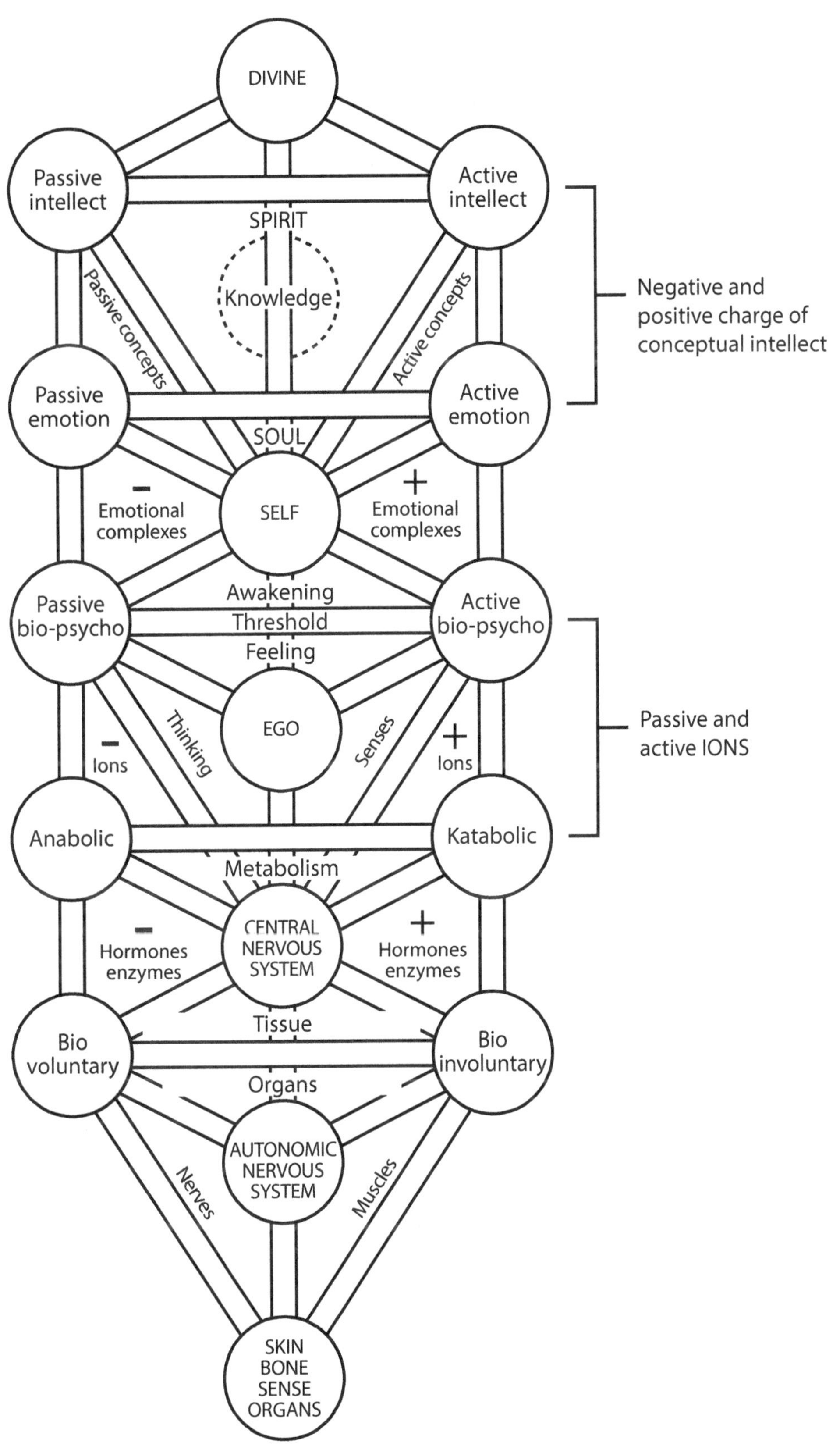

Diagram 17

To discern the differences for someone who is not familiar with neurophysiology and this material, it can be quite challenging. Let me give you some examples from Kabbalah (which, as an age-old tradition, has always worked upon these systems of neuroplasticity).

For example in the case of the functional method:

Kabbalistic meditation (Hitbodedut) is one way to generate an immediate effect on your internal neuro-chemical system. A classic meditation on the Tree of Life (Etz Chaim), which involves the image of the mind of God, the universe, the human soul, and all creation, is a very effective esoteric method.

Adam Kadmon is the anthropomorphic silhouette in the Tree of Life, representing the heavenly man (male and female). Adam Kadmon's picture reminds us of the inherent wholeness in our nature and existence. Within the Tree of Life, we find the whole neurological system, glands, neurotransmitters, and synapses. When we meditate by visualizing the Tree within ourselves, we actualize the memory of Adam Kadmon within the four worlds (from the Divine to the creative, the formative, and finally materializing in the world of action).

The suggestion this brings to the Kabbalist is the wholeness of being and consciousness of completion, integration, and unity. In other words: this is a healing meditation, bringing back our inner state to an experience of wholeness, as it has no immediate and direct focus on specific glands or neurological centres. Whether we are ill or out of balance, we use these meditations for purely mystical purposes. There is no emphasis on individual glands, as we do not know how many neurotransmitters should be released to achieve the desired effect in the body.

The same goes for the Eastern system, where there is no energetic concentration and focus on one or two chakras, but always on the complete system.

There are situations where our bio-psychological body (Assiah) is out of balance, and a different approach is desirable. If you look at diagram of the Tree of Life and Jacob's ladder, the side pillars generally show the principles of expansion (right pillar) and contraction (left pillar). By performing the above meditation, the Kabbalist not only comes to a therapeutic effect, but receives valuable information in a diagnostic sense.

You could experience, for example, how one pillar is heavier, lighter, lower, higher, absent, or present in whatever colour or appearance. From those insights, together with your own inner experiences inside your bio-psychology, you come to clear conclusions about your inner state.

For example, suppose you notice that your left pillar is heavy and your Gevurah is more active, while simultaneously, you suffer from anger, fear, or anxiety problems (with or without some auto-immune disorder).

In that case, there is a need to balance yourself by engaging the left pillar with the influence of the right pillar. Instead of swinging to the other side trying to find a solution in the other extreme, the Kabbalistic work is always about balance and harmony. On the path of neuroplasticity, this works in the same way.

It is not desirable to concentrate on one part of the Tree of Life without including the other. In personal situations where an illness is involved, this might not be so easy (from an emotional point of view). In most cases, the first impulse is to move away from the part (pillar, triad, Sefira) that is associated with the illness.

The second (or structural) method is somewhat more challenging, mainly because it will take time to develop new tissue and connections between different neurons and neurological centres.

The other problem is that we know some anatomy of the brain and nervous system, but we do not know enough about what neurons need to cultivate and grow. To study and be able to visualize the nerves and nervous system has its advantages though. In a Kabbalistic meditation, the method of visualizing and the faculty of the imagination are important: imagining the nervous system within, feeling its presence, and sensing how it functions.

Therefore, I am including in this book some images of the nerves and the nervous system, which help and aid you in this work.

Both forms of neuroplasticity may be clinically and theoretically divided, but metaphysically and practically they are so closely connected, that both systems are simultaneously stimulated with the exercises described above (as the ANS overlaps in the CNS). Of course, there are differences between these two forms explained through the metaphysical idea about states and stages, where states are momentary shifts of consciousness and stages are prolonged states of consciousness.

Stages on the Tree of Life, and in the life of the Kabbalist, can only be accomplished through successive states of consciousness. The Kabbalist initiates this path of neuro-networking by complementary states of conscious being.
To give you a better and clearer idea about this, I present you the following examples on the Tree of Life.

From the Kingdom to the Crown (Malkuth to Kether), the Sefirot express
Ten Names of Divinity that we may experience in the lower worlds as human spiritual qualities. In Malkuth, the practice is towards stability, manifestation, resolution, sensitivity, and incorporation of our being.
To truly be present in the physical body is a spiritual practice in itself.

To be fully present in the body and be attentive to its functions, like the senses, enhances the above qualities, and the neuro-chemical reactions in the physical body. With enough practice and repetition, the desired effect will also be noticeable in the hormonal-chemical parts of the body (Assiah).

Because matter and Spirit are not separate, the upward and downward causational motions come from the physical reality as well. Attention to the body through meditation increases blood circulation, circulation of oxygen, drainage of waste material, and many other beneficial processes. We do not need to teach the body to be sensitive, resolute or stable, because it has all these capabilities by nature; but we have to be consciously present within the body (vehicle) to stimulate and awaken them.

"Where our consciousness is, there is our energy", meaning that where we are, there is our potential to manifest the wholeness inherent in our nature.

Let us not forget that in our physical body, the Malkuth of Assiah on Jacob's Ladder (the final manifestation in existence), is the expression of four states of matter, as well as the manifestation of God, known in Kabbalah as the Shekinah.

The physical nervous system is present within this Malkuth. To be spiritually present, releases and stabilizes the neuro-chemical processes already present within the body. Now, if we include Yesod in our meditation, we emphasize a greater awareness of the vegetable or autonomic function of the nervous system. For this reason, we call this basic level of consciousness: the autonomic nervous system. The Yesodic principle is based on the deep unconscious force and form, regulated by circular (Netzach) and reverberating (Hod) processes. Yesod holds complex psycho-physiological structures (Yezirah and Assiah) that express themselves in well-defined patterns.

Some simple examples of these are bodily patterns like breathing, heartbeat, sleep activity, while the psyche processes countless mental-emotional automatic patterns that play significant roles in our lives. Only through recognition can we discover what these patterns are, and what they contain.

Apart from discovery, the meditation on Yesod sets our awareness on this extremely important neuro-chemical system upon which our physicality and energetic body are dependent. Within the unconscious of creation itself, and therefore within the personal unconscious life, intelligence regulates cosmic movement.

The whole Tree of Life expresses this unconscious intelligence, known in the Sefer Yezirah (book of formation) as the thirty-two paths or intelligences. All paths are expressions of the One Intelligence: the mind of God, which can only be known through its creation in space-time-movement.

It should be no coincidence that we have expressed ourselves through a physical body. The power and potential behind Yesod is this ongoing movement of life's energy (Chai) that animates all things, and reinforces all existing patterns and energy inherent within them. In some patterns we recognize as bio-psychological, the Chai (חי) has found its way into unhealthy forms. The effect of this manifests in the fourth world of Assiah as psychosomatic disorders.

Emotional disturbances on either side of our Tree of Life cause imbalance and chaos in the side triads, which in turn affects the corresponding triads in the body. On the level of our inner chemistry, hormones, enzymes, and peptides, our emotions will influence the body's neurochemistry.

Naturally, this is a neutral mechanism in our incarnate being. We should not conclude that such a force is evil. The choices that we make, which lead to disturbance and chaos, are the problem here.

As we have seen before, responsibility is an attribute of the soul, asking us to be self-conscious, present, and awake to ourselves and the world around us. Prior to any choice we make is the level of consciousness and corresponding intention. It is of great concern that we know "where we are" on the Tree of Life.

"Where you are is who you are".

To engage with the autonomic nervous system, cooperate with it, and bring it under our conscious influence, we have to apply the functions of that same nervous system. Breathing is the ultimate exercise in Kabbalah to regulate the unconscious system, because it deeply impacts on the whole nervous system. As such, the techniques that I wish to introduce here are for those beginning their Kabbalistic journey, and those further along the path.

Imagine that the totality of the human being and existence is depicted by the Tree of Life. In Kabbalah, the four worlds are four successive stages of Divine influence emanating from the ultimate Crown to the Kingdom. The Divine Name of Yod Heh Vav Heh (YHVH) is used to illustrate this process.

Now, if you are willing to experience the breathing exercise that involves the Name, sit down for a moment and relax.

There will be an in-breath that will sound like "Ya", the first two letters of the Name.

There will be a hold of two seconds, and a release or out-breath sounding like "Ve" (v sounds more like w). After the out-breath, there is a hold again of two seconds.

In other words: you are breathing in and out the Name of God, inhaling and exhaling the four worlds. You are breathing existence and thereby yourself in it.

After a few minutes of doing this technique, pause to realize how it feels, and its effects throughout your body and psyche.

There is, in most cases, a direct effect on the neuro-chemical system that you will recognize as feeling peaceful, in balance, harmonious, mild, and tranquil. This exercise can be done when you are in a state of disorder or feel fearful, anxious, or angry.

For the Kabbalist, there is no need to wait for an urgent moment. You can practice these techniques as a mystical preparation for the vehicle we are. The Tree of Life is the vessel for the Divine to live through and be. Of course, the Divine essence is already present, expressing itself in all the beautiful processes of the body and psyche at all times.

After discussing the Sefirot of Makuth and Yesod, we have this breathing technique to support our neuroplasticity adventure. The breathing rhythm creates electrical activity in the human brain that enhances emotional clarity and memory recall.

Please be aware that to have a fundamental and long-term effect on our inner (nervous) system, we have to learn new patterns and gradually introduce them into our unconscious.

These effects on behaviour depend critically on a few things, for example, whether you inhale or exhale, or if you breathe through the nose or mouth.

Different scientific experiments showed that individuals could identify a fearful face more quickly if they encountered the face when breathing in. Individuals also were more likely to remember an object if they encountered it on the inhaled breath, rather than the exhaled one. The effect disappeared if breathing was done through the mouth.

There is a dramatic difference in brain activity in the amygdala and hippocampus during inhalation, compared with exhalation. When you breathe in, there is a stimulation of neurons in two central nervous centres: the amygdala and hippocampus, within the so-called limbic system. In this system, the human brain remembers and is emotionally capable of connecting and reconnecting with others.

Both these human capacities are crucial in our Kabbalistic work of unity. Without memories and emotional responses to our environments, we could not come to a unifying and inclusive experience of ourselves in the world. Unifying and inclusive work is the work of love and healing. Within Kabbalah, all this can be achieved with these breathing exercises, as it stimulates both pathways in neuroplasticity.

Soul and self-consciousness
In different traditions of Kabbalah, the soul has several meanings and places on the Tree of Life. In Toledano Kabbalah, the soul is situated at the interface between the higher and lower faces of the Tree of life, namely, the triad of Chesed-Tifaret-Gevurah. The soul is the true human nature.

Such is the reality behind the appearance of the human presentation and performance. What is so easily called "the human being" is based upon a confusion and misinterpretation that's only related to the temporary disguise of the body and our personality (psyche). The soul is not within the body or the mind. The soul is the transparent core around which the subtle bodies and gross physical body reside. The soul is the vehicle of consciousness in which all appears and disappears.

The eyes of the soul are the eyes of God. Being able to look through the eyes of the soul allows God to behold Itself within the world. Besides the external world that you perceive about you, there is the personal body that you observe from the consciousness of the soul. All comes and goes within this consciousness.

As a soul, you are a temporary visitor to this passing world, travelling around, allowing God to become the audience of Its creation. From the senses of the soul, all changes under the observance of consciousness. Within the scope of your observation as God, you participate in the evolution and creation of the observed. Such is the Divine gift.

We know that from this consciousness, the nervous system responds together with all the parts of the cortex (brain) and the peripheral nervous system within the body. There is an effect that could be compared to seeing the dual pillars on the Tree of Life being equally stimulated and sedated, coming into perfect balance. When this happens, we know in Kabbalah that the human soul has positioned itself completely centrally within the Tree of Life. Through Kabbalah, we find the soul within.

There is no other place to find it, and true healing and happiness come from the realization of the soul. Having said this, the soul is not the end of the Kabbalist's work, but merely the beginning.

The soul lies at the Tifaret of Yezirah, or the heart of that same world. The central nervous system in the world of the body occupies the same position, and within the triad of Chesed-Tifaret-Gevurah, makes up the triad of metabolic processes. As the physical body metabolizes biological substances, the soul metabolizes the psychological inner life's processes. All this happens within the world of Assiah, and within Yezirah (the emotional side triads around the soul). In more popular scientific terms, some call these worlds bodies or fields.

All within these fields in the lower worlds (Assiah and Yezirah) changes form, and undergoes the process of becoming. Kabbalah is one of the many spiritual traditions that emphasizes the Tree of Life as its fundamental structure and design. The human being (Adam Kadmon) is made in the image of the universe, which is made in the image of the Eternal. Therefore, the human being is the totality of all the worlds, and all the fields therein.

Within this idea of fields and matrixes, the new biology speaks of morphogenetic fields (Rupert Sheldrake) as subtle forms or changing fields around the physiological and substantial body. All that changes in this subtle body/form/field causes changes within the gross material body.

Kabbalah teaches the same by talking about the world of the psyche or Yezirah, where a subtle body and substance, like a clay substance, gives shape and rise to a definite material world called Assiah.

This field seems to be electromagnetic, animating its force through all substantial phenomena. Allow me to point again at the relationship between the nature of the subtle-etheric body (which is electromagnetic), and the electromagnetic function and force of the physical nervous system. A physical body and its nervous system (consisting of the psychological-etheric and electrical systems) make up one field or world.

All these thoughts about our nature converge into the nature of the human soul.
In my previous book, the first volume of "A Kabbalistic view on science",
I describe the quantum suggestion that at the base of all matter lies a field that
contains endless space, and is empty and full at the same time.

This void explains itself Kabbalistically in Bohu and Tohu (Sefer Yezirah) as the
first void or emptiness from which all comes forth. This void or space holds
within itself endless possibilities, a potential without limit. The first form,
Kabbalah explains, is the shape of Adam Kadmon (or the Divine man),
representing the human soul.

While all other things in creation are made of the same material, but in different
varieties and forms, all is eventually the same thing: consciousness.

All is consciousness and all is the energy within that field, which explains itself as
the electromagnetic force that connects all things. The soul is the vessel of
consciousness, the field and the force.

Therefore, can we conclude: "Where consciousness is, there is the field, and there
is the potential force of endless possibilities".

The human soul is the vehicle for God to be present in creation, and to participate
and contribute as a Divine co-worker.

The holistic approach to spiritual living and healing lies within the depths of this
knowledge. Knowledge and knowing resides within the human being. There is no
other place to be and no other thing to become than oneself.

Kabbalistic (inclusive) work means that the apparent subjective is completely and
naturally entangled with the apparent objective. The relationship the soul has with
the world is of complete identification with who one is. Such should not be
confused with the identification with the personality and the world, where one
becomes constricted personally (Yesod of Yezirah). The soul is not personally
engaged with all things, but Divinely (Aziluth) identified with all others.

Now you could consider the following concerning neuroplasticity, as you may
think I am drifting away from our topic: through the scientific-spiritual search in
this book (where the knowledge of neuroplasticity and Kabbalistic-metaphysics
come together in the Tree of Life), we can change the nervous system!

This is because the study and practice of Kabbalah set in motion the principles of
neuroplasticity. It is said that when one studies and practices Kabbalah, there are
changes happening within the consciousness of the Kabbalist. Changes in
consciousness do cause changes in the neurological activity of the nervous system.
As the Kabbalist explores the Tree of Life and new levels of consciousness, the neural
network within the CNS is stimulated and activated for growth and development.

In Kabbalah, from a Divine perspective, there is no other than yourself. What one
perceives is who one is.

Consciousness is the witness of all things, as we have discussed before in the chapter about Quantum physics. The observer is simultaneously interconnected to what is observed. The observing consciousness (soul) of the human being, is one of the creative principles.

The second creative principle is imagination. Self-consciousness and imagination, together, form the potential and inner tools to create new ideas and concepts. No animal is capable of doing this, in the way a human being can.

Choice or free will comes from self-consciousness. From self-consciousness and free will, the imagination of the mind can become creative. As long as we live along the conditioned structures of our past, we will not gain entry easily into the level of self-consciousness and free will (soul and Tifaret).

As an exercise, we could imagine that the neural network in our CNS is finding new connections between neurons that have not yet been activated in your life. If you look at a picture of the brain, for example, you can imagine (see, sense and feel) that all the areas of the brain become activated as they are full of blood and with electrical-chemical activity.

You can practice this by imagining that through your Tree of Life energy is flowing along the way of the Lightning Flash (TzimTzum). Our psyche and physical body are very open and receptive to suggestion. Through self-consciousness and imagination, we can activate our CNS through suggestion.

Imagination is an implementation of the creative faculty of the human soul. The subjective suggestion overwrites, transforms, and actualizes a new situation of consciousness. This happens constantly on a subconscious basis. People often do not know that they have, and use, this ability of transformation. Our being influences the world continuously without our awareness of it. The soul, however, is the conscious operator of this process.

"As the soul is, so the world becomes".

To extend further upon these thoughts: by conscious involvement of the soul in life itself, one intervenes and remodels inner reality. On the material level, the first and most direct system to be influenced is, at the same time, the fastest of all systems in the body: the nervous system.

Again, it is no coincidence that the soul is part of the triangle with Tifaret at its centre (Yezirah), connecting the central nervous system in the Tifaret of the body (Assiah). If new information and data come through the nervous system in a consistent and prolonged manner, both the DNA and the genes may be influenced by this process.

In my first book I discussed biology and the genetic material in our bodies. I wrote that the DNA structure fixates the genes according to the perspective one has of the world. One's subjective reality and beliefs define the eventual physical DNA expression.

From the perspective of the soul, it is important that we know what we think, feel and how we act (to know and observe the content of our inner world). The soul can observe all these different perceptions of the body and psyche (body-mind organism), with the potential to give direction (free will) to these thoughts, feelings and actions.

"One's subjective reality becomes one's objective reality".

Worldwide spiritual traditions agree on the law of metaphysics which states that all is consciousness and interconnected (all is living and constantly changing; all is animated by Spirit). Reality is whole and one; that oneness can be realized by the soul, which has its place within that consciousness.

The first law in Kabbalah states that all is one and made from one substance, derived from one essence. From these wisdom teachings (which are unanimous in their voicing around the world), it may be concluded that the soul, which is the true human being, has the capacity in consciousness to reflect our personal reality and, if needed, to redefine that reality in accordance with our imagination. As souls, we can create our inner world in conformity with the images we use and reflect upon.

Tifaret is cultivated through:
- The work on self-identity (Who am I? What am I?)
- The work of intention (What do I want? What do I bring into the world?)
- The work of self-healing, by learning how to:
- Be self-aware (being conscious of being conscious)
- Practice equal mindedness (Histawut in Kabbalah)
- Take spiritual responsibility
- Practice free choice (place at the soul to choose from your own self)
- Use the senses as instruments of consciousness
- Be aware of how your Tifaret looks through the eyes of Yesod
- Practice image-making (Tifaret is the intelligence of the creative imagination)
- Practice energy raising through consciousness ("where your consciousness is, there is your energy")

Soul and wholeness
Every person wishes to be whole. It's the call of the soul.

Kabbalistic work is about bringing oneself back to a state of wholeness, and therefore enabling oneself to live in unity. Wholeness and inclusiveness mean being aware of the totality of your context and all facets of your life. One has to go from dependency to independence to relate to, and rely completely on one's inner life: the soul.

The soul is occupied with the truth within yourself, and your truthful relationship with the world. When you walk the path of integrity and honesty towards yourself, there cannot be any space for lies and self-deception.

Pillar of Consciousness
Pillar of Structure
Pillar of Dynamic
Anima Mother
Animus Father
COLLECTIVE UNCONSCIOUS
Super Ego Punishment
Ego Ideal Reward
INDIVIDUAL UNCONSCIOUS
Mortido
Libido
PERSONAL CONSCIOUSNESS
Kether SELF of DIVINE
Consciousness of DIVINE
Binah PASSIVE INTELLECT
Chocmah ACTIVE INTELLECT
Transpersonal Consciousness
Daath HIGHER KNOWLEDGE
Anti-Cathexes
Passive Concepts
SPIRIT
SPIRIT
Active Concepts
Cathexes
Gevurah PASSIVE EMOTION
Chesed ACTIVE EMOTION
SOUL
Conscience
SOUL
SOUL
Tifaret SELF of INDIVIDUALITY
Anti-Cathexes
Passive Emotional Complexes
Active Emotional Complexes
Cathexes
AWAKENING Pre-conscious
Hod PASSIVE ACTION
Passive Introvert Triad
Active Introvert Triad
Netzach ACTIVE ACTION
Liminal Treshhold
Feelings
Yesod SHADOW EGO IDENTITY
Thinking
Sense Data
Passive Extravert Triad
Actions
Motor Response
Active Extravert Triad
Malkuth BODY
Id-Nefesh Subconscious

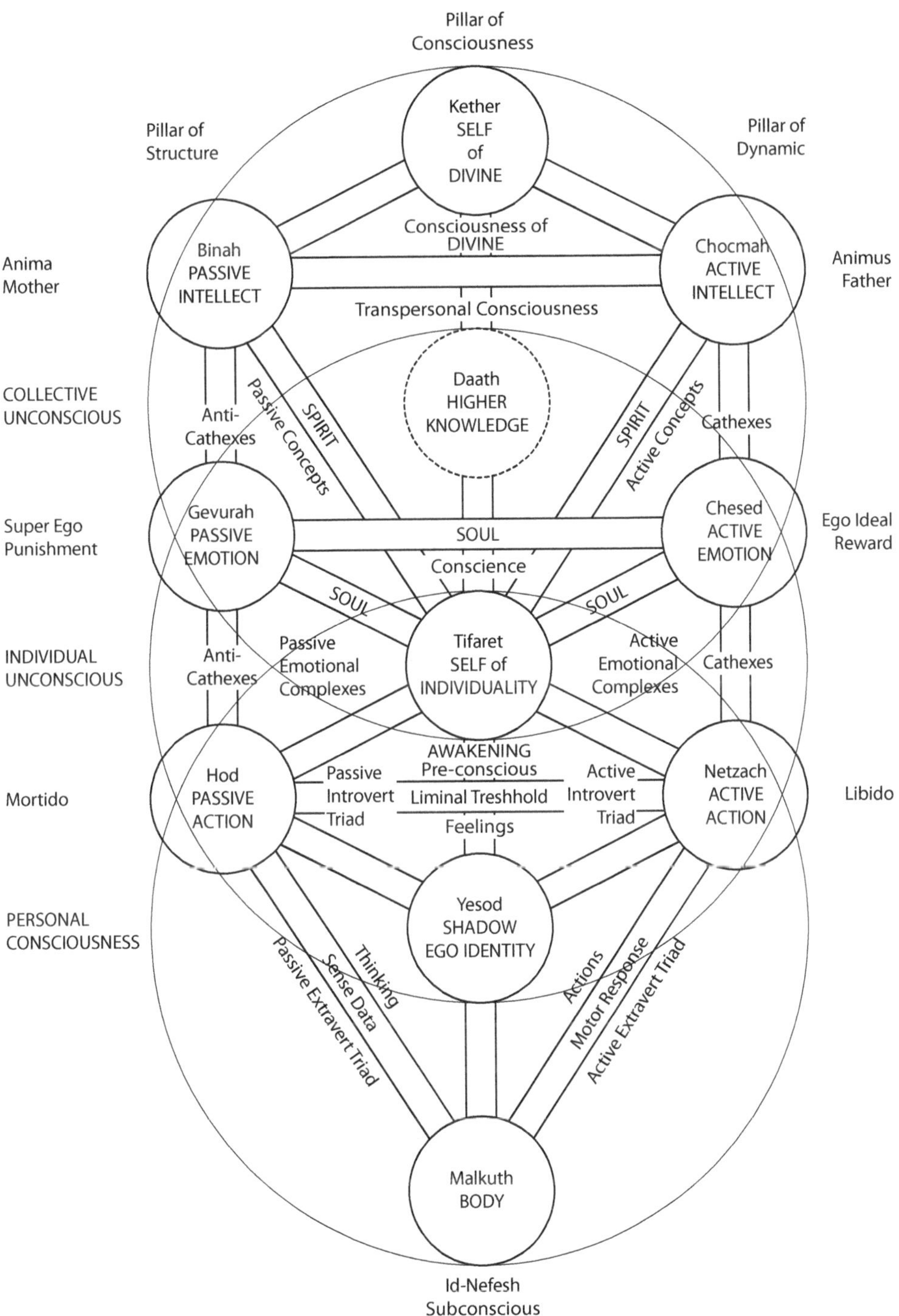

Diagram 18

Every individual, and every soul, is being stimulated and reminded that integrity is vital if one wishes to work on oneself, and recover from inner and outer wounds. The truth shall set you free. The soul that is slowly (but surely) developing towards inner truth sees the lies and excuses one has presented to oneself, and the impact they have on one's life.

Tifaret within us can be recognized as it guides us with care and gentleness, and with perseverance in the cultivation of truth. With truth comes the revelation of the shadow-side of oneself.

There is a reason why the human being represses and avoids certain aspects of oneself. The shadow is not something evil, but it refers to aspects of ourselves that we are not ready to accept. These hidden parts of our personality and behaviour do not "hide" for nothing; they are aspects that would be too painful to be acknowledged, and can't surface in our consciousness because of fear.

These blockages under the surface of our consciousness cause the nervous system to express the denial as ill-being, producing physical problems of all kinds: bodily pains, sleeping disorders and (chronic) fatigue, for example. Besides the somatic problems (body), there are psychological problems that are caused through repression.

The central nervous system, the autonomic, and peripheral systems, respond to how we are centered (or not) in our Tifaret. Three names or titles for Tifaret are: "the good, beautiful, and true". These titles are inner realities that derive from this center and energy, passing on this energy from the spiritual-psychological world into the bio-psychological world.

The shadow comes to the surface within the human soul through stress, anxiety, fear, anger, and many other repeating emotional states. Denied emotions become uncomfortable and cause distress: they are unwelcome.

Instinctively, human nature reacts with immediate resistance. This causes an inner fight against oneself. The soul wishes to accept what is happening, not avoiding any aspect of one's life. This is the integrated approach to healing in Kabbalah and neuroplasticity. All is included: even the pain and suffering. They have something to tell, talking with important meaning about what is going on.
For most of us, this is a confronting step to make: to come face to face with one's inner shadow directly. This exposure can be gradual, or sudden.

The holistic dimension explains how different levels are involved in finding causality and healing ourselves. Holistic or integral healing is taking place on all levels, and in all worlds within the human being.

The soul is the ever-present observer and witness on all levels, and in all worlds. The soul is the seat of healing. From this observing and peaceful, subtle watching, a new perspective dawns, making us realize through new experience that we need a new paradigm for living.

This means new thoughts, feelings, and actions. A new set of beliefs about ourselves, and the world. The soul is capable not only of observing, but also of keeping different perspectives at once: body, mind, and spirit. Holistic and integral means: comprehensive, balanced, and inclusive.

The inner life consists of thoughts, feelings, emotions, actions, values, drives, and instincts. The outer life is the direct environment, family, and cultural influences. Our personalities have learned to have a perspective on the world from the inner point of view, directed towards the outer world.

The interaction between the two worlds brings the human being to an understanding of the sense of "me" in relation to the outside world. The dynamic for every person is widely different, depending on many factors. To learn to have more perspectives on our life, and life itself, we need to:

- Enlarge the reflective capacity of our personality (Yesod on the Tree of Life)
- Embrace other possibilities beyond the known horizons we are familiar with
- To teach and train the ego-personality to adapt to other realities, coming from new perspectives
- Be open, therefore, to other perspectives, and do not close new reflections, but use what you have learned as a foundation of what you have known until today

Neuroplasticity is enhanced by direct engagement between the inner and outer worlds in developing new neuro-chemical pathways. Where neurons connect, new possibilities are brought into the potential domain of our body-psyche (world of Assiah).

New perspectives and viewpoints create space in your life. The personality should be asking: "Are you willing to take on new ways of seeing the world"? This openness and availability show a readiness to understand other points of view. It is the wish of every soul to find its place in the world. The soul aspires to find a place in the world, which is always a personal and subjective place. You create your place for everything in your life. All aspects of your life are necessary ingredients, that have made you the person you are.
Nothing has to be expelled or thrown away from you. On the contrary, all should be integrated and included. The soul, the human being, is perfect as it is: nothing has to be added, for all is present in potential. If there is anything that the human soul should get rid of, it is the idea that it cannot be itself, or is powerless by its nature. To "transcend and include" is meant to not only shift from one experience to the next, but also growing and integrating your old knowledge and experiences with the new experiences: all is inclusive. Integrate and include all that you have experienced and know until now. To exclude anything is to exclude something of yourself. To exclude something is to exclude God. The human soul and God are both whole and inclusive. Our work includes all levels, all lives, all states, and all worlds.

Four stages of the personality, four stages of Yesod
We live according to the cycles of outer and inner nature: we move with the seasons and the stations of the sun, and the fluxes of the moon. These cosmic cycles are of huge influence on our personal and daily routines.

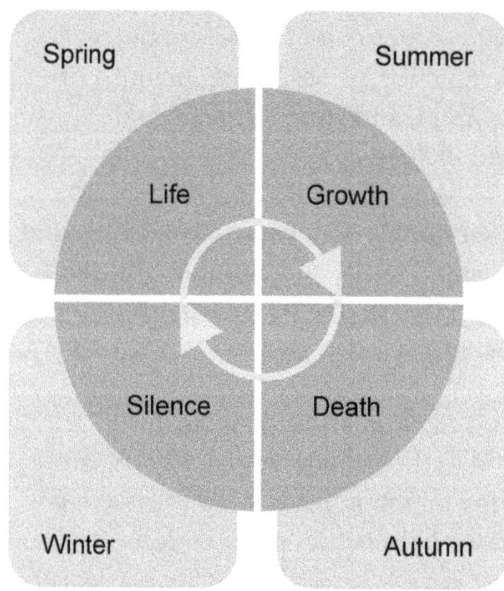

The stages of growing and fading light make people's moods change, and have an effect on the bio-physiological system (autonomic nervous system). These cycles operate mainly through the unconscious systems. There is no self-consciousness involved.

However, being aware of what is going on in these cycles can lead to great benefits in developing self-knowledge, rebalancing and recovering ourselves. Nature is very self-sufficient, being able to be harmonized by going through all the stages and seasons equally.

These four stages of one circle are equal to the nature around us in this world, and the same nature within the body and psyche. Both outer and inner natures go through similar stages. The human being can recognize these stages when being self-aware. This is achieved by seeing how our personal daily cycles move with the outer cycles of nature, and therefore, we can reflect upon, and anticipate them.

For example: a person can have a spring character, full of life, initiative, plans, and moving about like a young soul. This is the growing stage of nature when new life comes to flower and ideas fructify. A very necessary stage for renewal, fresh inspiration, setting initiatives in motion. If the person does not move on to the summer stage, nothing will come to pass, and the seed ideas will not flower in summer.

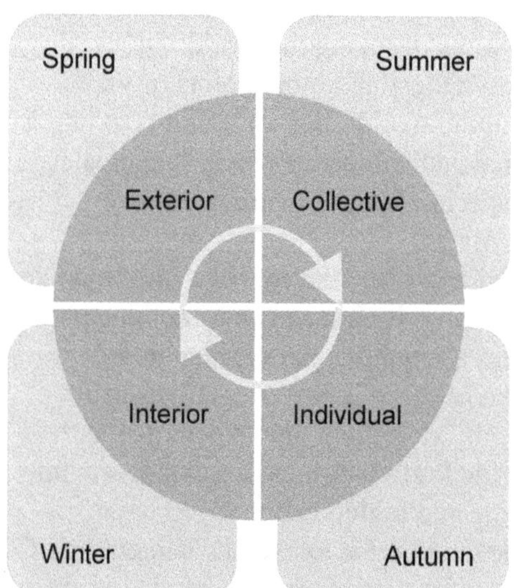

Likewise, when a person operates solely from deep introspection all the time, they reside in autumn and winter. The meditative and contemplative stage will leave a person isolated, and without the necessary interaction with the external world.

Fertility takes its course through the bio-psychological tides of spring. The spring stage is an exterior stage of living where "the bees meet the flowers", and nature moves about in an outgoing way. People move, literally, outwards from their homes to meet others, and youths meet for purposes of love and mating, engaging in rituals involved in attracting their partner.

In Summer there is full bloom, and effort towards the collective gathering of organisms and individuals. It is here where ideas and plans grow to their full fruit and show themselves as a substantial product: it is the season of light and revelation.

Autumn declares the stage of decay and necessary death, as the fruits have presented themselves for the good of nature, and served their cause. Now they have to deteriorate to make new soil for new life. There is a return towards the individual, turning within after two stages (or seasons) of exterior-collective progression. It is a stage for renewing force by meditation and contemplation; a reflective stage of what has been done and produced so far in the preliminary stages.

Winter calls in silence and rest. Here, all ask for stillness after the enormous activity of the three seasons of spring, summer, and autumn. Winter is completely interior, and invokes the urge to be away from the exterior world and expression. The organism and mind go into the winter sleep, comforting themselves into the subconscious realm. A very important stage of life through the seasons and daily routine, where one can incubate and digest fully what has been sown, grown, and reaped.

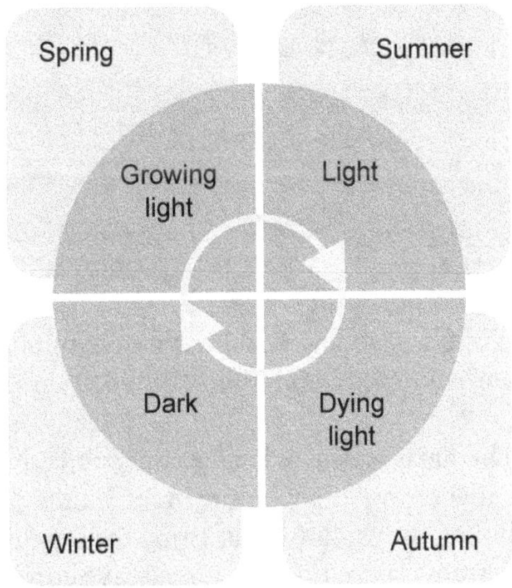

Light is very important to life and to the human being.

Besides the natural and biological sequence and progression of light and darkness, there is a definite effect on the psyche. People are vulnerable in a psychological way to the stages of light and darkness, and many recognize them, experiencing emotional fluctuations accordingly. What must be considered is that the human being reacts strongly to the four seasons unfolding through the 365 days in a year.

Nevertheless, the inner seasons within the bio-psychological organism also have seasonal cycles which unfold over a daily or longer cycle.

Variations are related to personality types, which help identifying oneself as a spring, summer, autumn, or winter person. One could also conclude from this classification of seasons whether one resides in more individual or collective, or interior or exterior modes of living.

Living towards the inside leads to more self-centered personalities (how one belongs to oneself).

Living towards the outside leads more towards ethnocentric personalities (how one belongs to a group).

Of course, generally, we can find traces of ourselves in more than one category; yet, a strong emphasis is often seen towards a quadrant in one of the seasons.

Apart from the seasonal and solar phases in our lives, we have the emotional and watery cycle of the moon, which goes hand-in-hand with the yearly cosmic cycle.

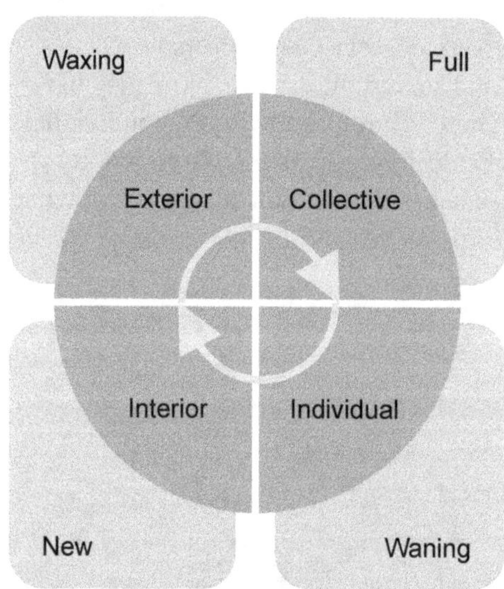

The moon has thirteen full moons per cycle: three stages of waning, new, and waxing moon. The full moon and new (dark) moon are, of course, more states than stages (as they have a relatively short time and effect upon the earth). The waning and waxing periods are like stages, and take the longest in one cycle.

Electromagnetism is the power of the moon, and its influence over the earth and its creatures (not only on a biological level, because many things move inside the animal and human body within the scope of the moon-power). Also, the psyche is much influenced, rising and falling within consciousness, and giving obvious signs of emotional and sensitivity changes.

The lunar states and stages are subjectively related to how our personal inner situation wavers with the moon's tides. Sensitivities are familiar signs of lunar fluxes, in which we can enjoy the heights, and suffer the depths of the watery current. These tides do not always correspond to the phases of the moon.

We should understand that there is also an inner moon cycle that travels through personally installed currents. Throughout our lives, we develop our lunar tides in the four stages of the moon. As with the previous seasons (solar tides) of the inner human, there are inner lunar stages. Our spiritual life and healing (regeneration) are interesting and important to observe, to see whether the seasons correspond with the lunar tides.

The lunar path is the first step to take within any personal and spiritual work, to get to know the structure and energy of the personality. Lunar work is about identifying our personal domain: learning to know the difference between inner and outer worlds, and the individual and collective mind.

The second stage is the solar work, which involves joining the path of integrity and honesty, to reach the self (sun or Tifaret) in ourselves. We discussed this in the section about Tifaret and the soul.

As Yesod is central to the vegetable level of the human being, we have to investigate our digestion by scanning our physical-vegetable level, and psychological-vegetable level. Both systems digest physical or psychological food: what they absorb or take in.

The question then arises: "What physical and psychological foods do I easily digest, and which ones are difficult or cause me painful problems?"

Relations to the elemental kingdom are relevant, specifically the four elements that give meaning to observing body types and personality types.

These are often classified under the physiological names of endomorph, ectomorph, and mesomorph. Feeling, thinking, and doing types are the psychological equivalents of the elementary-physical.

Here are some questions for the Kabbalist, relevant to these three types:

Contemplations:
- Individual: What are my thoughts? What do I see in me, myself? What is my identity?
- Interior: Ask about things, situations, and motives coming from within.
- Exterior: Ask about the body, behaviour, etc.
- Collective: Ask about family, life, work, society.

Feelings:
- Individual: What are my feelings? Are they about me?
- Interior: What are my feelings about… (things, situations, motives)?
- Exterior: What are my feelings telling me about my body and behaviour?
- Collective: What are my feelings about my life, family, and society?

Actions:
- Individual: What are my actions about?
- Interior: Are they about things and situations? Do I react upon them?
- Exterior: Are they involved with my body and behaviour?
- Collective: Are my actions triggered by life, family, and society?

If we reflect upon these three types of human functioning that appear, disappear, and reappear in our experience, we notice that they are temporary states that come and go. Our memory functions as continuity, but on closer inspection, we can see that these memories can be extremely fragile, false and temporal. These states are states of consciousness and, therefore, states of human experience.

States are related to stages of human development, which can be measured by lunar and solar cycles influencing our human experience. The art of living is to move with these stages, comparable to how animals and plants move with the seasons when the year changes every three months. These life cycles or stages have an interior equivalent that does not always run parallel with the physical-cosmic cycles of the seasons. However, the metaphor and the actual potential of the seasons are real, and proven to be experienced.

Move with nature instead of moving and working against it. Be aware that nature's outer rhythms and cycles are expressions of your inner nature: your inner rhythms and cycles. Nature provides all necessities to be well, healthy, and balanced. Practicing this awareness in our daily routines makes us move and flow in stages that complement the seasons.
All of this will enable us, not only to work and produce, but also to prepare for the next cycle, and rest properly. Our first civilizations were very much occupied with these inner and outer cycles. For farmers, for example, it was vital to tend to the land, for the sake of flora and fauna, and the preservation of the community. There was a close watch on the elements, the seasons, and other natural phenomena.

The modern human should do well to re-learn this skill in the 21st century, where domination is cognition and intellect. Our modern dependence on thinking has lead us to control nature and other humans. Nature can be regulated in accordance with nature, but never controlled.

Let us be educated so our physical body can listen to the cosmic cycles and rhythms; let oneself be regulated by the universal system (to live with the cosmos through understanding the cosmos). Educating the soul to see the whole of oneself, not by mind, but by aligning to the natural system; not as separate and opposite forces, but as complementary forces.

Nature and the outer seasons guide us for inner regulation and growth:
- Spring: growth, newborn processes, "sowing" plans and ideas, working out ideas
- Summer: reaping of fruits, creativity, expression of self, maturing of plans and ideas
- Autumn: going within, focusing on self and interior, searching for meaning, resting outwardly
- Winter: releasing and letting go, detaching, surrendering, making space for silence

These movements revolve around the centre, which is the core of the human soul. There, all is silent and unmovable. From here, the human being, who is the soul, can sublimate life. Nature does not endlessly repeat itself in a circular motion, but there are changes in time-space-movement. The old becomes new, and the One transcends and includes life and death in an eternal dance.

The four stations (or seasons) are levels on the Tree of Life that correspond to the psychological levels recognizable in humanity. The first level of Malkuth is the physical experience of the body. Here, our occupation is with the physical needs to be fulfilled during our physical life. The body speaks its own language, clearly expressing the intelligence of the elementary body—the four states of matter.

The second level is Yesod, where the psychological world is known through a complex, subtle composition of impressions called the ego-personality: the awareness of "me", often expressed at the egocentric level of life, which is also at the level of the life force (Nefesh).

We locate the function of automatic responses to the exterior world within the great triangle of the vegetable nature. Simultaneously, there are uncountable physical and psychological reactions taking place in the interior that correspond to the exterior. Here, we develop a sense of belonging to a group and its dynamic: this is the ethnocentric level of life.

When the range of experience expands with and beyond these levels, one can live life beyond the personal and ethnic perspective, and one can behold a world-centric view, while still being in the positions described above. This view includes all of us, other than only taking care of oneself and one's group. Now it is about all groups as being one community.

Being soul-centric is when one realizes that one is the observer of all these levels, yet one does not completely move with these experiences. The observer or witness is outside of the objects observed, and does not engage with them directly (including the objects of one's own life). The subjective soul is in all of our human experience. The soul knows "who looks through you, and who it is, that is experiencing the world(s)".

When all the former levels are experienced, and we access the world of the metaphysical knowledge (Briah), we become aware on the level of the Spirit, which is at the level of the cosmic and universal-centric consciousness on the Tree of Life.

Here, the relative worlds of time-space-movement are held in the consciousness of the transpersonal view. All the previous levels are ruled and orchestrated through the universal law: the transpersonal world of the Spirit.

Spirit is our universal nature, transcending and including all levels (and does not exclude anything). Spirit integrates in a synchronistic and holistic way, and engages all towards synergy and wholeness. This is the level of Daath, the so-called "meta-level".

The level of unity is what lies beyond and within all previous levels. On all levels mentioned, one knows and experiences unity.

The four personality types

Four personality types:
- Sensing is practical and structural
- Intuiting is full of ideas and sees
  new possibilities
- Thinking is cognitive and calculating
- Feeling is about sentiments
  and values

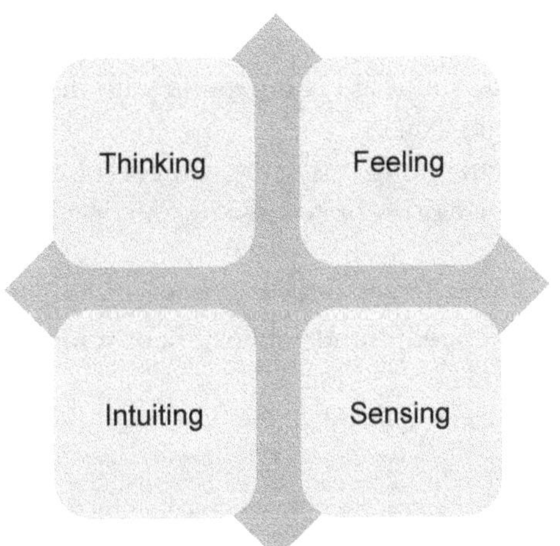

These four types are, to some degree, aspects of our personality. Some are more dominating than others, but all play a part in the character's whole. The prominent part of our personality is called the ego, and it has an important function in the relative world.

The ego is conscious of the objects around us in relation to who one thinks one is. Image reflection of the ego is an appearance in an interior mirror which reflects ideas, judgements, feelings, and memories that construct a self-image. This is often confirmed through the exterior world, to which the ego responds very strongly. The ego does not witness itself, as it is completely within the experience it has momentarily. The ego is the experience.

The ego cannot separate itself from experience. In situations within daily life, the ego is the issue, it is the thinking and feeling, unable to separate oneself from the consciousness that forms the background of each following development.

The self is often called the witness or observer; it is the ever-present awareness. The witness is the observer of the ego. From the ego, we identify with the qualities of the ego itself, whereas from the self (of the psyche), the ego is another object for observation.

Both ego and self, have the capacity for awareness:
- The ego is aware of objects and environment
- The self is a witness of all objects and of the ego

The self is the presence of consciousness that sees and knows from moment to moment.

The ego assumes that life is continuous, like a movie playing from start to finish. The start is our birth, and we have to face death in the end. This may be true on the level of the ego, because the ego can only witness time from a linear point of view. How the ego constructs the personal world is also seen in a transpersonal way by the observer.

Instead of a continuous evolvement, there is an experience from moment to moment: movement, but from an Eternal perspective, where the life of the body and ego are temporal phenomena in space-time. The observer-witness is timeless, always observing without judgement (prompted from the impulses that come and go in the world of the body and lower psyche).

These states are comparable with the categorization of Beta, Alpha, Theta, and Gamma states.
Extrapolating this same categorization to Kabbalah, we can find the first three lower worlds or bodies: Assiah, Yezirah, and Briah.

- Assiah: Gross states of consciousness (physical-bodily movement)
- Yezirah: Subtle states of consciousness (breathing, movement within the energy centres)
- Briah: Causal states of consciousness (metaphysical consciousness)

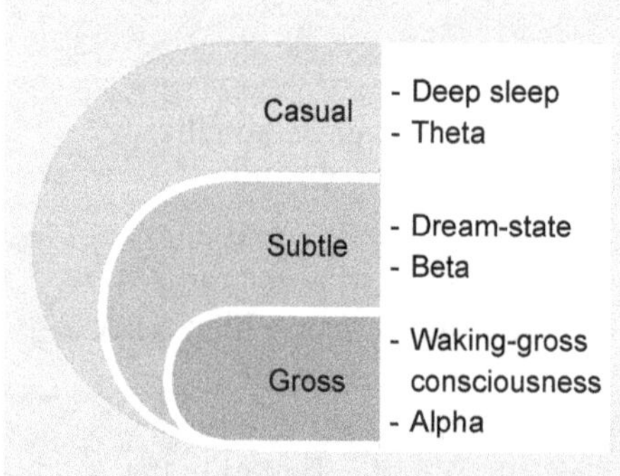

Sleep state belongs to the gross-subtle activity of the earth-lunar realm. The revitalization of the physical body and the subtle-psychological body (etheric), happens while being in a causal state. The causal state is non-intervening with time-space affairs. This state can be compared with the experience of deep peace, silence, and stillness.

On the Tree of Life in Kabbalah, the body (Malkuth) is the exterior world, cooperating the interior-lunar (Yesod) world. These two are formed by individual development through states and moments of consciousness (Hod), while on the other side, we see influence coming through stages in the group mind and the effects of cycles (Netzach).

This is the gross-subtle realm of human experience, which humanity shares with the mineral and vegetable level. Repetition and cycles are the rhythm and movement that make up the recognizable ingredients of personal life. Life repeats itself in endless cycles, which is demonstrated through the cosmic cycles of the seasons, and day and night. Our personality and biological body are two bodies of that same nature that respond to those cycles throughout the year.

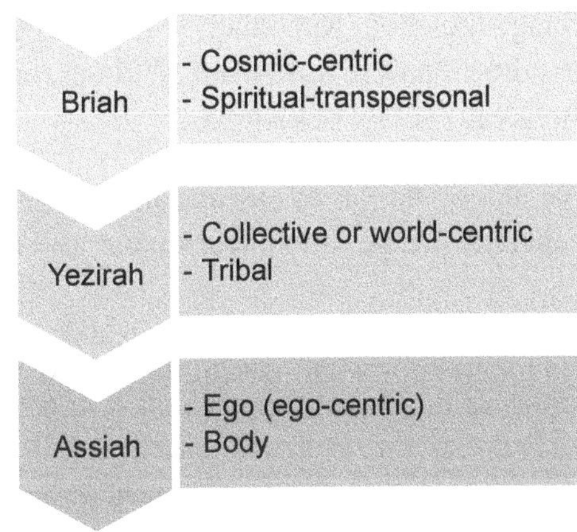

Besides this, the human has routine-personal matters which recycle in that great revolving movement. We integrate much of our personal experience into our daily cycles and habits so often, that we cannot separate them from each other; neither can we distinguish the patterns from our true being.

However, some personal patterns are not healthy or constructive, so learning to see them from a different perspective is worthwhile. This is all part of the work of the Kabbalist or a healing practitioner. In other words: how do we teach ourselves, or another individual who belongs to a common general group (vegetable level), to draw their attention and their sense of self away from that domain of gravity?

The Kabbalist is the participant in their healing-integrating process. The consciousness of the Kabbalist is what is involved in generating true changes, resulting in healing. It is the human being in the process of life. Our consciousness is the cause of all changes.

The causational level is the world of Spirit, which is always present, even when the human being is only aware of the body (gross) and mind (subtle). When we suffer our own consequences, it is our self (Tifaret) that is both our healer and provides a method for healing (inner teacher). Our being is the way.

Herein, the human soul is always concerned with the ultimate connection in life; its totality and wholeness. As such, the symptoms of some issues are not the most relevant, neither are diagnostic attempts to label our problems. The human being is about wholeness because the human being is whole in its very being. Such is our true nature.

We should always strive to work towards unity and wholeness, whatever the symptoms in our lives that cause distress and suffering. If we wish to be whole (healed), we should be whole in our self-image.

As we see ourselves in consciousness, we shall eventually become. How great is the power of consciousness and the capacity of the image-making mind, charged with emotions?

Image (zelem in Kabbalah) is important for the human being and its development in a time-space relationship. Without it, we cannot know the world we live in. Image gives rise to identity.

An image testifies to our identity on earth as separate beings amongst other separate beings. The mirror image gives us identity in comparison to other beings.

We know from the causal level of consciousness, that the mirror image (in likeness) is a temporal reflection of something else. We, as human incarnates, are a reference to something beyond the superficial appearance.

Beyond the superficiality appears another being: a loving reality on which all worlds are founded. It's no surprise that in many spiritual traditions, breathing is used to realize that breath sustains life. Suppose that you are breathing with awareness, and that your breath is felt and seen (from within) as a stream of life and love. Your breath becomes love, and your breath is love.

Love is without boundaries, and therefore, you can breathe boundaries that are self-constructed in your body and mind (gross and subtle) away. Instead of experiencing limits through negative inner patterns, you infuse yourself with goodness through love, inside your physical and subtle vehicle, through breathing.

A prerequisite for this method is to be available and receptive to let love in, as self-love is necessary in generating the stream of living consciousness that transports love through your whole being.

In doing such a spiritual technique, a possible way to take this further is to be receptive on the in-breath, and surrender or let go on the out-breath. Out-breath is letting go of unwanted and disturbing thoughts and feelings. First, accept all that is inhaled during in-breath, and then breathe away the accepted with the out-breath.

Much more can be added concerning this technique, like affirmations and sacred words (mantras), visualizations, and other invoked emotions. These techniques work well even while standing up and walking. Breath within meditation provides clarity and stillness.

Balance and harmony
Kabbalah expresses our conflicts on inner and outer levels of living through the competition between two opposing forces (represented by two outer pillars). Like two pillars supporting an entrance, they have to be in equal balance to carry the mass coming from above, and have enough strength and stamina to withstand the pressure on the bases. This last description explains that existence rests upon physical nature: the expression of all processes into matter.

Malkuth is the Kingdom and physical nature, yet contains in itself, like a vessel, all essences and potential in all its forms (right and left pillars).

Essence is the nature of the unseen, extra-sensitive higher (inner) worlds. Apart from the supporting function, the pillars have a connecting function, reaching from below to above, and vice versa (for as it is in heaven, so it is on earth; and as it is on earth, so it is in heaven).

Therefore, the pillars should always be in a multi-directional equal balance. The connection is vertical in body, mind, and spirit. The horizontal axis is the interplay of continuous forces, alternating between the left and right pillars: the opposing and dual forces inside and outside.

The middle pillar contains spheres that station between these dual forces, always being challenged to bring these two opponents into a balanced position. Balance is not an inert momentum or situation, as nature always moves.

Balance and harmony are movements in equilibrium, like scales that are in balance by equal weight, with the axis at the centre, which is still and carries, as it were, the weights on both sides equally. Harmony, therefore, can be called perfect justice and measurement.

Harmony and balance are the names or titles of the sphere or Sefira of Tifaret: beauty and harmony. In the macro and microcosm, Tifaret is the inner and outer point of balance, having a central position between above (macrocosm) and below (microcosm), and in relative nature, between left and right pillars. Physical nature (gross) and subtle nature (etheric-psyche) are often sufficient for reaching and maintaining harmony between opposites. In physical and etheric nature, we call this: homeostasis.

There is no self-awareness involved in this self-regulating process. However, when these vehicles cannot reach such states of balance, other levels of being (consciousness) need to be involved.

The relations between opposite natures in the universe and human nature are endless in variety.

Motion and inertia are dual manifestations of one being, but as consciousness is constantly present within the fluctuations of these opposites, the one being is difficult to identify with, let alone recognize.

Motion and inertia (respectively, Chocmah and Binah) appear in more concrete and recognizable forms, for example, in effort and surrender, which can come together in the quality of flow.

Between masculine and feminine, we come to the androgynous being (the relational versus the personal). Whatever the opposite character in dual manifestation, we are invited not to control these forces, but to regulate our lives through them. If we take the Kabbalistic Tree and observe Hod and Netzach, the quality of reverberation and cycles comes our way.

These somewhat abstract symbolic names are more easily translated in Hod as planning, logistics, communication, and time management.
In Netzach, as interpersonal skills, empathy, sensitivity, and emotions.

These Sefirotic qualities have their effects on the middle pillar in different worlds. In Malkuth, they cultivate stability. In the physical body, they monitor and regulate inner balance (homeostasis). In Yesod, the personality finds stability between the inner and outer life, finding oneself within and without.

A healthy personality is flexible, and can practice the necessary boundaries and limits. Imagine seeing yourself in the interior mirror of Yesod: this is where we can receive an image of ourselves (zelem), including the qualities of the right and left pillar on the Tree of Life. Our feminine quality is one of giving and image making. Our masculine quality provides energy and moves us to change. Daily reflections from our memories and experiences come and go within the mirror of Yesod.

Both these functions are continuous in our experience within the stream of time, connecting experiences and relating to them. The animal soul within the human being provides a healthy and balanced leadership. Tifaret uses Hod and Netzach in service and dedication to life, expressed through the self. Tifaret observes the process that comes out of the dynamic between both side pillars, and anticipates from self-consciousness. Tifaret takes responsibility for one's life and actions, considering the law of cause and effect.

Everyday interactions of life are essential for the spiritual soul (learning the effects of inner life and its interaction with outer life, both personally and professionally, provides ample opportunity to practice continuous balance in all circumstances). This soul work is essential for life-recovering activity in many ways:

- Gives service to others
- Generates structure in life from the consciousness of time
- Generates social involvement
- Generates emotional and affectionate participation
- Generates body activity and interaction

The physical and subtle bodies are related to the earth and the moon. This esoteric work, as mentioned in detail before, includes the earth and lunar stages of our inner work.
Human consciousness fulfils its function in accordance with the earth and our physical body of the senses, including the subtle world that supports and nurtures the natural body (Assiah).

The subtle body is the energy aggregate for the physical body. Both body and psyche need care and attention, yet they also need to be supervised by the monitoring centre of the soul and Tifaret.

The earth and lunar work involve:

- Identifying with interior and exterior states
- Identifying with individual and collective states
- Finding one's place within the world (belonging)
- Finding the effects of the moon phases in life
- Discovering the elementary kingdom within

Questions that need to be asked in our Kabbalistic endeavour are:

- What states are predominant and which are dormant?
- In what lunar phases do I generally find myself in?
- What do I see as fantasy and reality? What is my self-created world in contrast to the objective outer world?
- Which pillar on my Tree is dominant and why?
- What information comes from my body? What does it communicate to me?

These are levels of the mineral, vegetable, and animal of our being: the lower face of the Tree of Life. This is the personal part of our Tree of Life. Within these, we function as persons within the world, and we move in states through stages in our life. States are momentary and often short lasting, while stages come in natural periods of life. Stages come with age (for example, puberty), and develop according to cosmic circulation and tides.

People change, which is an organic process, as all things move within the stream of time. This change can be conscious or unconscious. Nature goes its way, even if there is no conscious involvement in the process.

Wise it is to swim with the currents of nature, and respect the natural phenomena as they occur and present themselves. Again, not to control, but to regulate life.

In Kabbalah and many other spiritual traditions, we aim to educate ourselves and others using counseling and therapy, developing ourselves towards wholeness and a vision of unity. The use of these skills not only allows us to see the parts, but also the whole of our being. We are potential, and our deepest being needs to actualize that potential.

Whenever we work towards holism, we work with synergy and need self-awareness, free will, and an open mind. The observer within has to wake up, as that self-aware consciousness is our self-created faculty. As the universe is a macrocosm observing itself, so is the microcosm. The observer opens the world of possibilities and potential to our consciousness. The witness or observer is operative from its silent viewpoint, to create by simply observing (for observation from this level implies active participation with creation).
It would be more accurate to say that one is both creation and the creative process. One is not living in stereotypical and rigid movement, but is creatively and fluidly accessing new ways of thinking, feeling, and behaving.

Neuroplasticity awaits these activities, where the three ways of thought, feeling, and action are brought into conformity. When these three activities blend into one stream of action, the nervous system does respond with a powerful neuro-chemical reaction, one much more powerful than if you were only thinking or feeling something.

There is always a combination of three ways of thought, and we must bring them into active consciousness. It is from the central nervous system that we can enforce and animate these three ways together.

Perspectives

Through inner work, self-awareness, and observation, the Kabbalist may realize that this is an open-ended universe without limits. The microcosm is as the macrocosm. This suggests that the universe and humans are open ended, gifted with endless potential. Therefore, there is always an answer to every question, and there is always a solution to a problem.

This attitude towards ourselves and the universe rests upon knowledge that the universe and the soul are not deterministically and mechanically fixed. There is not "one objective" reality as Aristoteles (Aristotle) suggested, but there is an ultimate subjectivity based upon the force behind the creative potential within the confines of the observing soul. How one sees and beholds the universe, one's life, and the Divine, so it becomes.

There are different types and levels of consciousness, and modern science provides more classifications, based on measuring brainwave activity. Average, daily thoughts are labelled as Beta waves (outer sympathetic waves).

Concentrated focus or inner attention (parasympathetic waves) are labelled Alpha and Theta waves. These higher frequencies in brain activity are enriched by consciousness in its pure form as presence. Being-ness is presence, and is equal to consciousness without specific form. While there is no attachment to form in pure consciousness, there are no disturbances in the brain's electromagnetic field of the brain.

Remaining in a presence state of pure attention is called meditation. This state of consciousness, stimulates the auto-immune system, the neuro-chemical circuit, and regulates the bio-physiological attunement.

This meditation state is true healing and regeneration, causing changes to occur in alignment with consciousness. As it has become obvious through many ancient and modern sources, consciousness (the Now) is the only thing that can change something. Even more so, the observing consciousness itself is the change that occurs by sheer observation.
Like in Kabbalah, the lower three worlds are integrated into this explanation. When being in the present moment (Now), a subtle-psychological-etheric form is generated on the subtle conscious level, which will manifest itself on the material plane.

When a physical substance (like a neuropeptide) is released in a conscious manner (Tifaret), the act is creative and works through the three lower worlds, or levels of consciousness. Holism works in this way when the whole being is asked to participate in the act of becoming (whole).

In truth, and beyond all doubt, the human being is whole and undivided.
The inner systems constantly work towards healthy synergy and integration.
By choosing to work and participate with ourselves consciously, we can accomplish many great things through being congruent within. Discernment (Gevurah) is of vital importance if advancement is to be made on the path towards the self: discernment in thought, feelings, and action, which shape behavior.

There can be no excuse anymore when honesty (path from Yesod to Tifaret) is the leading factor in life, letting self-responsibility take over our decision-making.

Sometimes we have to ask whether our current choices are still helping us to grow as a person. If the answer is no, we have to re-orientate our beliefs and choices. Our patterns and conditionings are not wrong, but they can become obstacles in the way of development if we are not careful.

For instance, making unstable and random decisions leads to a loss of energy, which could be better managed, or even avoided, by following an inner conscious strategy for living.

Let us call this: "economy of energy". This economy of energy is regulated by making clear our true necessities in life through:

- Deciding not to lose energy unnecessarily
- Not thinking unnecessary thoughts
- Not performing unnecessary activities
- Not getting emotionally involved in situations where it is not needed

Choose to involve yourself in moments and situations to provide energy or preserve what is within you. Many people lose enormous amounts of energy through random thinking, or just being completely oblivious of what they think.

Here are some simple ideas for the Kabbalist to work on different levels:

- Body (triad of action) - get adequate rest, sleep, food, and exercise
- Mind (triad of contemplation) - make a continuous commitment to health and goodness in your mind
- Feeling (triad of feeling) - cultivate loving emotions, and care for yourself and others (forgiveness)

When you are aware of these three specific roads to walk, you will notice a change. Awareness is the key out of resistance and thus out of suffering.

According to the model of the four worlds in Kabbalah, our mind-emotions form possible resistances in our action and behaviour. This results in a fighting attitude towards life, with strife and competition (to have to prove oneself). Resistance and friction cause negative bondage to other persons, situations, and objects.

To take away these resistances is to take away the negative relationship.
As a result, we are free to choose healthy and constructive relations with people and things outside and inside of us.

Most resistance is happening within the human being (the wars in heaven occur within us).

Often, external persons and situations represent the issues that are going on in our psyche.

Resistance against others, situations, and objects in life are extremely energy wasting. Imagine this: two people are standing up, one on either side of a door. One is trying to shut it, and the other is trying to open it at the same time… one pushing and the other pulling… they will be wasting a lot of energy for no gain! If they just agreed on what to do, the door could go in either direction.

We ourselves (the human being) are the greatest obstacle and cause of resistance in our own lives.

We should learn or be taught to recognize and identify such obstacles, which is only possible by seeing the context of ourselves and our lives. Most of us have fractured views of our being. We rely enormously on the conclusions of our thinking mind, which functions on these fragments (based on memory and momentary impressions). These separate parts in our psyche generate a fragmented self-image, leading to a fragmented behaviour. Context is putting all the fragments together, and seeing them in a coherent whole.

Outer and inner life are inextricably interwoven, as the inner world gives rise to the outer world, and the outer world gives rise to the inner world. Kabbalah tells us about different parts of the human soul (Adam Kadmon) by looking at the Tree of Life (its paths, relationships in triangles, and the four worlds). It is the work of the Kabbalist to come to a realization of unity and wholeness, on this journey of the healing of the soul.

Potentially, the wholeness is already there, and nothing needs to be added to become whole and complete. We are being asked to undertake the work of self-realization by inner investigation and inquiry. The fragments are part of the whole; they are most valuable and necessary for completion. Wholeness means completeness.

Being healthy is the experience of this wholeness-completeness. The self of the human being is the awareness of this wholeness; all parts are related, and complement each other. The self is the inner center. This is what the human being wishes to return to: the essence that lies deep within. To realize the true human being… herein lies our true happiness.

Another way to describe this is to regard the human being as wearing different clothes or bodies. These are the worlds that are worn as garments around the essential core. Completion comes from the experience of all fragments and their meaning-relationship, together with the knowledge of the observer-witness.

Observer
As it was already established earlier on, the observer is the Divine beholding itself in existence (essence beholding existence or soul beholding the created).

Because the different parts of ourselves have different demands (as there are different levels of will in the natural human being) sharing in the great consciousness of Being, we experience a continuous change in who we are. We know ourselves going through time, but hardly ever in the present moment (in the awareness of consciousness, as the observer or the soul).

The soul is the Divine perspective that realizes that its perception is itself.
The soul is the one who rediscovers itself through the recognition of who is who.
We can only find ourselves from the centre outwards, and not from the
circumference inwards.

The healing of ourselves is possible through the soul. We go from our soul
towards wholeness, because the soul is the centre that composes the earlier
mentioned fragments into an integrated whole. This is the purpose of the soul in
its very essence.

The soul is healing. The soul always works towards wholeness. The soul is the
observing consciousness that beholds itself in creation. The soul in itself is
timeless, but it perceives all phenomena in time-space as being itself.

Whenever you identify with your soul, you are seeing through its eyes and
listening through its ears. Having placed your soul with your physical body as
a vehicle of consciousness, you are healing.

You have incarnated into your denser vehicle to walk the earth, having descended
from the stars and beyond. It may be that you see yourself not as a healer, but as
the healing itself. This holistic view is the experience of the oneness permeating
the worlds. From such a view, we can naturally see the parts of our being that
disturb or obstruct us from knowing the whole of our being.

Apart from this soul quality, form is energy, and energy is form. Spirit is both and
neither. The soul (as the observer) experiences Spirit as both manifestations.

The theological discussion of whether Divinity has form loses its relevance after
this profound insight of Spirit. Kabbalah talks about the Heavenly or Briatic
Father and Mother as the two creative opposites: force and form. In reality, these
two cannot be separated, as they are always kept in the Eternal embrace of
the One: Kether.

The body's soul lies within our heart centre (Tifaret on the Tree of Life). Without
any doubt, self-consciousness comes from the soul, and is often titled the "spider
in the web". You are the spider, and the web is your world. You are at the centre
when observing, and the web is what you observe. In case you are not the central
observer, you are in the web, entangled within the observed. Being constricted in
the web of life means participation, yet without self-knowledge.

To take this metaphor a little further, we know that the spider at the centre of the
web has an equal distance to all sides of the circumference of the web (feeling all
sides equally in its tension). Whenever there is something in the web, the spider in
the centre can "observe" everything that is going on (regardless of its location).

However, when we are out of centre, situated somewhere else in the web, (we)
the spider cannot feel (observe) all that is going on in the web. Being at the center
of the web is like being the whole; being elsewhere in the circumference is like
being the fragments or pieces of the whole.

The secret contained within this piece of spiritual teaching is that, eventually, the human soul realizes that the centre of our being and the world is in all places simultaneously. From that wisdom, the soul knows that in every part is the presence of the whole. In all fragments is the living wholeness. Herein we can find balance and harmony in all things. Using the physical body as an object of study, the individual gradually becomes an undivided creature whose being extends beyond one's physical boundaries.

Kabbalah and the Tree of Life can be used to diagnose our internal struggles and problems. The Tree is like a mirror: as the universe mirrors the Eternal, the microcosm (or human being) mirrors the universe. The inner world mirrors the outer world, meaning that we can find a mirror image of ourselves when looking in the outer world.

The two pillars are twin mirrors of our duality; both show us the extremes in our nature, and the consequences come out of our choices. One pillar is active as the other is passive: action and rest, liberation and fixation. They are the two upholding foundation pillars from where the dual forces are awaiting to be applied.

As all is dependent on the polarity of the pillars. The principles are in all space-time and in all action. Our choices are our own. The outcome of our choices, and their effects, are our responsibility. We are responsible for choice and effect.

The cause of many self-inflicted problems is due to our choices, and not so much to our circumstances. Human choice is often misdirected by not knowing ourselves, and choosing options that are not good for us.

Again, what is often lacking (besides self-knowledge) is the knowledge of the context in which we live, and respecting natural rhythms.

The Kabbalist is their own therapist and counsellor, seeing themselves as a whole being, with a self-approach that is individual and creative. The human soul is the beginning and the end of the process of healing (not needing an external therapist).

As Kabbalists, we are on a path of self-discovery, wishing to find our strengths and wisdom. In our essence, we can (re)discover our innate ability for healing and regeneration.

The message for the Kabbalist is: make yourself and your direct environment a safe place for nurture and growth. A secure place for expressing your true feelings, where you can be vulnerable and expose who you are, including fears and desires that might otherwise be hidden. In other words: to make yourself free in the place that is your own.

When counselling yourself from this holistic and Kabbalistic perspective, there are many entrances to take: love, attention, comfort, nature, music, self-image making, forgiveness, integrity, accepting pain, respect, trust, beauty, nutrition, etc.

Let us look again at the cycles of life from different perspectives:

In Kabbalah, this is the solar cycle situated around Tifaret on the Tree of Life.

Tifaret corresponds with the sun, and therefore, initiates the four seasons on earth. These four solar cycles correspond with four stages (or cycles) in the human consciousness. Each day, we encounter the seasons as they pass through the stages of day and night, light and darkness. The solar influence of the seasons asks us to be aware of the four changes that occur in the cycle of a year, and the daily cycle of human experience.

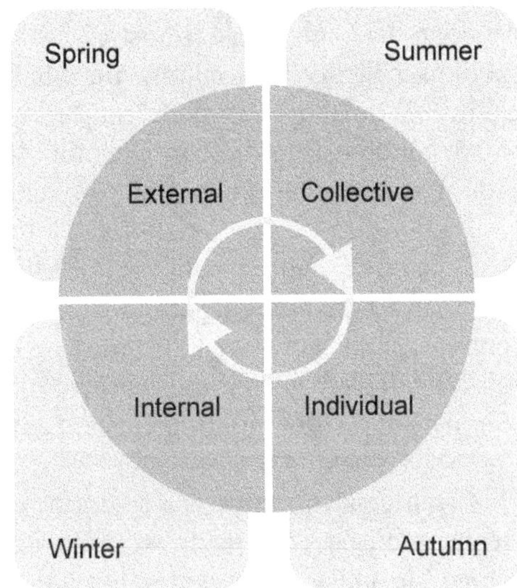

Biological-physiological nature reacts to the flux and reflux of these solar tides. It sets in motion corresponding enzymes, peptides, and hormones, detonating reactions that conform with the phase of the cycle. The cosmic phases are directive, and lead as a creative-macrocosmic causation. Such a hierarchy does not automatically imply a fatalistic relationship between the micro and the macrocosm (stating heavens or macrocosm as the only source of influence).

As far as we can recognize from our human advancement, there is a creative participation with the heavens or causational world (which we can see through cultural, scientific and metaphysical development). According to the perennial philosophy and esoteric teachings of East and West, including Kabbalah, we understand that the human being consists of more than one body. While we have experiences in the physical and psychological worlds and their respective bodies, the causational-Briatic body is encapsulating both of them.

Widely known in spiritual teachings is the hermetic axiom: "what is above is what is below", and vice versa, meaning that we are not separate, nor far away from the heavens (or causational body).

Inherently, the above informs us that a part of the human soul is of the heavens, and that these levels are within reach of the same consciousness. To engage and know these levels is to meet them face to face in daily life naturally, by becoming aware of them in ourselves through conscious observation on earth.

Earthly life continuously and consistently testifies of the heavenly directions and cycles orchestrated by cosmic intelligence. Evidence comes to us through outer nature and the information the physical human body provides.

Spiritual practice invites us to observe these cycles and processes as ephemeral phenomena that appear and vanish within the "eye" of the silent witness: the soul.

Again, to become whole (holistic view) and work towards healing and unity, we should aspire to come to know the whole of ourselves and the context in which we live. Wholeness definitely can be seen only from the perspective of the self, which contains the whole in potential. In Kabbalah, the self is associated with Tifaret, the sun that orbits itself, around which all other objects (planets) turn.

Being in one's centre or bliss is to be like the sun, knowing ourselves to be in the centre, instead of moving about in endless cycles. Tifaret is the silent and still centre, like the sun in analogy, moving around itself, around its axis. Kabbalistic sources tell us that Tifaret is a mirror of something Transcendent, which is a complete and still unity (represented as the point in the circle).

This Transcendent centre is Kether (the Crown), meaning that whenever we reach the consciousness of Tifaret, we come into touch with the Transcendent reality behind life and all of its cycles. From the experience of Tifaret (knowing that we are a mirror image of the Eternal and Transcendent), we may remember the affirming saying: "Holy art Thou, O God, all the worlds fall silent before Thee". Or we could add to that mystical experience: "All the worlds fall silent within Thee".

Make contact with your Tifaret, and observe the solar cycles within view: the external and internal seasons, and their corresponding effects.

The influence of the Moon (Yesod) is also cyclic, and runs parallel with the solar cycles. These are the vegetable cycles of the outer and inner nature. Physical cycles of this kind should be compared with the vegetable nervous system, functioning in an equal manner to how outer nature operates. The bowels or stomach area of the physical body informs us about this lunar-cyclic system. And psychologically, this watery dimension exposes deep emotional and subconscious patterns.

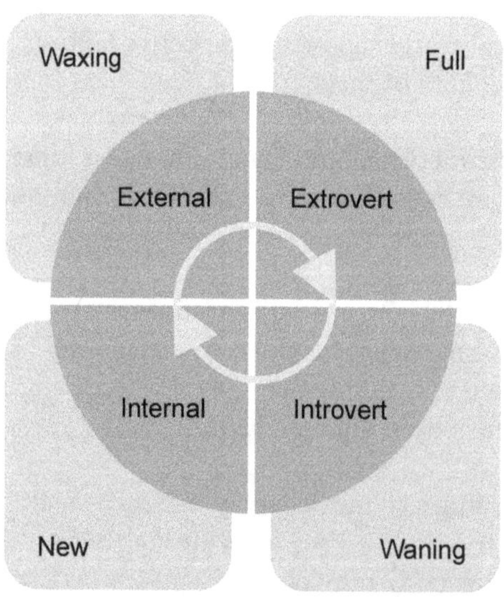

The subtle body not only energizes the physical body in four stages (phases), it also directs the psychological-emotional moods of the person.

These moods rise and fall with the subtle currents within the subconscious realm (which reflects itself within daily consciousness, and has taken root in the ego (Yesod) of every individual's Tree of Life).

Malkuth is the definite and unmistakable creative consequence of all that descends down the Tree of Life.

Cross-model plasticity: what is it?
After some extensive writing about Kabbalah and the different levels on the Tree of Life and Jacob's Ladder, let us return to the theory and practice of neuroplasticity.

The whole metaphysical teaching and application of Kabbalah is the work of neuroplasticity. Through practicing Kabbalah, we learn that our conscious participation in the awareness of life-processes makes an immense difference. We learn the difference between action and being, growth and transformation. Whether the Kabbalist is aware of this fact or not, the mechanism and principles of neuroplasticity are operative within the mystical work of Kabbalah.

Let's try to draw ourselves closer to the intimate knowledge of mysticism within Kabbalah, and the science of neuroplasticity, so that we can become aware of how both disciplines work together.

Neuroplasticity is based upon the neuro-chemical experiments of association and synthesis within the human being. We can learn through many pathways, and also by means of many more didactical methods that we can apply. We see at an early age that children do not all learn in the same way, dependent on many different conditions and backgrounds.

Culture, education, family, environment, constitution, etc., play a role in the formation of the ego (Yesod), which is the psychological foundation of learning within the personality. Most education systems are directed towards a frontal mode of teaching by bringing cognitive, motoric and relationship-skills (social and affective), and knowledge to the children's attention.

Now, teaching theories not only favours frontal brain stimulation, but also acknowledges that there is a psychological inner knowing within each child, which directly relates to recent findings in neuroplasticity. Yesod (lower psychological state of awareness) and Malkuth on the middle pillar possess many attributes and qualities for learning.

The physical body carries the four elements and five senses, which are tailor-made for living, interacting, and communicating with this world (earth). Our world of Assiah, the physical body, is made in harmony with the outer (or natural world), of which our physicality is a part.

It is the same with our psychological vehicle in Yezirah, on the lower face of the Tree of Life, where Yesod has the dominant monitoring function. With its personal, psychological and energetic capacities, Yesod is a match for the world of the psyche, within and without. The etheric field corresponds with this part of our psyche, which is part of a larger etheric field encapsulating all life.

From these levels on the Tree of life just described, we can learn and experience. However, we cannot learn from a level we have not achieved. Being only in the body and lower psyche keeps us limited to those levels of understanding.

To access learning that is related to Tifaret on the Tree of Life, we need to engage with associative and synthetic learning. Making associations in learning means that no piece of information is separate from another. Returning to the children at school, they have math, geology, biology, history, chemistry, and gymnastics classes. But… are these subjects related?

One way of describing intelligence is making connections between all possible phenomena of life. Why? Because they are interconnected!

To see a bigger picture and move our being towards associative learning, we should make constant connections between ourselves and the world around us. It will be no coincidence to see that the nervous system works only through associations. No information is irrelevant. No data are left out: all have something to say and contribute to complete an experience of wholeness.

The Kabbalist has been given this beautiful model of the Tree of Life and Jacob's Ladder, which guides us organically, and spontaneously, towards an associative approach to life in their geometry and symmetry.

All thirty-two paths (Torah) are connected and related, forming a complete whole wherein all worlds (realities) are represented. Within the four worlds of the Kabbalah, there are four perspectives of reality: the literal (Assiah), the metaphorical and symbolic (Yezirah), the metaphysical (Briah), and the mystical (Aziluth).

Another way of describing these stages of consciousness through the worlds is: "from the mundane (Assiah) to the metaphorical & mythical (Yezirah), to the metaphysical & miraculous (Briah), to the mystical (Aziluth)". To leave one world or perspective out of our Kabbalistic work is to miss out on associations that make up the completeness of reality (all four worlds).

Of course, the Kabbalist and scientist alike have to start somewhere, and preferably in the world(s) they know. Therefore, the Kabbalistic work starts at the bottom of the Tree of Life in the worlds we are familiar with (Assiah and Yezirah). Associative connections can only be made through our level of consciousness.
This said, learning through associations enhances and stimulates our capacity to learn quickly, and to make other associations faster, and more efficiently.

The nervous system works this way, especially the inter-neurons or glial cells, motivated to grow faster and generate new connections. As the inner work progresses and the Tree of Life and Jacob's Ladder are "climbed", the possibility to connect information and experience from the personal face of the Tree with the transpersonal or metaphysical face develops.

This personal and transpersonal connection is crucial in Kabbalistic work, as the higher face (where we learn about the metaphysical-creative side of our existence) teaches us about the archetypal background of our personal life. Metaphysics (Briah) explains the principles in the universe and how they work in the macrocosm and microcosm.

Bringing the lower and upper faces into each other's sphere of experience is a Kabbalistic way to associate on the vertical level. To put more emphasis on the separate Sefirot, and "walk the paths", is another way of association.

Another way of learning about associations is to thoroughly study and meditate on the Tree of Life. Each Sefira has countless correspondences, as there are four worlds to be found in each Sefira. These emanations have correspondences with physical nature (trees, stones, plants, animals, elements, etc.), psychological concepts, emotions, feelings, thoughts, and memories.

The Tree of Life embraces all the metaphysical principles through the archetypal domain and Divinity in the Sefirot. We discover manifold symbols and connections in dreams. But… do we know how to interpret them?

The more we have knowledge and experience (Daath) of Kabbalistic associations, the more we can connect the Tree of Life with all its paths to our nervous system. Knowledge and experience of Jacob's Ladder is the best way of integrating cross-modal neuroplasticity in your life. Association is the way of endless connection and relationships.

However, Kabbalah teaches us that horizontal relationships and connections are worldly connections, which is "half of the story". We need the vertical level on the middle pillar to make true spiritual associations.

Let us remember that Kabbalah comes from the root "Qibel", which means to receive. There are two ways of interpreting the word "reception": the oral tradition, and the mystical path of the Kabbalist (fourth way).

Oral tradition means the transmission from "mouth to ear": from teacher to student. The mystical reception is the vertical way of being available to the source, making ourselves a vessel for the Divine to shine through. Interestingly, in the nervous system, there are vertical and horizontal neurons. Neuroplasticity of this cross-model kind is almost identical with the way of Kabbalah.

From the associative part, we go to the other elements of the cross-model plasticity, which is synthesis. Association and synthesis can almost not be separated in this neurological change and transformation process. With and after association comes synthesis, making all the associative work inclusive and integral.

We could associate two Sefirot with each other through working the path between. But… how do we integrate that within the whole Tree of Life, and within our experience?

Connecting the different experiences and metaphysical knowledge in our consciousness of self (Tifaret) is the way of synthesis. If you recognize what I mean here, you may reflect on your inner work to see the association (or synthesis) within.

These connections enable you to make bridges across knowledge and experience, combining these experiences and cross-fertilizing them, to see a larger view of reality and behold the different Kabbalistic worlds simultaneously.

On Jacob's Ladder, this point of synthesis in different worlds is the place where the three lower worlds meet, also called the "Seat of Solomon".

Divine level: potential for
pure consciousness & ground of all being
Spirit level: potential for fundamental creativity
from archetypal domain
Creative or discontinuous insights
Soul level: potential for free will and the agent of
Divine consciousness
Self: potential to
be authentic
Animal level
Will to make or break
Sensitivity to create
Vegetable level
Conditioned psychological behaviour
Situational creativity

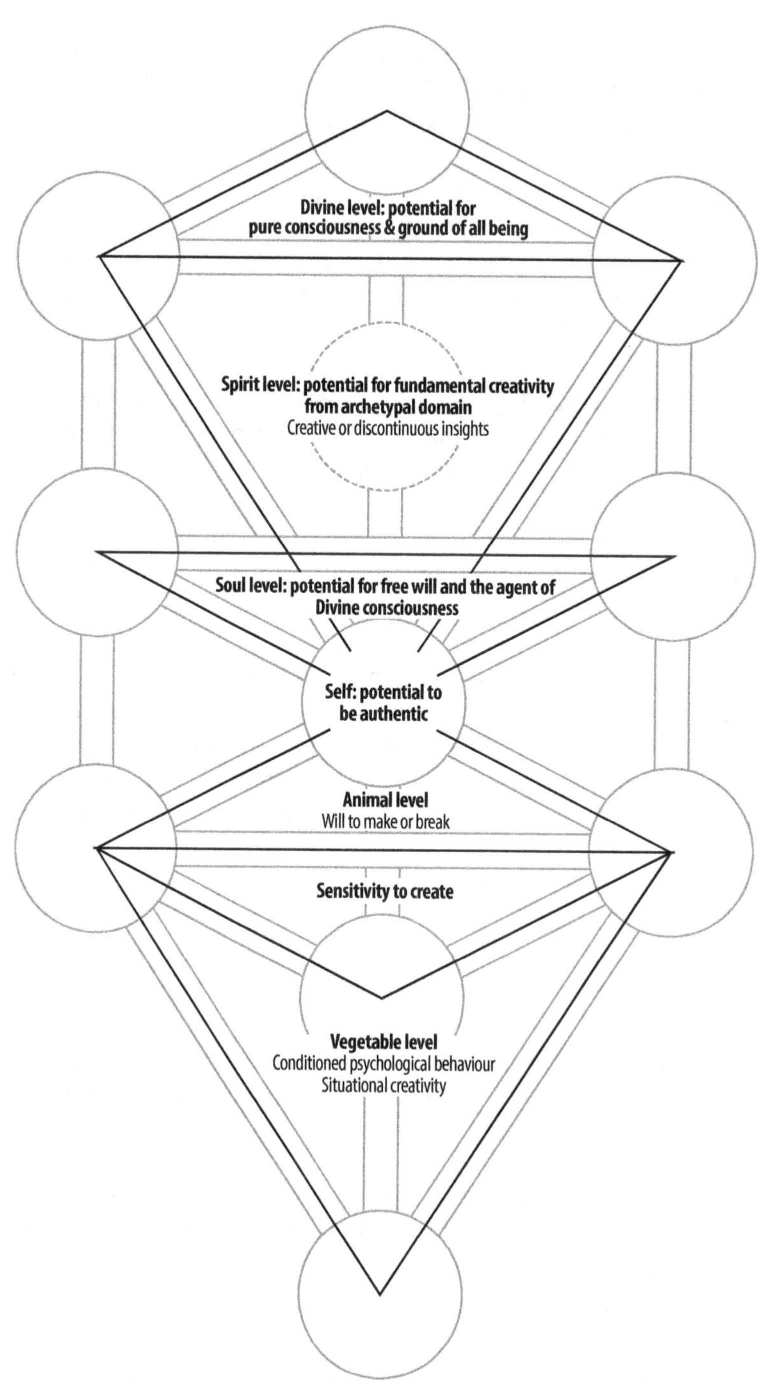

Diagram 19

We have spoken before about the place of the central nervous system on the Tree of Life. Being located at the Tifaret of Assiah, it has these particular properties of harmony, balance, and beauty.

In more concrete and neurological terms, it is the place of associative function and synthesis. To enhance and stimulate the cortex and central nervous system in the ways described above is to generate new pathways of association and synthesis. Cross-model plasticity is an efficient learning model for both the cortex and the central nervous system. The power of this method is so strong and efficient, that through the central nervous system and cortex, we can overwrite genetic coding. The possibilities are endless, considering the number of nerve cells in the human body.

Imagine roughly about 86 billion to 100 billion neurons with even more glial or interneuron cells. Over the last few decades, much more focus has been put on these glial neurons, functioning as transmitters and messenger cells with an intelligence of their own.

Glial cells can make a massive difference when it comes to empowering certain functions in the central nervous system: they support the nerves, transport nutrition and oxygen, and seem to have an auto-immune system as they remove dead cells.

Besides all this, the central nervous system, and the whole nervous system itself work towards purpose and destination. This makes sense as in the nervous system the potential of a neurological impulse needs several repetitions (action-potential) to come to a "destined" result. The nervous system works towards purpose, otherwise, it loses function. The more the system is stimulated and trained through purpose and destination, the more it will intrinsically develop.

In Kabbalah, the work is directed towards a specific or individual fate, which is a life of conscious choice and responsibility. Not surprisingly, individual fate lies at the triangle of the soul. General fate is what we share with humankind in a lifestyle and consciousness of consumerism and superficiality. We recognize this consciousness as the vegetable level (greater triad of Malkuth, Hod, Netzach).

Therefore, a person's psychological-spiritual destination and fate correspond with those parts of the nervous system, and their development in fate-destination.

Living from the vegetable triad only develops and stimulates (through our thoughts, feelings, and actions) the corresponding parts of the nervous system a general fate and destiny of the vegetable life (autonomic or vegetative nervous system). So, we can distinguish on the middle pillar of the Tree of Life the different levels of consciousness, and the corresponding cortical (brain) neurological centers in the nervous system.

The stage of consciousness that the Kabbalist is in tells us something about the potential for neurological growth. When spiritual work runs along the lines of destiny and destination, association and synthesis will become more apparent.

Cross-model plasticity will be activated when working from the soul level where the Kabbalist:
- "Metabolizes" psycho-spiritual processes through association and synthesis
- Makes choices based on free will, directing life on the path of individual fate
- Takes responsibility for one's life, and bears the consequences of past choices
- Integrates past, present, and future into a practical path of destiny and purpose
- Occupies Solomon's Seat, where Mercy and Justice have equal places

Imagine that these soul qualities improve the nervous system, stimulating those specific centres and cells (glial cells) that work towards cross-model plasticity. Our place within the soul has a very particular effect on our nervous system.

In the early development of the nervous system (prenatal and postnatal), the nervous system generates an enormous number of neurons, many of which die after not being used, while others are "shut down" as they are not stimulated or ready to function. By activating cross-modal plasticity through the proper psychological-spiritual pathways, new tissue growth and the awakening of the old and sleeping cells is activated.

Neurophysiology
This is an image of a nerve cell. They come in different forms, but they generally have this shape. Some see a head and a tail in the image: the head is the nerve body within it the nerve nucleus, and attached to it you see the tail, which runs towards another head of a neighboring nerve cell. Everything that you see in this picture is a neuron.

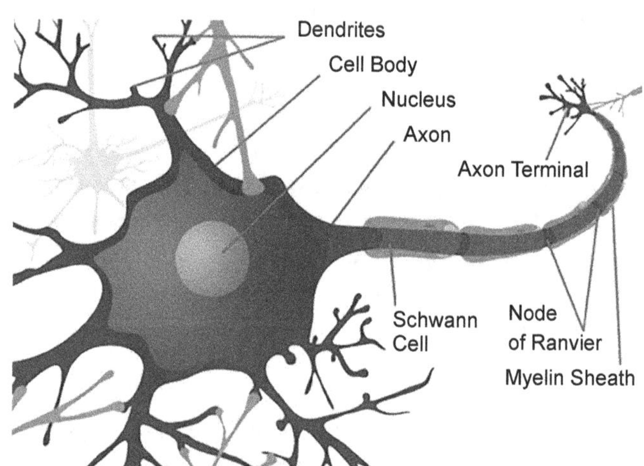

At the beginning and end of every neuron, you find these dendrites, or little antennas that connect to another neuron. This is the place of transmission from one neuron to another. At the end of the neuron's tail we find an axon terminal, where information travelling through it will be transferred unto the next neuron. This part of the axon terminal is called "pre-synaptic" because it is located just before the space between the two neurons.

The part where it connects to the cell body and the next neuron dendrites of the next neuron (the subsequent neuron's end) is called "post-synaptic". There are little holes (called vesicles) at both endings of the neuron that connect one neuron to the next. In these vesicles, neurotransmitters are stored. Vesicles are essential for propagating nervous impulses between neurons, and are constantly recreated by the neurons. The area in the axon that holds groups of vesicles is called an axon terminal.

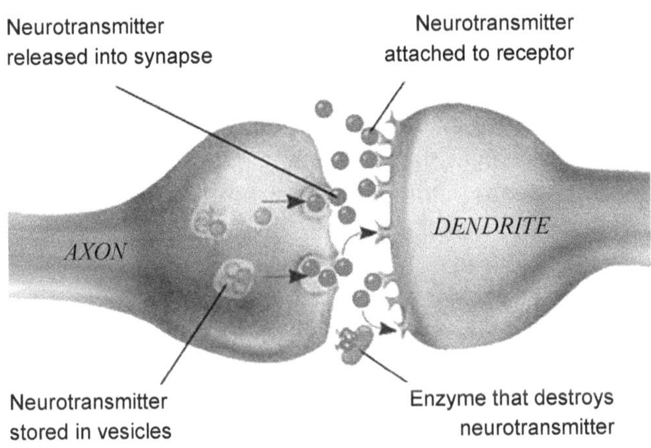

A neurotransmitter is a type of chemical messenger which transmits electro-chemical signals across a gap or crevice, which we call a synapse in neurophysiology (this is comparable to a neurological junction connecting to a muscle cell, tissue, an organ, or a gland).

Neurotransmitters are released from these vesicles in synapses into the synaptic space or cleft. There, they are received by neurotransmitters of the next cell (post-synaptic).

Neurotransmitters come in all shapes and forms. There are transmitters for every possible signal you could imagine. You could think about motor or sensitive transmitters, enabling us to move (motor) and feel (sense). Besides these more physical transmitters, some transmit the electrochemical equivalent of emotions and feelings. Some cause excitation, while others cause inhibition.

If the signals are strong enough at the end of the pre-synaptic nerve end and a buffer of transmitters is laid down in the vesicles, there will be an action-potential. This process is called a summation, and it takes place at the terminal or the end station of the neuron. The opposite option is also possible. The summation won't occur in case there is an inhibition of impulses at the pre-synaptic end.

For the Kabbalist, it is not a big step in our imagination to see this story unfold between two Sefirot and a path (Navitot) between them. One Sefira is the cell body of one end, while the other Sefira is the next neuron cell body (post-synaptic). The path situated between these Sefirot is the neuron's axon.

The analogy makes perfect sense, although physically, it seems to have no comparison. In this way, we can regard the paths on the Tree of Life and Jacob's Ladder as nerves between the ten Sefirot. What would be the use of this for the Kabbalist or the exploring scientist?

First of all, to work along the lines of neuroplasticity and the rather complicated way of cross-modal plasticity, we may think we need to obtain all there is to know about the nervous system (that we memorize every neuron, synapse, neurotransmitter, etc.). Although it may be helpful to visualize the nervous system as it really looks (as far as we know), there is no need to become a neurologist to start working on the principles of neuroplasticity, especially using the aforementioned analogies and metaphors from the Tree of Life.

Instead of only applying the literal knowledge of the nervous system (Assiah), we can use the Kabbalah with the Tree of Life as a map of the inner nervous system.

As described before: it is possible to represent the nervous system within us by analogy and symbol through the world of Yezirah.

The Tree of Life represents all of existence and the anthropomorphic image of Adam Kadmon (humanity or the human being). Therefore, our spiritual image is also an image of our natural body (Assiah) within the natural world. The Tree of Life contains the complete nervous system as it was called forth (Aziluth), created (Briah), formed (Yezirah), and made (Assiah).

To change ourselves or even transform something, we have to depart from an inner state of consciousness that is at least one step higher than the level we wish to alter or change. In neuroplasticity, this is equally true, considering there is a similar hierarchy present in the nervous system as it is on the Tree of Life and Jacob's Ladder.

Imagine that each Sefira is like the soma (or body) of a nerve cell. In each body we find a nucleus, which might be easily and metaphysically compared to the point in the circle of each Sefira.

Each Sefira after Kether (Crown) reflects that first emanation, and thus, reflects a point in a circle. You may remember that within the Kabbalistic cosmology, Kether is the unique One (nequida or point) that by an act of will extends itself into a line (Chocmah), which can be seen as the axon of the nerve. At every junction where path and Sefira touch and connect, we have the earlier discussed pre-synaptic and post-synaptic areas of the nerve.

The whole analogy can be taken much further: remember that the paths on the Tree of Life are connections of energy (Chai) and consciousness. This is exactly what nerves transmit in the nervous system: consciousness and energy.

There is a saying: "Where your consciousness is, there is your energy", and this is not just a metaphor but is factually true.

Let us now use a practical example from Kabbalah, working with the Tree of Life and applying the neuroplasticity principles. The way of Kabbalah is the path towards unity and wholeness. Each of the qualities of the Sefirot is internalized in this work.

Take, for example, the Sefira of Chesed, the emanation of compassion and mercy. Imagine that we do a meditation starting from Kether, and following the lightning flash sequence, the creative process of Divinity into existence.

Sitting in a meditative state, visualize Kether at the top of your head (crown centre) with white light radiating out from it. Now, invoke within yourself the quality of Chesed: compassion and mercy. If this is difficult to do, try to go back into your memory where you have encountered these emotions in your life.

When you have established this state within you, seeing, sensing, and feeling it at your Kether, make the light (Kether) and the corresponding inner state of compassion and mercy (Chesed), to flow to the right hemisphere of your brain into Chocmah. Before this, visualize the circumference of the sphere of Kether; there, it touches upon the path leading to Chocmah. An electrical flow of compassion spills over, and streams this path from Kether to Chocmah.

Kether is the soma or cell body, moving its light and energy into the axon or path (diagonal line) towards Chocmah.

You may now take the time and effort to see the essence of compassion and mercy flowing down the axon/path, until it reaches the end of that axon/path in the vesicles of the pre-synaptic space, before touching Chocmah. As I explained before, a summation has to take place to make the current of this light truly reach the next emanation (cell body).

In Kabbalah, we do not talk about summation but about kavanah, which is a holy intention to move our will into existence. Kav is a Hebrew word for "line", translated as directed (sacred) willpower. Summation would be the neurophysiological equivalent of this metaphysical principle in Kabbalah.

Kavanah or summation is of one single mind and energy. There is nothing other than this energy flowing down this path. Only in this way is it possible to transfer the energy past the terminal (where the path touches upon Chocmah) into the post-synaptic location of the next soma or cell body: in this example, Chocmah receiving neurological (electrical-chemical) energy from Kether. The summation can eventually take place because enough electrical information is present to cause an action potential in the nerve.

Compare this to your own experience when you do not have enough "fire" and inspiration to move a thought or a belief within you. There will not be a movement coming from you. Only when enough and sufficient stimuli within you are present will there be a chance that you generate something new and creative.

Within this practice, just like within the nervous system, you have to repeat the light and compassion going through the axon/path, leading to the pre-synaptic place where the vesicles are present. We need several repeated impulses to make an action potential happen. That means, in this Kabbalistic meditation, that we need consistent concentration (kavanah) to arrive at the desired result of our work.

If you feel creative and ready for a challenge, try to see how the energy (compassion and mercy) is transformed into little substances (from energy into substance) that travel through the channel between the cells.

From the scriptures, we know that first "was the Light, and the Light was with God, and from the Light came the Word (the call, or Kav, to move the Light which extends into a line), and the Light was made flesh". The energy (light) and intention (Kav) are transformed into their substantial equivalent: the particles in the vesicles.

So, with repetition and practice, the light will extend itself within your vessel.

The sequence of the light and energy travels on from Chocmah to Binah, as you persist in seeing, sensing, and feeling the light coming down the Tree of Life (and following the lightning flash onto the next Sefira).

As you concentrate on the right side of your head, the sphere of Wisdom, you build up compassion and mercy within Chocmah, until an action-potential takes place. See and feel a burst of light emerging from the soma or cell-body, making its way horizontally towards the emanation of Binah.

Once more, take your time to build this specific energy in the axon or path, and transfer it with your mind towards the end of the axon, or the pre-synaptic space before Binah-Understanding.

Here, the same happens as you sense, see, and feel that the little holes, called vesicles, make little substances of compassion and mercy out of the energy you just passed through the axon/path.

Small "packages" of compassion and mercy are now carried over the terminal into the space between the end of the path and the next cell (neuron), touching the post-synaptic part of Binah. In this place, the process repeats itself, and the substances enter into Binah, which is stimulated and responds with energy and light (in the form and experience of compassion and mercy).

In this way, you can complete the Lightning Flash (Tzimtzum) all the way into Malkuth. Always make sure that you finish what you started, completing the light into manifestation and existence, materializing the light on the earth.

This is what the nervous system wishes: to manifest itself through lightning! Its working method is alternating, as we can see in the nerve (on the axon, the electrical charge goes up and down), and how electricity moves in nature (physical lightning flash during thunder).

To this extent, you can apply every quality of the Sefirot, charge the paths, and connect the whole Tree of Life (and all the worlds) within you.

There are a few biological principles involved when it comes to neurophysiology and neuroplasticity. Just as we have a law in metaphysics, so we have a law in physics and physiology.

First of all, the stronger the facilitation and stimuli in the nerve, the stronger it will fire and cause an action potential

Secondly, the stronger the energy connection (electricity) is between two (or more) cells, the stronger the connection becomes

Thirdly, when axons and vesicles are repeatedly stimulated, they become a potent pathway for future neurological activity

"Those nerves that fire together, wire together" is a saying in neuroplasticity.

If we look again at these three rules, it becomes apparent that these principles are neutral, not working towards something good or bad within us. That is just the way the nerves work.

We have to (and we are allowed to) give conscious input and meaning to this process. As in the exercise described above, the Kabbalist engages with these neurophysiological principles, applying meaning and consciously directed energy to it.
Nerves work roughly in two ways: by excitation (right-side pillar influence) or inhibition (left-side pillar influence), meaning that it is possible to stimulate a process or sedate the nerves. Synapses are open to both processes, waiting for input from the "outside".

In other words: we have substances and ions (charged atom or molecule) that work towards activity (excitation) or passivity (inhibition). Some physical examples of ions within the body are: sodium, potassium, and calcium (active); chloride, fluoride, and bromide (passive). These ions are often classified as "positive and negative" because of their electrical charge, but not as a moral classification.

There are a few emotional states that cause changes in the human being. They are often classified as higher or transpersonal emotions. To integrate these emotions into this model and method of neuroplasticity moves us into healing and experiences of wholeness.

Examples of these emotions are:
- Gratitude
- Love
- Compassion
- Forgiveness
- Stillness

These emotions have healing properties and act as remedies against stress, pain, fear, anxiety, depression, and many more psycho-physical forms of suffering. Briatic archetypal essences are brought down into symbolic substance through these emotions because they hold strong relationships with the world. Without personal and physical relationships, these emotions would not have any use.

From a neurophysiological perspective, the limbic system is the seat of memory and emotions. We know by now that these brain regions are not completely fixed in their topography.

Senses within the cross-model
Cross-modal plasticity functions through sensory stimulation and interaction with our environment, especially when these stimuli resonate with beauty, love, truth, and similar higher values and properties. You can think about pieces of music, a work of art like a painting, poetry, and dance, but let us not forget the greatest artist of all: nature.

Sensory input in these examples is a higher spiritual quality hidden in the natural world. Nature is a powerful alchemist and transformer, inviting us to grow and develop our innate neurological and organic being. The natural world is always moving (moved by spirit), exploring, and finding new ways to thrive.
If we listen to the intrinsic intelligence and the messages nature provides for us, we can grow with nature. This vital relationship is a revelation, both in the field of popular neuroplasticity, and within the current ecological concerns about the environment (and our beautiful planet).

"Nature within is nature without = nature without is nature within".
In Kabbalah, there are many methods to work with the exterior five senses as a means of engaging with Divinity in the natural world (Assiah). The five exterior senses that belong to the physical body are the tools for measuring the outside natural world.

In relation to the inner natural world, there are the five interior (psychological) senses. These five interior senses in the world of Yezirah make it possible to see, hear, smell, taste, and feel on the subtle dimension of our psyche. Remember that the world of the psyche is called Yezirah in Kabbalah, which comes from the word Yazar, meaning: "to gather". That is exactly what these inner five senses do in the psyche: they gather information about the interior world.

What these senses perceive can be as vivid and alive as detecting the biological world around us with the physical senses. By using these instruments of exploration, we make it possible for the Holy One to (re)discover itself through many of its Beings. For the Kabbalist, it is a known mystical axiom that the human soul is the "eyes and ears" of the Holy One.

Bringing this into the field of neuroplasticity, and especially with cross-modal plasticity, I would like to remind us that the senses (interior and exterior) are moving towards association and synthesis (integration) all the time.

Now, if we intentionally use the senses, being aware of "who is looking", and even more "who is looking at whom", we are on a fascinating mystical track within neuroplasticity.

Self-awareness has an equivalent state in the neurological system. First of all, in the frontal or neocortex, the centres are responsible for the sense of "I".
What I mean by "I" is what we refer to, both in psychology and Kabbalah, as the ego: a partial sense of identity that has a limited scope of oneself and the world.

Nevertheless, the ego and the physical body have a natural relationship, brought about by, and constructed through the developing stages (from baby, infantile, adolescence, to maturity).

Together, they have a mode of self-awareness that corresponds to the natural physical and psychological world (Tree of Assiah).

The whole "game" of life becomes more interesting when we start to ascend, resting within the pre-awakening triad of the human-animal (Hod-Tifaret-Netzach), or even Tifaret with the connection to the soul.

From Tifaret, the awareness of self-consciousness dawns, bringing to the surface the meta-phenomenon of "being aware of being aware". Seated upon the Throne of Solomon is knowledge of who is looking, and who it is that we see (the consciousness behind the soul's consciousness). Imagine… what will it do to our nervous system if we cultivate this kind of consciousness?

Let us remember that the work of the Kabbalist is the work of unification. Therefore, to realize what it means if God beholds God ("I am that I am") provides the Kabbalist with the ultimate experience of association, synthesis, integration, and unity. The effects in the lower worlds will be the equilibrium of the side pillars (harmony, justice, mercy), and all those qualities leading to a synthesis between oneself and the world.

The consciousness of "who is looking" may come from the Tifaret of the psychological world and the place where the three lower worlds meet (the seat of Solomon), but it has nothing to observe when the senses are not installed to make it possible to know "what or whom we are looking at".

On the other hand, the senses are only partially operative, depending on the level of consciousness that is awake within the human being. From this, we can see that the senses may be instruments of the physical body, but they become instruments of higher consciousness as soon as those levels are accessible.

The five physical senses (as well as the senses of all four worlds in Kabbalah) are present in nature to perceive ourselves, and the world we live in, as an expression of Divinity.

Brain training
There are many different ways of training the brain and its neurological functions. Our experiences continually shape our brain activity and potential. There is enough evidence in neuroscience to prove that training cognitive, sensitive, motor, and other functions have significant effect on our organs and the organism.

Learning a language, for example, has proven to increase inter-neuron connections and synapse forming. Bilingual people have an increased amount of grey matter in their brains.

Grey matter refers to the unmyelinated neurons (those without the sheath of the specific material that isolates the neuron), and other cells which are important to the central nervous system functioning. Grey matter is present in the brain, cerebellum, spinal cord, and brain stem.

Mastering two (or more languages) increases the thickness of the brain areas linked to language, and causes changes in the architecture of the white matter that interconnects neurons. In some studies, it was clear that when a person loses their language skills (not through injury, but by not using the learned language), there is a reverse effect in the brain and nervous system. Training should be maintained to keep the results steady.

Language between different cultures and societies is not the only language that increases brain growth and capacity. Symbolic language is more primal and stimulates older parts (arche-cortex) of the brain. The limbic system, where language has a role to play (together with memory and accompanying emotions), is important to mention. More than verbal language, symbolic language moves the imagination and asks for associative ways of understanding.

In other words: verbal language does not connect the human being to transpersonal and cosmic concepts. Poetry, of course, is the exception, as it uses linguistic means to express symbolic emotions and meaning.

Most interesting is the combination of verbal language and symbolic language, where the Kabbalist works towards associative and synthetic ways of learning and knowing. All languages stimulate neuro-imaging, including music.
As the Kabbalist trains their sensory and motor skills, they enhance the white and grey matter of the nervous system. Reading music, of course, is another way of learning and practicing symbolic language.

Navigation professionals like taxi drivers, air traffic controllers and the like, have a thicker and more developed hippocampus (a part of the central nervous system that plays a role in short-term and long-term memory, and consolidation of information) due to the intensive training, these people undergo. The same results are found with people who practice intensive and complicated sports like Karate, Tai Chi, and gymnastics.

The brain is a highly adaptive and malleable organ, answering to the demands of its user. The more the aforementioned skills and knowledge are applied, the quicker one can learn new skills, connect and associate to other areas of study, and become more creative. The brain is like a muscle: the more it is used and put into practice, the stronger it becomes.

Younger brains have more plasticity. As we age, we lose plasticity, just as we can experience muscle wastage if we stop using a muscle in our body. The body will only fuel parts of the brain that are being used.

The brain uses twenty-five to thirty percent of our nutrients, and as it cannot conserve energy, it has to be extremely efficient. In reality, this explains why we find it hard to break habits or form new behaviour (because our brain has to work incredibly hard to create new pathways).

Chapter 6: Kabbalah-Quantum-Plasticity

In this final chapter, we bring together the different disciplines we have talked about in this book, to truly understand and deepen the experience of this Kabbalistic adventure.

Z'ev ben Shimon Halevi, the teacher of the Kabbalah society who brought the Toledano tradition into the last decades of the 20th century and the first part of the 21st century, said to me once: "The Kabbalist is interested in the truth".

To find out what that requires, the Kabbalist has to dedicate their life to a lot of meditative work and inner searching. The four worlds in Kabbalah and Jacob's Ladder explain and present to us four different ways of seeing reality, and therein, even a fifth way: a fifth Tree within the scheme of Jacob's Ladder representing a totality of the four worlds together in the middle pillar, running through all the worlds.

The truth may be seen from that psychological point of view, where being yourself is the relative truth of "who I am". Of course, this interpretation doesn't end there. The worlds within worlds are revealed like a mirror within a mirror: there are deep reflections that are behind every truth we discover.

God beholds God in the mirror of existence, and makes every sentient and living being a mirror for God to behold Itself. Every subjective experience is also God beholding itself into that mirror of existence. Every reflection is a part of that truth. While God is the whole truth, Its creation does present, at least, a part of that truth.

It may be easier to regard our personal life (and life in general) as a mirror that reflects a part of that truth. But if God is the totality of all being, death is also a state or stage within the experience of truth.

As I have explained before in this book, life and death are two sides of the same coin. They are not states of being, but rather stages or processes occurring simultaneously. Like the two pillars on the Tree of Life, they are intrinsically connected and complement each other. Not one after the other, but both simultaneously and in a synchronistic manner.

Quantum physics shares with us the ultimate weird conclusion that life and death are two possibilities at the same time, held within the consciousness of an observer (Schrödinger's cat).

In Kabbalah, the micro and macrocosm include all the worlds on Jacob's Ladder, including humanity and all of nature, the heavenly and metaphysical, and the above or within. In the quantum world, the micro and macrocosm are also everywhere. It is that Eternal world within space-time where all happens simultaneously and where the wave and particle coexist.

Things can be in two realities at once. All are entangled, and all is dead and alive at the same time. All are held inside that world of potential where nothing has

come to pass (yet). This Implicate order is the Divine world of Aziluth.
The Divine world is therefore present in all the worlds.

In every single moment of your life (and death), the Divine is within and around, and yet, it is never there. It is a world or place of pure potential and probabilities: all is possible in this realm of Divine wholeness.

To know a part of this world is to know its fullness and entirety. If God is truth, then there is no place in existence where truth does not reside. Truth is everywhere and nowhere. God is everywhere and nowhere.

The universe and the world we live in, even the physical body and the psyche, are fields of potentiality. We like to think that our world is stable and reliable, based on mathematical formulas and the laws of physics. The worlds within and without are radically different from what we normally feel and think.

The cultures we have built upon this earth are not the only realities. There is just one chosen reality in a universe where uncountable realities can take place at any moment. This is the reality behind all realities. The truth behind all truth.

The experience of truth is not something static and fixed. Truth itself is that "thing" upon which the whole relative universe is based and changes all things, and yet, it remains unchanged.

The microscopic world changes all the time within our micro and macrocosmic worlds. At the foundation of matter, all is unstable and prone to the conscious observation of the universe itself. Creation happens, and does not happen, all the time, waiting to unfold from the same consciousness of the whole of creation.

Our physical biology, psyche, and nervous system (all chemical and electrical systems) react upon the quantum changes and measurements coming from consciousness. Because consciousness is the ground of all being (all thing and all creatures), it is also the ground of all changes within the universe.

The world of Aziluth, or the Implicate Order (David Bohm), is constantly behind our ever-shifting universe. Scientists have discovered that there are also constants to be found within the physical universe and the laws of physics.

Isaac Newton discovered the constant of the gravitational force between two masses (called the constant G). In spiritual terms, this would be the law of constant attraction between the opposites (side pillars on the Tree of Life) in nature. We know that there are endless varieties of opposites in nature. Therefore, there is an endless interplay in the universe, where gravity has an enormous role.

In a more poetic way, we could imagine that the constant of gravity as a natural law and force is the physical equivalent (Assiah) of the psychological and emotional law of love. There is a constant attraction of opposites going on. Gravity also shows the force that brings smaller objects towards bigger (heavier) objects.

The second constant discovered in physical science (by Albert Einstein) was the speed of light in a vacuum (also called the constant C).

Max Planck came up with the third one (called the constant H), a quantum-physical constant. In a sense, we could say that the results of his research explained that energy is not continuous, but discontinuous.

Energy or waves (spiritual side of nature) is the probability in the quantum stage or state. Light is also made up of waves or energy (photons). At the same time, light consists of particles and has mass and weight (although very little). Bio-psychology says that every thought, feeling, and action causes a quantum change within the field of probabilities that causes a wave to move and formulates a new arrangement of particles.

In a metaphysical sense, light has the same properties, and every thought (as an expression of consciousness) is made up of energy and particles.

In the nervous system, we can see this again by how this system works on the macroscopic level (whole organism), through light or electricity and particles or hormones (the chemical pathway).
What happens within the smallest particles of matter during our lives? An atom is like a grain of matter (an invisible building block of matter). The classical idea was that the inside of an atom was like a solar system: a nucleus in the center, and some "planets" (or electrons) orbiting around the nucleus in fixed circles.

But it is not so on the quantum level and inside the atom. If atoms turned endlessly in the same orbit, they would lose energy and burn themselves out. Therefore, electrons can be measured because of their energy, but not because we know how they look. This is the same with the higher worlds in Kabbalah (Briah); we cannot see these realms (for they are essential, but have no substantial existence).

However, our physical existence does show us that there are unseen worlds that sustain our physical universe. Moreover, because of this relationship between these worlds or realities, there is an interdependency between them. An entanglement shows us that these worlds coexist, and rise and fall out of each other.

The structure of our physical world is eventually related to (or even based upon) the particular size of an atom. This physical state of our reality is probably also dependent on the changes of the electron in an atom when it shifts energy states.

The changes in energy states can be compared to what Niels Bohr would call: the changes of the electrons in their orbits around the nucleus. An atom is held endlessly in the world of infinite probabilities of Aziluth (Implicate Order), while it may simultaneously collapse in another physical charge and state.

The possibilities an atom has to change energy level per second, is infinite. This means that a state of matter is in all potential states at the same time, and it can change at any moment into another state of matter. This makes physical existence a random event in potential, an ever-moving play of energy and matter.

However, there is more to physical existence, and how it is created. Chance would not result in the precision and exact measures of this universe. Einstein, therefore, came up with the theory that photons are made not only of waves, but also of particles. These particles still have energy (wave) and momentum.

But… what if physical quantum reality is a wave of matter (sometimes called a "wavicle")?

The spiritual-metaphysical principles of Chocmah and Binah (the creative parents of existence), resonate with the quantum ideas of wave (Chocmah) and particle (Binah). Although they are depicted and described as separate on the Tree of Life, they are inseparable and always one.

Even when they appear in physical existence as matter (particle) or energy (wave), but still, they are both states at the same time. The wave within every particle guides the motion (momentum) of how it behaves. It is almost as if the wave is there to give a certain subjective quality to the atom and its behaviour. In human terms, we are almost inert and passive if no emotions or passions make us move.

On a psychological level, it could be possible, by analogy, to say that the wave inside the atom directs and guides the electron, just like our emotions and feelings guide us (for better or worse) in our psyche. Waves and particles are opposites in our minds, but they complement each other in Kabbalah and esoteric philosophy. Waves are the potential that makes up this universe like a space full of probabilities, a universe of chance.

The particle universe seems to be the opposite, declaring that all is fixed when the potential wave has collapsed into a state-particle. This is the deterministic idea behind the physical universe where all is made from logical and predictable equations.

Quantum physics and Kabbalah do not follow either one of these ideas, ending up in a dualistic universe that doesn't match our reality and truth. Existence is created moment by moment out of chance and determinism. These are both held in the embrace of consciousness, and the position of a third factor that we call in Kabbalah: the conscious observer (Tifaret). The human ability to choose comes from the observer, called in Kabbalah: Free Will.

To look at the quantum reality in the same way as we look at the physical universe and its laws, is impossible to do. Quantum physics works differently than the laws of time-space and causality as we know it.

This is strange because there is a macro level at the level of Assiah, which is the appearance of all organic nature in the mineral, vegetable, animal, and human nature. Inside these expressions of material nature, there is a micro-level, which is the quantum level. Although they have everything to do with each other, and even seem to be made from the same stuff, they do not behave in the same way.
What happens on the quantum level of matter does not necessarily happen on the macro level of physical reality.

Can there be an objective quantum reality within quantum theory? Some quantum scientists (like Niels Bohr) say that this is not the case, and that the quantum world is ultimately subjective. This is the same as saying that the causal world of Briah in Kabbalah is purely subjective, and that every causation cannot be measured or known (which would make the whole path and work of the Kabbalist redundant and futile).

If all is purely dependent on the observer only, it would mean that the universe only exists when we are aware of it. All the things we are not conscious of cannot collapse and actualise into a particle state to become something. This is why, in Kabbalah, there must always be an observer of this universe to make the universe happen; otherwise, there would not be any creation.

Is God the ultimate observer in existence? And does existence depend upon God's observation?

Some quantum ideas might answer these questions by suggesting that the universe exists, whether the universe is observed or not. Through observation of the human being, we can discover the connections between our total organism (macro world) and the subatomic world (micro world), which are found in Assiah.

Does a self-conscious being like the human soul make changes in the quantum field? And does the soul indeed cause a collapse in the wave function? If not, this would mean that the soul cannot influence the downward movement in the four worlds that we know in Kabbalah, and therefore, eventually manifest in the world of Assiah (so no downward causation).

Niels Bohr (among other scientists) stated that there is no such thing as a quantum world, but only quantum phenomena, which are the results of our observations. These observations could come close to the hypothesis that the quantum domain is the world of Aziluth (or the Implicate Order), which is awaiting an observer so that the Divine potential can come into being through the successive worlds of Briah, Yezirah, and Assiah.

Einstein said that all beings influence the universe as observers, and therefore, the quantum world. In Kabbalah, this could mean that all creatures created (made in the image of the Divine, each on their own level), are conscious beings that function as the eyes and ears of God. They are all, on each level, consciously observing the universe, and sustaining or moving the universe as it is. Erwin Schrödinger had the same idea as Einstein: we cannot separate the macro and microcosmic worlds within quantum physics.

In quantum reality, whether it is a world or a field, several possibilities may occur on the macroscopic level (Assiah). Although things may appear as dead on the quantum level, they may be alive in our classical macroscopic world and reality. Quantum reality has different possible outcomes whilst something might have collapsed from waves into particles (parallel existences on the quantum side of things).

In the higher worlds of Kabbalah, there is more than one possible outcome in the endless possibilities that are waiting to collapse. That outcome must first be observed before it becomes "something" in the manifested world.
That "something" has a potential manifestation of countless probabilities.

Consequently, the explicate order (Assiah) is never finished nor complete, as the implicate order of Aziluth is always present. All possibilities do indeed evolve in a deterministic fashion by creating all possibilities simultaneously!

This is not limited to our personal space and environment. All is made up of the quantum world (Aziluth), and is present at the same time (Eternity).

There is no past or future in the quantum world. All is there, and evolves at the same time. When the quantum world is involved with the "classical world" of space-time and movement, one event collapses parallel to the collapse of many other potentials and probabilities. There are still endless possible outcomes of the same event.

Aziluth (or Divinity) is all things at once (Eternal), and it is all things that were, are, and shall be. In the world of Aziluth, nothing ever changes in that Eternal consciousness. Even when potential collapses into actuality (Assiah), the world of Aziluth is unchanged and holds all in that same space or potential.
Although something might have manifested (collapsed), there are parallels to that manifestation: endless probabilities, besides the thing that has come into space-time-movement.

When you are reading these words, there are countless possibilities about your situation. All that happens and does not happen depends largely on consciousness. When there is no change in consciousness, no new collapse is expected in the quantum domain or implicate order.

The quantum field has to be "stirred", like a stone being cast into the water, making circular waves from the centre outwards. Let us meditate on this magnificent topic, and include the other subjects from this book.

Use the guided meditation below to tune in and align yourself with the words as they are described before you.

Meditation

Sit quietly and close your eyes.

Start regular breathing and relax all the levels of your being. Imagine that you can breathe through your whole body. Not just your lungs, but all the physical elements of your physical vessel. Feel, sense, and see that you breathe through all that is made up of the element of earth: your bones, muscles, skin, organs, nerves...

You breathe through the elements of water within you: blood, and the water in the cells... breathing through the element of air: all the gaseous substances... and through the element of fire: all that gives heat and warmth, and your electric mechanisms.

Breathe through this emanation of Malkuth, your physical existence.
Next, move upward in consciousness and reach the Sefira of Yesod in your body: the pelvic area. Now you see, sense, and feel the sphere of the moon and the subtle or etheric body. This subtle sphere is around and within the physical body.
The vital soul and all your daily thoughts, feelings, and actions are present here. This is the vegetable level of your being. Breathe through all this subtle-lunar body.

Make the two bodies breathe gently together.

Rising in consciousness, you reach the level of the Sefira Tifaret, where you are at the higher part of the psyche, in connection with the self and the soul. Herein lie your self-consciousness and free choice. Breathe through your Tifaret, and the influence of the sun within you.

At the level of Daath, you come into the transpersonal or cosmic dimension, where you behold stars and infinite space within you, at the level of the head. Breathe through this cosmic body that surrounds and penetrates you.

At the top of the middle pillar within you, you arrive at Kether, the Crown on top of your head. Here you breathe through the Eternal Light that is within all the bodies and beyond.

Now, you become aware of the world of Aziluth, which is not only an image on the diagram of Jacob's Ladder, but is a world that is everywhere in space and time. Aziluth, the Divine Presence, and the realm of quantum probabilities (or the Implicate Order) are within you, and all around you; as far as the eye can see or your mind can imagine... and beyond.

Follow this infinite world that is everywhere at once. Here you engage with past, present, and future within the Eternal moment of now. You are everywhere at once. You are in the past, present, and future. You are all possibilities at the same time. You are unmoving, but all movement comes from you.

This infinite Light that you are begins to show itself as innumerable points of light on an invisible surface. You begin to define yourself as sparks of light that shine and radiate towards one another. All the light that you perceive now is the same, although you appear as multiple sparks on the inside of a space.

These sparks are possibilities that position themselves somewhere in a potential space and time.

Then your consciousness converges into one spark of light that you notice somewhere floating in your space. It is like a twinkling star that dances in a void. All of this is you.

You bring your whole being and consciousness into this single spark of light, and you become like a sun. You can now feel the potential for creativity as you become self-aware as an individual spark of light, and choose from the endless possibilities. All the four worlds are still there.

Take a moment to become aware of this state, and the fact that you have reached the consciousness to apply free will.

While you descend further into your being, you reach the Sefira of Yesod within (the sphere of the lunar influence and the bio-psychological forces). Here, the light of the sun, or star that you are, begins reflecting electrical processes within your psyche. You start to realize that the boundaries of your psyche are far beyond your personal psychology. They stretch as far as the quantum world, infinitely.

Your psyche contains all possible outcomes that ever were, are, and shall be. Personal thoughts, memories, impressions, inner actions, and feelings, are just a tiny part of your whole psychological dimension. Inside of you, there is a subtle communication going from one end of the universe to the other, as if there is no time and space, and all is present non-locally and eternally.

These processes flow down into your physical existence, where you become a being made up of four elements and five senses. All that has gone before, and all the possibilities, collapse into this unique vessel or body. There you encounter a complex system of electrical and chemical impulses that find their way through the quantum field within you.

Now, you experience a final collapse in your physical manifestation. Still, you know that all is possible, and your current collapse is not final. You are all states at once. You are alive and dead. You are past, present, and future.

Feel, sense, and see all the biological systems operating in your body. They are there all at once, working in perfect harmony within the potential world of Aziluth, where all is possible and probable; yet, this is the manifestation at this moment.

Feel all the neurological processes within you: the electrical and magnetic activity that functions like a huge network within a confined part of your existence, the physical body. See how this electromagnetic network and energy connect with the etheric body, which also works through the same energy and force.

All bio-rhythms and cycles within your manifestation work under the will of the world of Aziluth that chose you to be and become. This is the quantum reality within your manifested personal being.

You are the Immanent of the Transcendent. You are the all within the great
Nothingness. You are the outcome of the endless and infinite realm of the
quantum (Aziluth) world. You have manifested the Transcendent, which has
become a centre within its existence. Let this moment last for a while.

Gently return from your meditation, coming down into the physical body.

Let all the images dissolve, and become aware of your breath through the physical
body. Feel the gravity as you sense your body sitting on the surface underneath
you. Feel the temperature of your body and the space around you.

Open your eyes to the sensitive world, and write down any experiences you wish
to remember.

Conclusion

Kabbalah has shown over the centuries that life does not just happen to us, but that we are players in this great game into which we were born. There is more to the human being than only this physical body.

Having said this, the body itself is the key to all the other (unseen) worlds that are part of our reality. All the worlds come together inside the body you are living in. We are born as co-creators, able to cause changes in our own lives.

The mystic does not mean to influence things magically, but to honour and apply the gifts of the universe and the Holy One. This book shows us that we are not just spectators of our own lives, but we are participants in the passing show.

We move along this wonderful road, from birth to death, and beyond. Meanwhile, in these discoveries, we may realize that our reality is not that linear, and that the definition of a human being is quite limited in this stage of our knowledge.

Quantum physics brings us the philosophical and mystical ideas that we are made up of matter that is Spirit at the same time: the two pillars on the Tree of Life, where we are simultaneously dead and alive.

Our consciousness makes us occupy a very interesting position as creative beings with the innate ability to manifest the potential universe into being. Life and death are not that linear, and not that simple either. It seems there are no hellos and no goodbyes!

The universe seems to be ultimately subjective, and all changes and reacts to the way the universe is beholden through consciousness.

The cosmos is a vast network with no boundaries, and is endless in its intelligence and wisdom. All connected, all is one. The law of entanglement shows us that we are not separated, and that all is in contact and communicates with each other. Distance and size do not matter at all!

Space-time is relative, and is only experienced in the process of how the Eternal becomes manifest. Still, a manifest universe is held in the embrace of the Eternal, and is not separated through our theories.

Neuroplasticity brings us closer to our microcosm and the amazing abilities of the physical body. As a mirror of the macrocosm, the nervous system is also endless and limitless in its potential. It seems that the only limitations we find are the ones that we give to our system, or the boundaries that we shape through our ignorance about ourselves.

The nervous system is truly a mirror image of the macrocosm, where all is held together by a fine network of communication that functions like a supercomputer. Every part of that whole system is intelligence itself.

Kabbalah says the same thing about existence and the Tree of Life: all is One, and nothing should be added or taken away from it. Creation might be an ongoing process that is never finished, but it is complete and whole, from start to finish.

And please, do not forget about the body itself; it is a spiritual gift for us to remember and experience that this life, and all of existence, is a manifestation of God: the One Who is All and Nothing, a Limitless Light.

May we all remember this on our spiritual journey.

www.ingramcontent.com/pod-product-compliance
Lightning Source LLC
LaVergne TN
LVHW081717210726
843527LV00006B/320